SYRIA

T0304469

SYRIA

Civil War to Holy War?

CHARLES GLASS

OR Books
New York · London

© 2025 Charles Glass

Published by OR Books, New York and London

Visit our website at www.orbooks.com

All rights information: rights@orbooks.com

First printing 2025

Library of Congress Cataloging-in-Publication Data: A catalog record for this book is available from the Library of Congress.

British Library Cataloging in Publication Data: A catalog record for this book is available from the British Library.

Typeset by Lapiz Digital. Printed by BookMobile, USA, and CPI, UK.

paperback ISBN 978-1-68219-606-9 • ebook ISBN 978-1-68219-607-6

For Lucien,
with love from Dad

CONTENTS

Foreword to the Second Edition—*Aaron Maté*   ix

Foreword to the First Edition—*Patrick Cockburn*   xv

Introduction   1

Chapter One. A History Lesson   11

Chapter Two. Aleppo, September 2012: The Citadel   27

Chapter Three. Aleppo, Autumn 2012: Olive Oil Soap   39

Chapter Four. Damascus, Autumn 2013:
Arab Spring, Syrian Winter   53

Chapter Five. Tadamon, Damascus, Winter 2013:
A Fraternal Bloodbath   65

Chapter Six. Aleppo and Damascus, September 2014:
A Shattered Mosaic   75

Chapter Seven. Damascus, Summer 2015:
Friends Like These   85

Chapter Eight. Damascus, Autumn 2015:
War Drums' Sad Rhythm   103

Chapter Nine. Kessab, Autumn 2015: The Battle for Kessab   117

Chapter Ten. Damascus, Winter 2016–2017:
Camp of the Defeated   133

Chapter Eleven. Damascus and Aleppo, Spring 2017:
Morning Chorus   145

Chapter Twelve. Palmyra, October 2017: Zenobia's Throne   169

Chapter Thirteen. Homs, January 2018:
    Another City Demolished   185

Chapter Fourteen. Washington, D.C., May 2018:
    Tell Me How This Ends   193

Chapter Fifteen. Damascus, December 2018:
    The Blood Cave   227

Chapter Sixteen. Damascus, February 2023:
    A Tourist in Syria   255

Epilogue. December 2024: Death in Damascus   265

Acknowledgments   273

About the Author   277

FOREWORD TO THE SECOND EDITION

The overthrow of Syrian president Bashar al-Assad followed a more than decade-long war that claimed hundreds of thousands of lives, created millions of refugees, and tore apart the birthplace of one of the world's oldest civilizations.

Syrians who had suffered under the Assad family's fifty-four-year autocracy rejoiced at its downfall and in the emptying of the country's torture-ridden prisons, which symbolized the Baath Party's harsh reign. Yet the demise of one authoritarian, repressive system did not guarantee that Syrians would avoid another. Assad was replaced by Hayat Tahrir al-Sham (HTS), a direct offshoot of Al Qaeda's franchise in Syria. Although the Sunni fundamentalist HTS pledged to respect Syria's cultural diversity, members of minority groups—among them Kurds, Alawites, Shia, Christians, and Druze—had ample grounds for fear: HTS and allied sectarian militias had terrorized civilians across all walks of life throughout the war.

Meanwhile, Syria remained at the mercy of multiple foreign powers who, throughout the bloody conflict, had always pursued their own agendas at the Syrian people's expense. True to form, Turkey and Israel capitalized on Assad's fall by seizing even more Syrian territory and, in Israel's case, wiping out much of Syria's military infrastructure.

With five decades of reporting inside Syria and the wider region, Charles Glass is a leading chronicler of the country's ongoing tragedy. In this book, which draws on his first-hand coverage of the

Syrian war since it erupted in 2011, Glass provides a vital account of how a conflict that began with pro-democracy protests as part of the Arab Spring descended into one of the twenty-first century's worst humanitarian disasters.

It is not only his rich experience that distinguishes Glass among Western reporters covering Syria. Whereas establishment media outlets have generally offered simplistic narratives that present Syrians as a monolith, Glass has given voice to all sides of the war. These include people who took to the streets in March 2011 protesting the Assad government's repression and corruption, but who became isolated as foreign-backed sectarian elements took hold of their struggle. Glass also gives voice to a constituency the Western press widely shunned altogether: those members of Syrian minority groups who, notwithstanding their criticisms of Assad, saw the sectarian insurgency armed by the US and its allies as a greater threat.

In this respect, Glass also deviates from the Western media norm by exposing how the US and its allies fueled the carnage in Syria for cynical ends. Chapter Fourteen of this book, which is based on a seminal article first published in *Harper's Magazine*, brings Glass out of the Syrian warzone to Washington, D.C. In the heart of the world's top hegemon, Glass applies his critical lens to the government bureaucrats who, unbeknownst to most Americans, played a major role in provoking and prolonging the Syrian cataclysm.

Capitalizing on the 2011 protests against Assad, the US partnered with Israel, Gulf monarchies, Turkey, and other NATO states to fuel a sectarian insurgency that sought regime change. The CIA-led operation, codenamed Timber Sycamore, proved to be "one of the costliest covert action programs in the history of the C.I.A.," the *New York Times* later reported. Leaked National Security Agency documents revealed a budget of nearly a billion dollars per year, or around one out of every fifteen dollars of CIA spending. Drawing on a massive arsenal sourced from across the globe—including the looted stockpiles of the government it had helped overthrow in Libya—the CIA armed and trained nearly ten thousand insurgents, expending "roughly $100,000 per year for every anti-Assad rebel who has gone through the program," US officials told the *Washington Post* in 2015. Two years later, one US official estimated that CIA-funded militias "may have killed or wounded 100,000 Syrian soldiers and their allies."

The roots of this campaign date back to the George W. Bush administration. According to former NATO commander Wesley Clark, the Bush team marked Syria for regime change alongside Iraq in the immediate aftermath of 9/11. A leaked cable sent from the US Embassy in Damascus in 2006 assessed that Assad's "vulnerabilities" included "the potential threat to the regime from the increasing presence of transiting Islamist extremists," and advised how the US could "improve the likelihood of such opportunities arising." The following year, Seymour Hersh reported in the *New Yorker* that the US and Saudi Arabia had agreed to "provide funds and logistical aid to weaken" Assad's government.

Syria was an important member of the Iranian-led "Axis of Resistance" to US and Israeli hegemony in the region. Situated between Iran and Lebanon, Syria provided a land bridge across which Tehran could funnel arms to its most potent military ally, Hezbollah. This strategic depth played a critical role in Israel's failure to defeat the Lebanese movement in the 2006 war. For architects of US policy, neutralizing Assad held out the prospect of dealing the resistance axis a decisive blow. "The best way to help Israel deal with Iran's growing nuclear capability is to help the people of Syria overthrow the regime of Bashar Assad," a State Department email to then-Secretary of State Hillary Clinton explained in 2012.

For Syrians, the cost of this US-backed regime change campaign was catastrophe. While the Obama administration claimed to be arming the "moderate opposition" fighting Assad, Joe Biden accidentally revealed the true story. In September 2014, he told a Harvard audience that "there was no moderate middle" fighting Assad's government in Syria. Instead, Biden explained, "hundreds of millions of dollars and thousands of tons of weapons" were supplied to an insurgency dominated by "Al Qaeda and the extremist elements of jihadis coming from other parts of the world."

Biden's public slip that the US and its allies had supported an Al Qaeda-dominated insurgency came more than two years after another critical admission was made in private. In a February 2012 email, Jake Sullivan—who went on to serve as Biden's national security adviser—wrote to Hillary Clinton: "Al Qaeda is on our side in Syria." Three years later, "our side" took a major step forward when Al Qaeda in Syria joined with CIA-armed groups to seize the Syrian province of Idlib. "Idlib Province," Brett McGurk, a top US official for the Middle East, later remarked, "is the largest Al Qaeda safe haven since 9/11." At the time, Idlib was ruled by Abu Mohammad al-Jolani, who would ultimately lead the successful ouster of Assad.

Although the CIA program was formally shut down in 2017, the US continued to torment Syrians by other means. When President Donald Trump ordered the withdrawal of US troops from Syria's northeast in 2019, top Pentagon and State Department officials simply ignored him. That military occupation allowed the US to plunder Syria's most valuable oil and wheat reserves, further impoverishing ordinary Syrians in government-controlled territory. As Dana Stroul, later a senior Pentagon official under Biden, explained that same year, "one-third of Syrian territory" was now "owned" by the US government. According to Stroul, possessing this "resource-rich" region—which contains the country's "hydrocarbons" and is its "agricultural powerhouse"—gave the US "leverage" to shape the "political outcome in Syria" according to US objectives.

The theft of Syrian resources was part of a broader US strategy to stop the devastated country from rebuilding. By "preventing reconstruction aid and technical expertise from going back into Syria," Stroul explained, the US could ensure that the government-controlled areas where most Syrians lived would remain as "rubble." Accordingly, in June 2020, the US imposed sanctions that "crushed" Syria's economy and "exacerbated fuel and food shortages for everyday Syrians," as two Trump administration officials later gloated. Upon ending his role as UN Humanitarian Coordinator for Syria in 2023, El-Mostafa Benlamlih noted the obvious: "American and European sanctions, despite all claims to the contrary, punished the poor and vulnerable."

Targeted by a US-led dirty war, sanctions, and military occupation; hollowed out by its rulers' corruption, brutality, and inertia; and increasingly isolated as key allies Iran, Hezbollah, and Russia became consumed with parallel conflicts against the US and its Israeli/Ukrainian proxies, the Syrian state as it existed under Assad finally collapsed.

For those seeking to understand how this seismic event came to be, and how a better future for Syria might yet be forged, Charles Glass's first-hand account of the complex and widely misunderstood Syrian war is an invaluable resource.

—Aaron Maté, January 2025

FOREWORD TO THE FIRST EDITION

The war in Syria has long needed a good book to explain what and why it is happening. Few events in recent history have been subjected to so much inadequate and partial reporting and there are few writers who have the perception and experience to illuminate this terrible tragedy. Charles Glass is one of them: he knows Syria, Lebanon and the region extremely well and has been an eyewitness to its crises and wars since the 1970s. He has essential recent experience gained through his travels to Damascus, Aleppo, Homs, and other parts of Syria since the conflict started in 2011 and a popular revolt rapidly transformed into a sectarian civil war.

It is difficult to write sensibly and with balance about a struggle in which all sides, including much of media, is so partisan. From the early days of the Arab Spring, not just in Syria but in other countries caught up in these complex developments, journalists often crudely demonized one side and portrayed the other as unblemished democrats. Obvious contradictions were ignored: how, for instance, could the Syrian rebels be the secular democrats they purported to be when their most important supporters and financiers were Saudi Arabia, Qatar, and the oil-states of the Gulf, whose rulers are the last theocratic absolute monarchies left on earth?

The media was not alone in its self-deception. Leaders in the US, Europe, and the region assumed that President Bashar al-Assad would fall in 2011 or early 2012 because they had just seen Muammar Gaddafi overthrown and killed. This was despite the fact that, at his weakest, Assad controlled thirteen out of fourteen of Syria's provincial capitals. Only full-scale US intervention, more along the lines of Iraq in 2003 than Libya in 2011, would have overthrown him. Rebels pretended that all they needed was some heavy weaponry and a few US air strikes to win, but this was never the case.

The Syrian war is today frequently compared to the Thirty Years War in Germany in the seventeenth century and, unlike many such historic analogies, this one reveals an important truth. As in Germany four hundred years ago, there are now so many players with divergent interests in Syria that the conflict is becoming impossible to end. Syrians have less and less influence over the fate of their country. To understand all this is not easy, and anybody who tries to do so must combine deep understanding of the region with up-to-date knowledge at ground level from one of the most dangerous places on earth. In this study, Charles Glass tells us more about the reality of Syria and its future than could be gained from any other single source.

—Patrick Cockburn, 2015

INTRODUCTION

The war that overwhelmed Syria in 2011 faded from the headlines a few years later. Interest diminished with the realization that Syrian President Bashar al-Assad had defeated the rebellion against him. But while the rebels had lost the war, they did not give up. Outside powers continued to fund them, as other foreign states maintained their support of Assad. The war that should have ended in 2017 with Assad's victory finished at the end of 2024 with his humiliating defeat.

Syria evolved from one war to many. The first phase began in March 2011 amid the euphoria of the Arab Spring that toppled dictators in three other Arab states, Tunisia, Egypt, and Libya. Dera'a, a remote farming town at the edge of the southern desert, became the uprising's birthplace. A long drought had reduced crop yields, and the government failed to ameliorate the peasants' plight. The torture of youngsters, whose only offense was scrawling graffiti on walls, led to demonstrations that inspired idealists in Damascus and Homs to echo Dera'a's cry for reform. The government suppressed rallies whose slogans evolved from changing policies to changing leaders. Each side blamed the other for drawing first blood. As the violence escalated, the government accused outside powers of fomenting rebellion. At the time, one protest organizer told me that the government had no right to complain about foreign meddling when it had interfered in Lebanon, Iraq, and Palestine— resembling America's outrage over external interference in its elections, when the CIA had rigged the vote nearly everywhere from Italy to Iran to Chile. The dissidents unwittingly invited a foreign onslaught, pleading for assistance from states that were anything but democratic. The Sunni Wahhabi regimes of Saudi Arabia and Qatar rained largesse on groups whose outlook mirrored their own. Turkey's fundamentalist, albeit elected, government gave preference to militias allied to the Muslim Brotherhood with which Recep Tayyip Erdoğan's Justice and Development Party (AKP) had forged links when both were underground movements seeking to destroy secularism in the Muslim world. The secular governments of the US, Britain, and France underwrote much of what became a religious uprising. Ostensibly on behalf of non-sectarian demonstrators seeking democracy, they funneled the aid through religiously based regional powers. Sectarian bigots dominated the rebel field, making it impossible for Syria's many minorities—Kurds, Arab Christians, Armenians, Druze, Ismailis, Shiites, and Yazidis—to participate in a revolt that sought to expel or annihilate them. The Salafists objected to Assad, not as a dictator, but as a member of the Alawite sect of Islam that they branded as heretical.

Iran, as theocratic as Saudi Arabia, rushed support to longtime ally Assad without requiring him to make his country an Islamic Republic. In addition to weapons and battlefield guidance, Iran dispatched Hezbollah's effective and combat-ready shock troops from Lebanon. Having fought and defeated Israel over twenty years in south Lebanon, Hezbollah was more than a match for nascent and disparate rebel bands. With Hezbollah on one side and the Salafists on the other, the war took on an increasingly sectarian tinge—reflecting the regional polarity between Iran and Saudi Arabia. While Assad's secularism had little in common with Iranian rule by Shiite clergy, their strategic alliance dated to their shared hatred of Saddam Hussein in Iraq from the time of the Iranian revolution in 1979.

Russia, which had sponsored the Syrian military and intelligence services since the 1960s, also moved to rescue Assad during his hour of need. Russia interceded with troops when Assad was at his weakest, turning the tide for him at the end of 2016. If the US objective in Syria was to drive Russia and Iran out, its policy of arming a jihadi opposition only strengthened Russian and Iranian influence.

From December 2016, when the Russians enabled Assad's army to retake the eastern portions of Syria's commercial capital, Aleppo, Assad seemed secure on his throne, and the rebels struggled to survive while governing the province of Idlib in the north. American attempts to roll back Russian and Iranian gains made Assad more dependent on them. When the crisis came in November 2024, Russia and Iran deserted him – both because he was not cooperating fully with them and because they had turned their attention away from Syria.

§

The Syrian capital was, for the most part, secure throughout the conflict, although rebels controlled a large swath of its populous semi-rural outskirts until 2018. Siege, bombardment, and negotiation persuaded the rebel factions to abandon the last suburbs they held in the eastern Ghoutha. Many left in buses for Idlib, the de facto jihadi capital under Turkish Army protection, while others surrendered their weapons and took their chances living with their families under the government. The "reconciliation" process of surrender or exodus followed a pattern set in other Damascus suburbs, Homs, and

Aleppo, sparing army and civilian casualties when the rebels had no option but to withdraw or die. Wherever the fighting stopped, civilians returned to rebuild their houses.

In other corners of Damascus, including the Palestinian refugee camp of Yarmouk, fighters of the fundamentalist Islamic State in Iraq and Syria (ISIS) held out for a short time after their comrades left eastern Ghoutha. They threw their last punches, as they did in the short-lived capital of their caliphate, Raqqa, before they vanished to plot terror attacks against infidels everywhere.

§

The Kurds cultivated an ambiguous relationship with the government after 2011. At first, the Kurdish Democratic Union Party (PYD, *Partiya Yetikia Demokrat*) confronted the government in three Kurdish pockets—Afrin in the west, Kobani in the center, and Qamishli in the east—dotted along the Turkish frontier. The PYD and its military wing, the People's Protection Units (YPG, for *Yekineyen Parastina Gel*), were not seeking to change the regime so much as to take advantage of unsettled conditions to achieve local autonomy. The Syrian Army, trusting in the inevitability of its return, withdrew to concentrate on more important battles.

The Kurds used the respite from security service attention to experiment with grassroots democracy in Syria's northeast corner that they call Rojava, or West, for Western Kurdistan. Mythic Greater Kurdistan covers a vast area from the Mediterranean Sea east across Syria and Turkey into Iraq and Iran. Although irredentist ambitions appeal to only a tiny minority of Kurds, they explain in part why Turkey, Syria, Iraq, and Iran agree on one issue only: the Kurds must never carve an independent state out of any of their lands, lest they achieve independence in them all. Modern nation states that claim

4

self-determination for themselves and deny it to others are guilty of hypocrisy, hardly a new concept in international relations. Other dreamers in the Mideast display their ideal maps of Greater Syria, Greater Israel, Greater Turkey, Greater Armenia, and a Greater Iraq that includes Kuwait and parts of Syria.

Syrian administration remained in Rojava with the government sustaining its claim to sovereignty by paying civil servants and teachers. Flights continued between Damascus and Qamishli. Complicating this modus vivendi in 2014 was the invasion of the region by ISIS. ISIS, later rebranded the Islamic State (IS), threatened everyone: the Kurds in Syria and Iraq, the Syrian and Iraqi governments, Iran's allies in Damascus and Baghdad, America's stake in Iraq, and Russia's stake in Syria. The Kurds of Syria developed a military relationship with the United States, while they cooperated with Damascus in civil affairs. The US absorbed the Kurdish YPG militia into the so-called Syrian Democratic Forces (SDF), supplying arms, training, funds, air support, and logistical backing. The US accomplished its mission when the SDF captured ISIS's capital, Raqqa, in October 2017. Despite their victory, US forces did not leave. American officials declared new goals: preventing Iran from dominating Syria, excluding the Syrian Army from an expanded Rojava, and controlling the Syrian-Iraqi border. In 2018, the US abandoned the Kurds—not to Assad but to a Turkish onslaught—while committing forces to keep them out of Assad's grasp.

Just as the US approved Turkey's action against Kurds in the northeast, Russia had permitted ethnic cleansing of Kurds in Afrin province of the northwest. The Kurds, after all, were American, not Russian, allies. As Turkey launched its assault on the Afrin Kurds, the Syrian government dispatched paramilitaries and arms to the

Kurds. But it did not commit its army to fight a neighbor with four times its population and a NATO-standard military numbering at least eight times as many troops. Turkey's conquest of Afrin led to the exodus of around two hundred thousand Kurds and the looting of Afrin city by Turkey's fundamentalist proxies.

Turkey maintains a troop presence in Idlib province, which jihadi and other rebel forces who enjoyed Turkish protection seized from the government in 2014 and 2015. Its long-term goal in holding onto Idlib, where the pretext of controlling the Kurds does not apply, turned out to be, not only to prevent the Syrian Army from returning, but also to enable the Hayat al-Tahrir Sham militia to seek total victory. Unlike Assad, who bided his time and resisted negotiating with Turkey, the rebels united their forces and expanded their territory southward—all the way to Damascus, as it turned out.

At the presidential palace in Damascus in the spring of 2018, I asked one of Assad's senior advisors how long the Turkish Army, then on the verge of conquering the Kurdish town of Afrin, was likely to occupy northern Syria. The response was fatalistic: "They have been in northern Cyprus since 1974."

Turkey invaded Cyprus to prevent the island republic's *enosis*, union, with Greece that Nikos Sampson's coup d'état threatened. Sampson's disastrous eight-day rule laid *enosis* to rest for good. Yet Turkey did not withdraw. Moreover, it planted Turkish settlers in former Greek homes the way Israel installs its Jewish citizens in the occupied West Bank and in the Syrian Golan Heights. The last time Turkey invaded Syria, under Sultan Selim the Grim in 1516, it remained for four hundred years.

§

Israel has kept a wary eye on developments north of the Syrian territory it occupies in the Golan Heights. Its enemies are Iran and Hezbollah, which played a decisive role in the Syrian war. Israeli warplanes and rockets have hit hundreds of Iran and Hezbollah targets, as well as civilian areas, in Syria since 2011. At the same time, Israel facilitated the movement of rebel militias along its frontier with Syria and offered medical treatment to wounded jihadi fighters. It became obvious that Israeli prime minister Binyamin Netanyahu intended to keep his promise "to stop Iran" in Syria and, in October 2024, he launched another of Israel's Lebanon invasions to destroy Hezbollah.

§

The closest Syrian area to Israeli-occupied territory is Jebel Druze, the Druze Mountain, that perches 1,800 meters above sea level about 115 kilometers south of Damascus. Its basalt foundation provided the black stone used for building houses until cement put its ugly stamp on the region. Oak and olive trees grow in abundance. The population is for the most part Druze, descendants of settlers who left Lebanon to escape a French expeditionary force in the mid-nineteenth century. Belonging to a syncretic quasi-Shiite sect that differs from other Muslims on many theological issues including their belief in transmigration of souls, the Druze chose to stay out of the Syrian civil war. Their region avoided much of the violence that devastated other parts of the country, as did Afrin before the Turkish invasion. Long resentful of over-centralized rule from Damascus dating to the French Mandate between 1920 and 1946, many Druze saw an opportunity in the peaceful protests of 2011 to achieve a measure of local control over their affairs.

Some took part in demonstrations in 2011 demanding reform of the Syrian state. From Lebanon, where most Druze live, Druze leader Walid Jumblatt urged his Syrian co-religionists to help bring down the Assad regime that had assassinated his father in 1977. The Syrian Druze did not listen to him. By the end of 2012, the anti-Assad opposition loomed less as an ally than as a threat to their existence when fundamentalist sheikhs in the mosques were calling for the rape of Druze women and murder of Druze men.

In the Druze capital of Suweida, I met writers, politicians, and teachers, all of whom noted increasing instability in the region. They also feared violence encroaching onto their mountain from the fundamentalist Sunni militias that controlled the neighboring Dera'a province. ISIS, Jabhat an-Nusra, and other jihadi forces occupied areas adjacent to Druze territory, resulting in clashes between Druze and Sunni villages. The Druze pushed the jihadis back, but they did not go into Dera'a province to confront its Sunni Arab majority. Yet, when jihadis from the north seized Damascus and forced Bashar al-Assad to disappear, the Druze cheered the demise of his regime as much as the jihadists themselves.

Aref Hudaifa, a Druze writer and translator who has lived in the village of Al Kafra near Suweida since his birth more than seventy years ago, gave me a lavish lunch and spoke of the past. Having witnessed many wars and revolutions, he clung to the hope that his country would return to peace. "The Phoenix is a Syrian myth," he said. "It dies, and then it goes back to life. Syria will regain life. But how long will it take?"

§

My first visit to Syria was in 1973, my most recent in 2024. This book, while providing some of the country's history over those fifty years and before, is primarily a record of my research there during the war that began in 2011. That lingering conflict appeared to offer little hope of a conclusion until, to universal surprise, rebels overthrew the Assad dynasty that had ruled Syria for fifty-four years. He ended up in Moscow, and they occupied his palace in Damascus.

CHAPTER ONE

A HISTORY LESSON

A terrible war has been raging in Syria since 2011. It is not the first contest for control of that mainly Arab country between the eastern Mediterranean and the Iraqi desert. No one has asked the Syrian people, in whose names all parties to the conflict claim to speak, what they want for their country. The only attempt to ascertain their opinions came in 1919, when Dr. Henry Churchill King and Charles Crane headed an American delegation to determine what the people of Syria wanted in the territories that the Ottomans had recently evacuated. Britain and France, which had only contempt for the wishes of the natives, boycotted. From June 10 to July 21, 1919, the King-Crane Commission travelled from one end of Greater Syria to another, received 1,863 petitions, and met 442 delegations from the various ethnic and sectarian groups. They found that 80.4 percent of the population wanted to keep Syria—the historic Greater Syria of Lebanon, Jordan, Israel, and little Syria—united. Seventy-three-point-five percent wanted full independence. Fifty-nine percent favored a constitutional monarchy under the Emir Feisal bin Hussein of the Hejaz, who had led the Arab uprising against the Turks. So, what did they get? No unity, no independence, and no Feisal.

The French expelled Feisal and imposed the so-called League of Nations Mandate over little Syria and Greater Lebanon in 1920. The British kept Palestine and Transjordan. Rebellions began immediately. Damascus was always at the heart of the rejection of disunity and foreign rule. French Général C. J. E. Andréa wrote in *La Révolte Druze et l'Insurrection de Damascus, 1925–1926*, that "the Arab heart beats more strongly here than anywhere else." His observation preceded by twenty years Egyptian President Gamal Abdel Nasser's dictum that Syria was "the beating heart of Arabism," a phrase quoted from time to time by Syrian President Bashar al-Assad as posthumous benediction from the last, possibly the only, great Arab nationalist leader.

Damascus was the capital of the first Arab empire, the Omayyad, in the seventh century. When its Sunni legions completed their conquest of Syria, they turned their might on Persia, a precedent not lost on the Shiite rulers of contemporary Iran. The Omayyads annexed all the territories from India west across North Africa to Spain, making theirs the most extensive imperium the world had known. Though illustrious, its duration was a mere ninety years. Thirteen centuries later, Damascus became the capital of the first independent Arab kingdom to emerge from the defeated Ottoman Empire. Its tenure was a bare five months, from March 1920, when an elected Syrian Congress proclaimed Feisal its king, until French forces expelled him on July 28. Damascus's seventh-century empire and twentieth-century kingdom, though vanished, inform the myths to which the city's inhabitants cling in turbulent times, as these are.

No event looms larger in modern Syrian history than the Great Syrian Revolt of 1925. Syrians recall it as a nationalist revolution against foreign occupation, while to French Général Andréa, in his memoir of its suppression, "*C'est du banditisme tout pur.*" That insurrection erupted unexpectedly, like the rebellion against Bashar al-Assad in March 2011, during a drought in the Hauran, a plateau rich in wheat and vines beside a rugged basalt mountain south of

Damascus. Similarities between the rebellions of 1925 and 2011 are many. Both started with petitions and non-violent demonstrations over discontent with local governors. Both caught the authorities unaware. Both spread to Homs before engulfing the rest of the country. Both received weapons from Turkey, Saudi Arabia, and Jordan. Both comprised rival factions of secularists and Islamists, democrats and theocrats, tribesmen and city sophisticates, Syrians and outsiders. Both, despite provoking bombardment from airplanes and heavy artillery, enjoyed initial success. The first was defeated, but the second triumphed—for the time being.

Every Syrian government since the final departure of the French Army on April 17, 1946, has claimed to incarnate the spirit of the Great Revolt. Yet each Syrian government found itself in the position of the French, governing and modernizing a country that tended to resist both projects. France's high commissioners, like their indigenous successors, failed to absorb the greatest lesson of four centuries of Ottoman trial and error in Syria: to govern well, govern little.

The Turks, while introducing haphazard and occasional reforms and hanging fomenters of sectarian strife, barely tampered with the structure of governance they inherited from Rome, Byzantium, and the Omayyads. That is to say, they left the tribes and sects to their local chiefs. The French, as well as the assorted civilian and military regimes that followed in their wake, were more ambitious.

Governing Syria has never been easy, as the commanders of punitive expeditions from Titus to the Ottomans' last general could attest. Two years into the French Mandate over Syria and Lebanon, a Scottish traveler, Helen Cameron Gordon, toured the country and described conditions that would daunt any sovereign, foreign, or local. She wrote:

Her inhabitants are made up of at least a dozen different races, mainly Asiatic; and worse still, of about thirty religious sects, all suspicious and jealous of each other. Amongst Christians alone, there are seventeen high dignitaries with the title of Patriarch, and other leaders politically minded and steeped in intrigue: Moslems, Druses, Ismaelites, Nosairis [Alawites], Yessides [Yazidis] and various sub-sects too numerous to mention. Influence, that is pernicious, is brought to bear upon them from outside, which they are themselves unequal to combat, and sometimes prone to pay too much attention. Is it to be wondered that amongst officers of the [French] Army of the Levant, it has become proverbial that peace is only in the shadow of their bayonets and within the radius of their machine-guns?

France's *Armée du Levant* engaged in nearly continuous counter-insurgency from the moment it invaded Syria. Twelve hundred Arab fighters, including Feisal's minister for war, Yusuf al-Azmeh, died resisting the French advance on Damascus in 1920. Syrians resented the intrusion of westerners who sliced their homeland into mini-states that would become Israel, Jordan, Lebanon, and a "mini-Syria" that was a fraction of itself. The Alawite minority under Salih al-Ali fought the French for a year in the northwest, as did a largely Sunni force led by a Kurdish former Ottoman officer, Ibrahim Hananu, around Aleppo. In the Hauran and its mountain, alternately called Jabal Hauran and Jabal Druze, the French skirmished often with King Feisal's former partisans, who made cross-border raids from his brother Abdallah's new principality of Transjordan. Many Druze fought them until 1922, when France granted a "Druze Charter of Independence" with local autonomy and an elected Druze Majlis or Council. By the time Général Maurice Sarrail, France's third high commissioner in four years, disembarked in Beirut on January 2, 1925, Syria had been subdued. Nowhere appeared quieter than the formerly turbulent Druze region in the highlands of the Hauran. The Majlis had even chosen a French officer, Captain Gabriel Carbillet, as governor in July 1923, when they could not agree on a Druze candidate. Carbillet was a man of the Left, anti-clerical and a Freemason, who determined to bring *égalité* to the Druze by enfeebling their aristocracy. Joyce Laverty Miller wrote in the *International Journal of Middle East Studies* in 1977:

> Carbillet proved to be an ambitious and zealous reformer. In the course of a year, he opened twenty-three new schools, equalized the civil laws, opened a court of appeals at al-Suwaida (the capital city of Jabal-Druze), constructed an extensive system of irrigation, built roads, disarmed the population, and used the forced labor of prisoners and peasants.

Among his achievements was to bring running water for the first time to Suwaida. He also built five museums, but his use of conscripted *corvée* labor caused resentment. So too did his collective punishment of Druze peasants and sheikhs alike, whom he forced to break rocks under the Syrian sun. Druze reaction resembled that of Lieutenant Colonel Nicholson and his fellow prisoners of war in *The Bridge on the River Kwai* to Colonel Saito's decree that officers, in violation of the Geneva Conventions, would do manual labor alongside other ranks. Like George W. Bush's neoconservative true believers in occupied Iraq, Carbillet had a vision. He asked, "Should I leave these chiefs to continue their oppression of a people who dream of liberty?" France introduced something new into Syrian life, something that lingers to this day. "Rigid control of personal movement was established," wrote Stephen Hemsley Longrigg in *Syria and Lebanon Under French Mandate*. "The use of schoolmasters as informers was everywhere practiced. Punishments, for offences sometimes trivial, were arbitrary and even capricious. The sensitiveness of Druze pride was repeatedly offended."

Like the Trojan War, the Great Syrian Revolt resulted from breaches of hospitality. As Paris stole his host's wife, functionaries from Third Republic Paris made a gross *faux pas* in the village of Qraya on July 7, 1922. Armed soldiers broke into the house of Sultan Pasha al-Atrash, who was away, to arrest a Shiite named Adham Kanjar on charges of attempting to assassinate the high commissioner, Général Henri Gouraud. Al-Atrash, a thirty-one-year-old hotspur with penetrating azure eyes and formidable moustaches, was the visual embodiment of the noble Druze warrior. He had served in the Ottoman Army before defecting in 1918 to Sherif Feisal and the British. When the absent Atrash discovered the French had desecrated his house, he demanded Kanjar's return. The French refused. Al-Atrash, as a notable whose prestige depended on his power to protect others, attacked a train he mistakenly believed to be carrying the prisoner to Damascus. The French retaliated by demolishing his house and ordering his capture. He fled, returning a year later under an amnesty.

The Observer, in an article on August 9, 1925, sub-headed "Quarrel with a Young Governor," traced the revolt's spark to a subsequent violation of the Druze code of hospitality. The "young governor," Captain Carbillet, had overseen the construction of the first hotel in the Druze capital at Suwaida and required travelers to lodge there rather than as guests in private houses. The *Observer* account continued:

> [Nesib] Atrash Bey pleaded that the century-old traditions of hospitality could not thus be broken, and finally roundly suggested that the Governor was financially interested in the fortunes of the hotel, and refused to yield, whereupon the notables guilty of having opened their houses to travelers were seized and sent to break stones on the roads.

The Atrash family appealed to the senior French official in Syria, newly arrived High Commissioner Maurice Sarrail, in February 1925. Général Sarrail, like Carbillet a rare republican and progressive in the French officer corps, declined to receive the forty-man delegation. When they persisted, he arrested their leaders. Nesib Bey al-Atrash was reported to have told the French, "Very well. Rifles will speak." The arrested Druze were sent to France's new prison in the desert at Palmyra, where Sarrail's secretary, Paul Coblentz, admitted that treatment "was certainly not always comparable with the methods used in similar cases in Europe."

In March 1925, Captain Carbillet went to France on leave. A more conservative officer, Captain Antoine Raynaud, filled in for him. Raynaud's light-handed governance made him popular, especially among the landlords. When a French parliamentarian, Auguste Brunet of the Radical Party, came to Beirut on what a later era would call a fact-finding mission, Druze delegates presented him with a petition calling on France to make Raynaud's appointment permanent. Brunet ignored the petition, and Sarrail once again rebuffed their deputation.

The Druze graduated from polite petitions to public protest. Their newly formed Patriotic Club staged a demonstration on the morning of July 3 in front of the Majlis in Suwaida, where Captain Raynaud was presiding over a council session. About four hundred Druze horsemen shouted demands, chanted war songs and brandished weapons, while refraining from violence. When French-officered gendarmes dispersed them, though, shots were exchanged between one Druze leader, Hussein Murshid, and French Lieutenant Maurel. Neither man was hit, and the Druze offered an immediate apology. Captain Raynaud, despite the fact that the demonstrators' goal was to retain him as governor, commanded the Druze to pay a large fine and turn over twenty young men for detention. He also ordered the immediate demolition of the house of Hussein Murshid. The Druze religious sheikhs intervened to prevent bloodshed, agreeing that the community would pay the fine and turn over the young men. But the destruction of a Druze house was not acceptable.

When French troops appeared at Murshid's house to tear it down, Sultan al-Atrash and hundreds of mounted and armed men forced them to withdraw. Raynaud sent a warning to High Commissioner Sarrail that discontent was leading inevitably to revolution. Sarrail dismissed Raynaud and assigned an officer from the Intelligence Corps, Major Tommy Martin, to fill his post pending Carbillet's return. Sarrail summoned five Druze chiefs, including Sultan al-Atrash, to Damascus. Fearing a trap, Sultan declined. He was not surprised when Sarrail arrested the others at their Damascus hotel and sent them to Palmyra.

Up to that time, the Druze had not demanded an end to the French Mandate, any more than Dera'a's demonstrators in early

March 2011 initially sought to depose Bashar al-Assad. Their request for one French officer to replace another implied recognition of the Mandate. Similarly, the Dera'a protestors' call in 2011 for the dismissal of a governor who had crossed a line by torturing children acknowledged the president's authority to replace local officials who violated the law and trampled on their dignity. When the rulers refused to listen, the people's horizons expanded to a future in which they would choose new rulers.

Captain Carbillet returned from leave on July 19, but Sarrail did not restore him as governor. The governorship had ceased to be the issue, just as Bashar al-Assad's belated dismissal of Dera'a's governor, his cousin Faisal Kalthum, came too late to pacify the rebellion against his rule. The Druze and their allies, including many Sunni Muslims and a few Christians, demanded nothing less than France's expulsion and self-determination in a unified Syria.

On the day of Carbillet's return, two French reconnaissance planes spotted Sultan al-Atrash's growing insurgent band in the village of Urman. The Druze fired at the planes, downing one and capturing its two pilots. This became the date on which the Great Revolt is said to have begun. Michael Provence in his excellent history, *The Great Syrian Revolt and the Rise of Arab Nationalism*, writes: "Neither rebel leaders nor the mandate authorities had a clear conception of the direction and seriousness of the uprising at this early point." Nonetheless, both sides escalated the violence.

The next day, Major Martin sent a force of about two hundred French and colonial troops under a Captain Normand to retrieve the two pilots and crush what appeared to be a local disturbance. Normand bivouacked on July 21 beside a village halfway between Salkhad and Suwaida, where Sultan al-Atrash's envoys asked him to return to Suwaida for negotiations to end the fighting. Normand declined. During the battle that followed, Sultan al-Atrash's Druze and bedouin warriors destroyed Normand's force in about thirty minutes. A few stragglers made their way back to the garrison at Suwaida, which al-Atrash attacked the next day, laying siege to the French in the old citadel.

The destruction of the Normand column galvanized latent opposition to the French in Syria. Young men from Damascus joined the colors, as did Arab patriots from neighboring countries. Abdel-Aziz ibn Saud, who with his Wahhabi followers ruled the Nejd desert and had recently conquered Mecca and Medina from Britain's Hashemite allies, sent arms and men. Mustapha Kemal Pasha, the Turkish leader who had his own dispute with France over Turkey's border with Syria, supported the rebels in the north. The French armed Armenian refugees, who had barely recovered from massacres by Muslim Turks, as well as minority Circassians and Arab Christians. The rebels cut French communications, severing rail and telegraph lines at different times to Lebanon, Iraq, and Transjordan.

To quell the uprising, Sarrail dispatched Général Roger Michaud, the *Armée du Levant*'s commander, from Beirut to Damascus. Michaud led a large force south toward the Druze capital to relieve his besieged countrymen. On August 2, when his force rested about twelve kilometers short of Suwaida, Sultan al-Atrash attacked with five hundred Druze and bedouin horsemen. The French drove them back, but, running short of water, began a withdrawal north the next day. Al-Atrash attacked again with greater force, annihilating the French column. Michaud's second-in-command, Major Jean Aujac, committed suicide in the field. Al-Atrash's men collected more than two thousand rifles, as well as machine guns and artillery pieces, from the dead Frenchmen. Reuters reported, "The French have evacuated Southern Hauran."

French Foreign Minister Aristide Briand nonetheless declared that the situation in Syria was not dangerous. France faced a graver threat in its Morocco Protectorate, where insurgents from the Rif Mountain were humiliating the armies of both France and Spain. Moroccan success inspired the Syrians, much as the downfall of the dictators in Tunisia, Egypt, and Libya would ninety years later. But the rebellions in Morocco and Syria had far to go.

Unrest spread immediately to Homs, where so-called "bandits" attacked outlying French positions and closed roads. The nationalist elite in Damascus, who had remained quiet, was forced to support the rebellion or stand accused of treason. On August 23, al-Atrash requested negotiations with Sarrail through his old friend Captain Raynaud. Just as Sarrail had invited Druze leaders to Damascus as a ruse to arrest them, al-Atrash's offer was a cover for an assault on Damascus. On August 24, more than a thousand men from Jabal Druze, the Hauran and the desert mustered on the city outskirts. Arguments among their leaders over strategy delayed their advance, giving French planes time to locate and strafe them. North African cavalry then drove them south.

Muslim soldiers from Algeria and Senegal began deserting the French army to join the rebels. So did local levies in France's Syrian Legion, including the Legion's commander in Hama, Fawzi al-Qawuqji, with all his men. The mutineers held Hama for two days, until ferocious French bombardment of the ancient *souqs* and residential quarters forced the town's notables to beg Qawuqji to spare the city by withdrawing.

As during the Syrian uprising that began in 2011, some rebel leaders claimed to speak for all Syrians—Arab Sunni Muslims, the various Shia sects, and Christians. But not all the participants shared that universal vision. In 1925, some raised the flag of jihad and attacked the Christian town of Ma'alula and massacred many of its

Aramaic-speaking inhabitants. One of the revolt's more able leaders, Said al 'As, wrote:

> This work was not legitimate and the revolt was exposed to doubt by their attack and their hostility against Ma'alula which alienated the hearts of the Christian sons of the one nation, our brothers in nationalism and the homeland.

As the nationalists regretted the assault on Ma'alula in 1925, their descendants condemned the jihadi assault on the same Christian town nearly a century later. Yet the effect of both was the same: to drive Christians out of a country where they had lived since the time of Christ or to force them into the embrace of the regime, French then and Bashar al-Assad later.

By early October, the rebels had the initiative, forcing the French to confront them at times and places of their choosing. Their next target was Damascus, which they entered on October 18. Typical of the disorganization within rebel ranks, the local commander, Hassan al-Kharrat, invaded the city before Fawzi al-Qawuqji's mutineers and Sultan al-Atrash's Druze-bedouin cavalry arrived. Entering the Shaghur quarter, Kharrat shouted, "Rise up, your brothers the Druze are here!" Most Damascenes, like their descendants in this century, did not rise up.

As his forces lost control of Damascus, High Commissioner Sarrail declared martial law and commanded the summary execution of Syrians found with weapons. French tanks raced through the souqs, wrote *The Times* of London, "at terrifying speed, firing to the right and left without ceasing." At noon on the eighteenth, as Sarrail departed for Beirut, he ordered warplanes and heavy caliber cannon to bombard the city day and night.

The *Manchester Guardian* correspondent interviewed a traveler from Damascus who "describes days and nights of unforgettable terror." The shelling destroyed the famous Souq Hamadieh bazaar, the Biblical "Street Called Straight," the magnificent Azem Palace and the districts of Shaghur and Meidan. French troops executed insurgents and those who protected them. *The Times* reported that French troops, having murdered two dozen young men in villages southeast of Damascus, brought their corpses to Marjeh Square near the city center. The paper's correspondent wrote:

> Instead of merely exposing the bodies for a space on the spot as an example to other malefactors, in accordance with Eastern custom, and then handing them over to their relatives for decent burial, the French authorities brought them to Damascus. There they attached them to camels and paraded them through the streets. The ghastly spectacle presented by the swaying corpses naturally infuriated the excitable Damascenes, as indeed the news of the official adoption of such deterrents will inevitably arouse the natural indignation of many Frenchmen.

The Times reported that the rebels then killed twelve Circassians serving with the French and left their bodies outside the city's Eastern Gate. "This was the reply, typical of the spirit of those whom it was intended to humiliate," wrote *The Times* correspondent in Damascus. Forty-eight hours of steady bombardment, as in Hama, saw the city's leaders begging the rebels to leave. *The Manchester Guardian* wrote, "The rebels remained in Damascus until October

20, and only retired because their presence was given as the cause of the bombardment."

By the time Sultan al-Atrash's forces arrived, Damascus was lost. He and his allies, however, took control of nearby villages and orchards in the fertile Ghoutha, isolating the capital from the rest of Syria. Animosity between Damascene civilians and rebels grew. *The Times* added that one Druze leader threatened "the residents of the Meidan quarter that as they had betrayed the Druses on Sunday by refusing to fight they would be the first to suffer from the next attack, which would be made very soon." The French also antagonized the population, devastating villages, machine gunning unarmed civilians, and looting houses.

As France gained ground, a Maronite Christian supporter of the rebellion accused them of a crime against humanity, writing, "The French army has employed poison gas against the Druze, which affirms French will to exterminate an entire people." No inspectors came to investigate the charge, but pressure on France grew to end the war or to abandon its Mandate.

As with the rebellion against Assad, rival leaderships emerged inside and outside Syria. Fighters ignored the external leaders, but they attempted operational coordination under Ramadan Pasha Shallash. Shallash, a bedouin prince, had served as an officer in both the Ottoman and Feisal's armies. Genuine rebel unity, however, proved as elusive as it would after 2011. In his study, Longrigg describes the rebel leadership in terms that could apply to the subsequent insurrection:

No statesman with a truly national appeal, no considerable
military leader appeared, no central organization controlled
events, little correlation of effort or timing was visible. The

Government of Syria [Syrians appointed by the French]—
ministers, officials, departments—gave no countenance
to the rebellion, those of Great Lebanon and the ʿAlawis
still less; and the greatest part of the public abstained, if it
could, from overt help to a movement which damaged and
alarmed it.

French military setbacks were causing severe repercussions at home.
Pierre La Mazière, a senator of the Democratic Left, wrote in *Partant
pour la Syrie* that "we have lost so much money, so many lives, so
much prestige that—Ah, if only we could get out of Syria without any
of the rest of the world noticing it!" Much of the world demanded
that the League of Nations end the French Mandate. To hang on, the
French government changed leadership in Syria. Général Maurice
Gamelin replaced Général Michaud. A disgraced Sarrail was recalled
to Paris, and Senator Henry de Jouvenel became the Mandate's first
civilian high commissioner. He immediately put out feelers to Sultan
al-Atrash, paid subsidies to village elders to support the French,
offered amnesties to rebels who gave up their arms and travelled to
Ankara to bargain with Mustapha Kemal Pasha, the future Atatürk.
In exchange for a small parcel of Syrian territory, Turkey cut the
arms flow to the rebels.

Disputes among rival rebel leaders crippled their movement,
and foreign backers pulled them in different directions. Rebel chiefs
deposed and arrested their military commander, Ramadan Shallash.
He escaped, surrendered to the French and helped to suppress the
rebellion he had led. France escalated its military campaign with
aerial bombardment in and around Aleppo and a ground campaign
under newly promoted Général Andréa that routed Druze and Sunni

forces in the Hauran by the late spring of 1926. "The French flag flew over Suwaida," concluded General Andréa, "but there wasn't a single inhabitant left in the town." As with the Americans in Vietnam, destroying villages counted as saving them.

In 1927, Sultan Pasha al-Atrash took refuge in Transjordan and then with Ibn Saud in what would eventually be the Kingdom of Saudi Arabia. The Druze warrior was permitted home ten years later, and he lived peacefully until 1947 when he launched another doomed revolt against Syria's newly independent government. In the current rebellion, the Druze have remained neutral.

The parallels between the rebellions of 1925 and 2011 are as instructive as the differences, which are many. In the 1920s, fighting did not spread to Iraq as the current war did when ISIS defeated the US-backed Iraqi Army and occupied the city of Mosul. While Wahhabis from Arabia fought for the rebels in 1925, there was no equivalent to ISIS that rampaged across Syria and Iraq to declare an independent caliphate governed under the strictest, if arbitrary, interpretations of religious law.

The French finally left, as the Assads did, but that took another twenty years.

CHAPTER TWO
THE CITADEL

Aleppo, Spring 2012

Archaeologists believe that human beings settled on the hilltop that became Aleppo—some 225 miles north of Damascus—around eight thousand years ago. Cuneiform tablets from the third millennium BC record the construction of a temple to a chariot-riding storm god, usually called Hadad; while mid-second-millennium Hittite archives point to the settlement's growing political and economic power. Its Arabic name, Haleb, is said to derive from Haleb Ibrahim, Milk of Abraham, for the sheep's milk the biblical patriarch offered to travelers in Aleppo's environs. Successive conquerors planted their standards on the ramparts of a fortress that they enlarged and reinforced over centuries to complete the impressive stone Citadel that dominates the twenty-first-century city.

"It is an excellent city without equal for the beauty of its location, the grace of its construction and the size and symmetry of its marketplaces," wrote the great Arab voyager Ibn Batuta when he visited in 1348. During the Renaissance, Aleppo was Islam's third most important city after Constantinople and Cairo. The modern Lebanese historian Antoine Abdel Nour praised it in his *Introduction à l'histoire urbaine de la Syrie ottomane*: "Metropolis of a vast region, situated at the crossroads of the Arab, Turkish, and

Iranian worlds, it represents without doubt the most beautiful example of the Arab city."

Its beauty reveals itself in the elegance of its stone architecture, redolent of historic links to Byzantium and Venice; and in the diversity of its peoples—Arabs, Armenians, Kurds, eleven Christian denominations, Sunni Muslims, a smattering of dissident Shiite sects from Druze to Ismailis, ancient families of urban patricians as well as peasant and Bedouin immigrants from the plains—that makes it a microcosm of all Syria.

Documentary records of Ottoman Turkey's dominion over Aleppo from 1516 to 1918 portray communities of Muslims, Christians, and Jews living in the same neighborhoods. Unlike Tunis, where Jews were obliged to rent living space, Aleppo's governors imposed no restrictions on house ownership by members of any religious group or by women. It was not unusual for large mansions to be divided into apartments in which Muslim, Jewish, and Christian families dwelled with little more than the usual rancor that afflicts neighbors everywhere. Unlike more xenophobic Damascus, Aleppo encouraged European merchants to trade and live within the city walls. The European powers, beginning with Venice in the sixteenth century, established in Aleppo the first consulates in the Ottoman Empire to guard the interests of their expatriate subjects. Reputed descendants of Marco Polo, the Marcopoli family, retained the office of Italian honorary consul well into the twentieth century.

In a neglected corner of the old Bahsita Quarter, behind several shabby office buildings, stands a testament to Aleppo's historic mélange. The Bandara Synagogue was built on a site of Jewish worship that predates by two centuries the 637 AD Arab-Muslim conquest of Aleppo. Its courtyard of fine cut-stone arches and domes resembles the arcaded cloister of the nearby al-Qadi Mosque. The Jewish community of Aleppo, like its larger counterpart in Damascus, gradually made its way to New York after the founding of Israel. The last Jews departed en masse in 1992, when then President Hafez al-Assad lifted restrictions on their emigration. Suddenly, Damascus and Aleppo were bereft of an ancient and significant strand of their social fabrics. The synagogue, restored by Syrian Jewish exiles, is the forlorn relic of a community that thrived for ages before vanishing under the weight of war between Syria and Israel. It is also a harbinger of what Aleppo's Christians see as their fate following domination by Sunni Muslim fundamentalists.

"Am I worried?" Syriac Orthodox Archbishop Mar Gregorius Ibrahim Yohanna, asked me rhetorically. "Yes. Am I afraid? No." The archbishop's concern is widespread among Christians of both Arab and Armenian origin, who claim to make up nearly ten percent of Aleppo's two and a half million people. (That percentage, while half what it was fifty years ago, may have halved again to five percent, owing to Christian emigration, low birth rate, and the steady influx of rural Muslims into the city. The Syrian government does not publish statistics by religion.)

The archbishop, who wrote his Ph.D. thesis at Britain's Birmingham University on Arab Christianity before Islam, insisted that Christians should not take sides between the government and its opponents. Unlike the Christians of Lebanon, Syrian Christians do not have their own political parties or armed militias. Mar Gregorius told me, "The only weapon we can use is to leave the country. I don't believe it's right." Those who are leaving, even if only for the duration of the conflict, provide a rationale similar to the one Syrian Jews gave me in 1992: they were escaping not the Assad regime, but the Muslim fundamentalists who might overwhelm it.

Instability brought on by armed rebellion, mass demonstrations, regime violence, and economic sanctions has unsettled Syria's many minorities. The Alawites—whose doctrines are related to those of the Shia branch of Islam, and whose rule is opposed on principle by many Sunnis, who make up some seventy percent of the Syrian population—are concentrated in the west near the Mediterranean. The Kurds live mostly in the east beside the Euphrates and the Druze in the south in Jebel Druze, giving each of those minorities a territorial base from which to negotiate their survival no matter who takes power. (In Beirut, just before I crossed the border to Syria, Walid Jumblatt, Lebanon's Druze leader, told me he had urged his fellow Druze in Syria to join the rebellion. "They swim in a Sunni sea, not an Alawite sea," he said, mentioning what happened to the Algerians who sided with the French during the war of independence: many were killed and the remainder found refuge in France.

The Christians, however, are thinly dispersed among Aleppo, Damascus, Wadi Nasara, Qamishli, and other parts of the country. Having witnessed the flight of nearly two million Iraqi Christians to Syria during Shia-Sunni fighting after America's invasion of 2003, they fear a similar exodus from Syria if tribal and sectarian war between Alawites and Sunnis traps them in the middle. Reluctant to leave their ancestral homeland, which they regard as Christianity's cradle, they are confronted with demands from both the revolutionaries and the regime to declare themselves. They have resisted as communities so far, although individual Christians are fighting for and against the regime. The Armenian Catholic archbishop of Aleppo, Monsignor Boutros Marayati, told me, "We cannot say one side has truth and the other does not, because both sides have faults." He added that 171 Armenians in Homs have died as members of the security forces or in crossfire, but not as deliberate targets of either side. Minorities who benefited from the policies of the Alawite minority regime hesitated to turn their backs on it during a time of crisis.

When I left Aleppo, regime security forces raided dormitories at Aleppo University. Each side, as with all previous clashes, provided a version of events that bore no relationship to the other's. Opposition groups said troops attacked students who had taken part in peaceful demonstrations, killed at least four of them, and arrested hundreds of others. Those sympathetic to the regime blamed rebel students from Homs and Idlib, who had transferred to Aleppo after violence closed their colleges.

Aleppo is tranquil most of the time. There are no soldiers on the streets, and the nightlife that was suspended out of caution in the first months of the rebellion has returned to downtown and the outdoor cafés along Azizieh Square. But Aleppins of all faiths wonder, for how much longer?

On April 13, Good Friday for the Orthodox churches, I spent the morning walking through the Aleppo Citadel. Families traversed a stone footbridge, supported by seven Roman arches over a dry moat, from a pedestrian plaza at ground level ascending more than two hundred feet to the Citadel entrance. On the stone pavement in front of a row of outdoor cafés, a man in a Nike baseball cap played soccer with his son and daughter, about three and four years old. A few families were having breakfast, others coffee and soft drinks. A man pushing a kiosk on bicycle wheels sold cotton candy. The aroma of apple-scented Persian tobacco, smoked through ornate waterpipes by women and men, hovered in the air. In the dry moat, a half-dozen preteens played soccer. Since the conflict began in March 2011, no tourists have checked into the ancient hospital that is now the five-star Carlton Citadel Hotel. Its restaurant terrace, however, is filled with Syrians at lunch.

In the spring of 1987, also at Eastertime, I made notes in one of the local cafés just as I was doing twenty-five years later. Thousands of Christians were then visiting one another's churches and exchanging flowers, without provoking so much as an awkward glance from their Muslim neighbors. Unlike wartime Lebanon, where foreigners were being kidnapped, Syria then seemed solid, unchanged, and unchangeable, like the Soviet Union at that time. The Assad regime had been in power since 1970, the Alawite minority since a coup in 1966, and the Baath Party since 1963.

The combined military-party-family structure of Assad's regime had survived the two-year uprisings by Sunni Muslims under Muslim Brotherhood leadership in this city and in Hama that ended violently in the spring of 1982, with the killing of thousands of Sunnis by Hafez al-Assad's forces. Israel decimated Syria's air force and armor when it invaded Lebanon that summer. The president's brother, Rifaat, attempted a putsch in 1983. Two years later, Syria resumed control of Lebanon with American approval. It acquired a Lebanese ally, Hezbollah, whose steady humiliation of the Israeli army in south Lebanon helped Assad to raise his standing in the Arab world.

For all his political strength and canniness, Hafez al-Assad had a weak heart that made his mortality a source of opportunity for his enemies (Israel Radio announced his death about fifteen years early) and apprehension for his friends. He groomed his toughest, oldest son, as did his fellow dictators in the hereditary republics of Iraq, Egypt, and Libya, to assume power as naturally as the crown princes of Saudi Arabia, Jordan, Oman, and Qatar. That child, Bassel, died in a car crash in 1994, so a younger son, Bashar, was drafted from his London medical studies to assume his brother's place as heir. On his father's death in 2000, Bashar, with his British-born wife at his side, promised reforms that he failed to carry out. The Baathist slogan,

32

"Unity, Progress, Socialism," still plastered on the Citadel in 1987, was already fading from the assaults of sun and rain.

Syrians seemed in 1987, if not content, reconciled to a fate that was preferable to the regime of terror they observed in Saddam's Iraq to their east and the anarchy of Lebanon in the west. (The Lebanese Druze leader, Walid Jumblatt, said of Beirut's gunmen at the time, "They don't even obey the law of the jungle.") The type of mildly dissident intellectuals that Saddam Hussein would torture to death before assassinating their families would receive a dressing down from security officials and sometimes a few weeks behind bars to restore them to the path of Baathist righteousness. Torture was reserved for more serious dissidents, the army's would-be coup-makers, and also, after 2001, suspected terrorists discreetly transferred to Syrian custody by the CIA. It was cruel, it was efficient, and, until students demonstrated against it in the remote southern border town of Dera'a in March 2011, it seemed as strongly established as Aleppo's Citadel.

When Dera'a's students opened the gate of protest, almost everyone suddenly became a critic of the regime. Even servants of the state complained of corruption among the president's immediate family and the security services' use of surveillance, informers, detention, and torture to maintain elite privileges. The foreign media officer at the Ministry of Information, an attractive young woman named Abeer al-Ahmad, surprised me by offering introductions to "opposition leaders." They were, however, the "official" opponents, candidates for parliamentary elections. The regime permitted the campaign, along with a new constitution and ostensible suspension of the long-standing state of emergency, in order to give the appearance of meeting the demands of the peaceful opposition led for the most part by youth in the streets.

The young, born too late to have seen the regime's brutal suppression of the Muslim Brotherhood's rebellions in Aleppo and Hama between 1980 and 1982, came of age during an era of superficial reforms. After Bashar al-Assad succeeded his father in 2000, government schools abandoned military-style uniforms for primary and high school students and granted everyone access to modern telecommunications. (Under his father, even international news agencies needed government permission to install a fax machine.) This illusion of liberty seemed to whet an appetite for the reality. Youngsters who did not understand the older generation's experience of prison and torture ignored their elders' caution by calling on other youngsters to join them in the streets.

In the spring of 2012, I interviewed Orwa Nyarabia, a thirty-five-year-old film producer and organizer of the Damascus Film Festival. He was working with younger colleagues to organize peaceful demonstrations and street theater to undermine fear of the all-powerful, all-knowing regime. He confessed to embarrassment at avoiding arrest while youngsters in his office spent short periods in jail. For him, the protests that erupted in Dera'a in March of 2011 were not surprising. "It's been cooking for a while," he told me in the coffee shop of the Omayyad Hotel. "In my domain, documentaries, we showed films on dictatorship in Burma and China. The censors passed it, but the audience came out discussing Syria." When his film festival asked audiences to vote for best film in 2008, the newspaper headline was, "First free vote in Syria." He said, "The regime blackmailed us with accusations that we were about political provocation. I told them I'm a total liberal businessman."

Most regime opponents, apart from the "official" candidates, dismissed the parliamentary elections of May 7, 2012, as irrelevant. Most recall a joke told about the referenda staged every five years by Hafez al-Assad to endorse his tenure. An official brought him the results: "Mr. President, you have won again with 99.9 percent approval. Only 450 people voted against you." The president glowered. The official pleaded, "What more could you want?" The president replied, "Their names."

Nyrabia said that when young people in Dera'a campaigned to ban smoking in public places as far back as 2005, "It was really to have a campaign." The opposition is finding its way, learning from mistakes and making new ones. It lacks the experience of the regime, as well as the armory of control. "Two weeks ago, I was talking to the leader of a militia," Nyrabia, who is half-Alawite and half-Sunni, said. "There is a danger of becoming sectarian. They are becoming anti-Alawi rather than anti-regime." The reason for this, he and his friends believed, was that Saudi Arabia provided arms and funds to those rebels closest to its own Wahhabi ideology rather than to liberal democrats. This, combined with threats against those who don't share fundamentalist ideology from Syrian mullahs broadcasting on satellite television from Riyadh, frightens the minorities more than anything else about the opposition.

So far, as of Spring 2012, the regime is holding out. There have been few defections of senior officials, less an indicator of loyalty than of cold calculation that the opposition is a long way from achieving power. Few soldiers have deserted the army to join the rebels. Some people from Homs told me of their anger at the rebels' Free Syrian Army (FSA), whose strength remains unclear, for making their city the crucible of the revolution, then abandoning the populace to its fate when the regime counterattacked. The UN estimates that approximately ten thousand people were killed during the fighting between March 15, 2011, and April 22, 2012; other estimates are higher and lower. Thousands more fled from Assad's attacks on places such as Bashiriya in Syria's northwest.

SYRIA

Like Vichy France, Syria today is divided into regime supporters, *résistants,* and *attentistes* who await the outcome before choosing sides. Most of those I spoke to in all three camps rejected military intervention by the US, Britain, France, and, especially, Turkey to solve their problems. Armenian Catholic Archbishop Maryati recalled that many Armenians in Aleppo came from the massacres in Turkey and were forced to leave their country in 1915. "They found in Aleppo a secure shelter, have the rights of any Syrian, and became part of the Syrian identity. They had many martyrs who defended Syria. Psychologically and spiritually, we have some worries—especially intervention by Turkey. We are afraid to be forced into a new emigration."

Even the non-Armenian bishops who spoke to me in Aleppo and Damascus dreaded invasion by the Turkish Army. Turkey, they pointed out, does not allow churches to conduct services freely as Syria does, and it prevented Arabs in Hatay province, part of Syria until the French gave it to Turkey in 1938, from speaking their own language. In Syria, they can speak whatever language they want. Muslim children make up the majority in most of Aleppo's Christian-run schools where much of the teaching is in French. As the Armenians fear the Turks, Alawites and Christians fear Sunni Salafists who chant:

Massihiyeh ala Beirut,
Alawiyeh ala Taboot.
Christians to Beirut,
Alawis to the coffin.

Syria's anti-imperial history dates from its violent rejection of the French occupation from 1920 to 1945, when the French destroyed much of Damascus and other cities to maintain their rule. The near-universal view is that the US, which until 2004 turned over terrorism suspects to Syria for brutal treatment, objects less to the regime's repression than to its alliances with Russia and Iran. If the US and Israel are contemplating an attack on Iran's nuclear facilities, it would make sense to sever the link between Syria and Hezbollah in Lebanon to limit Hezbollah's ability to respond with rockets against Israel. Some Syrians fear that the revolution has become a tool of the US, Saudi Arabia, and Israel to defeat Iran.

That was not why the uprising began or why so many have become part of it. The perception that outside powers are changing the revolution's objectives can only rob it of popular support, particularly at a time when the regime has the upper hand militarily and opponents resort to sending car bombs into security buildings and into busloads of policemen—attacks that kill as many civilians as soldiers.

One Christian, who proudly demonstrated against Assad in 2012, said to me in a whisper, "I shit on this revolution, because it is forcing me into the arms of the regime."

CHAPTER THREE
OLIVE OIL SOAP

Aleppo, Autumn 2012

This year, Aleppo will produce no soap. The late-medieval souqs in which craftsmen fashioned blocks of the famous olive oil and laurel *savon d'Alep* succumbed to a conflagration during battles at the end of September. The Jubayli family's soap factory inside the Mamelukes' thirteenth-century Qinnasrin Gate survived the inferno, but relentless combat has left it inaccessible to workers and owners alike. By late November, following the harvest in the groves west of Aleppo, residue from the olive oil presses should be boiling in vats and poured onto carpets of wax paper stretched over stone floors. Sliced into two-by-three-inch blocks, the bars would be stacked to dry for six months before being sold. Deprived by war of the soap, fabrics, processed foods, and pharmaceuticals its region has so long produced, Aleppo is drawing on reserves of basic commodities, cash, and hope. All are dwindling rapidly.

"You don't need to go to Aleppo," an Aleppin friend in Beirut told me. "All Aleppo is here." Aleppo exiles, mainly the industrialists who provided much of the region's employment, were congregating in the cafés along Rue Hamra, some pro-regime, others anti-regime, delicately preserving friendships despite political disagreements. Playing bridge and backgammon, they await the day when it is safe to return, if it ever comes.

When I was in Aleppo last Easter, those mercantile expatriates had yet to leave and their businesses were functioning. Aleppo's soap was plentiful in the labyrinthine souqs of vaulted stone near the Citadel. Most people shared relief bordering on complacency that their city was avoiding the violence engulfing the rest of the country. Aleppo's cosmopolitanism, they seemed to feel, made it different. The only pogrom against its Christian minority had taken place in 1851, when the number of dead was small, and the crime was never repeated. The city's relative prosperity kept much of the population satisfied, despite the suppression of political opinion.

Aleppo was Syria's workshop and marketplace, and its region generated as much as sixty-five percent of the national wealth apart from oil. Factories making textiles from Syrian cotton, as well as medicines and furniture, dominated the industrial zones outside the city and provided work to thousands. The regimes of Hafez al-Assad since 1970 and his son Bashar since 2000 had left the gracious city center with little to rebel against, even if the rural poor—driven into the suburbs by drought, unemployment, and ambition—had legitimate complaints that went unnoticed in the lavish villas along the River Qoweik. Many of Aleppo's inhabitants were old enough to remember the last time the city was the scene of a rebellion, in 1979. Its outcome gave them little hope that a repetition would be anything other than disaster. Yet with the revolt in the countryside creeping closer on all sides, the ancient city had no more chance of remaining aloof than a log cabin in the midst of a forest fire.

In normal times, the best way to travel the two hundred miles from Damascus to Aleppo was by road, with a lunch break in the gardens beside Hama's Roman aqueducts. When the rebellion expanded in May 2011 from Dera'a in the south to Homs, cutting the Damascus-Aleppo highway, flying became a safer option. In April of this year, my flight was uneventful as was my taxi ride along the main highway into town where I checked into the welcoming, late-Ottoman Baron's Hotel.

On my return six months later, Aleppo's airport was nearly deserted. Taxis no longer risked the trip from town without the guarantee of a fare, so I had arranged for friends to send a driver they trusted. He grabbed my bag and ran to his car, turned the key in the ignition, and made a hasty sign of the cross. Then he broke into a sweat. About a quarter-mile from the airport, an abrupt U-turn took us off the highway to a deserted access road. The few buildings here had been hit by high-velocity ordnance and all of them, except a warehouse that Syrian government troops were using as a command post beside sandbags and a limp flag, were gutted and empty.

About a mile on, a truck-mounted antiaircraft gun on a bank above the road loomed into view. The driver turned back onto the desolate highway. Suddenly, burned tires, cement blocks, and debris blocked the road and forced us into what would have been oncoming traffic, had there been any. Gas stations were wrecked, and gasoline trucks lay charred beside the road. Rough cinder block houses for the poor stood on either side of us, pocked by artillery. A few miles further, as we entered the city proper, the driver relaxed at the sight of pedestrians and a few cars. Near a traffic roundabout, people at a makeshift street market were hawking bright red and green toma- toes, huge potatoes, eggplants, zucchini, apples, and pomegranates. The driver pointed at the carts, which had not been there in April, and said, "They wanted freedom. Here's their freedom!"

The city has acquired internal borders. On my first night back, a friend walked with me to the edge of the safe Sulaimaniya neighborhood. Where once we would have walked easily from Sulaimaniya into adjoining Jdaideh without noticing any difference, Jdaideh had become another world. Cars had been parked to block the entrances to its streets, and none of its lights were on. Sulaimaniya's street lamps shone on modern cafés filled with men and women enjoying coffee, sweets, or narghiles. Jdaideh, only fifty yards away, had been depopulated since the rebels entered it a month earlier. Wherever the rebels went, the army attacked them and residents fled.

I wanted to visit the souqs in the morning, but my friend told me that continued fighting there made it impossible. Who had burned the souqs a few weeks earlier? "That was the Free Syrian Army," my friend said. "We are caught between two bad powers. As you know, I don't like the dictatorship. But these people are showing themselves as worse."

Another friend said of the rebels who had come to dominate large swaths of his city: "They entered Aleppo. Aleppo didn't enter the conflict." He is a businessman, happy to be quoted last spring but now insisting I not print his name. Members of his family have been kidnapped, and he has paid large sums at the end of tortuous negotiations for their release. Where Aleppins once feared the state's many *mukhabarat*, intelligence agencies, they have become wary of additional retribution from the Jaish al-Hurr, the Free Army, and its associated militias. Another friend said, "The opposition thought Aleppo would welcome them. It didn't, except in the outskirts, where the very poor and the rural people came in." While espousing the revolution, some in the poorer districts nonetheless sought to exclude the rebels from their neighborhoods. For example, in Bani Zayd, where many people sift through the city's garbage to make a living, the district's elders delivered a letter to the Free Army:

We cheered the Free Army. But what is happening today is a crime against the inhabitants of our neighborhood. For there are no offices for government security or the *shabihah*. However, the groups that have taken position in the neighborhood cannot defend it. . . . We, the elders of Bani Zayd neighborhood, are responsible for making this statement and demand that battalions of the Free Army which have entered the neighborhood leave it and join battles on hot fronts. . . . This would ensure the return of calm to the neighborhood and would end the random shelling [by regime forces] of a poor neighborhood housing thousands of displaced people.

Bani Zayd's residents were natural supporters of the revolution, but their commitment did not extend to tactics that exposed them to regime retaliation. The Free Army's inability to defend most of the areas it occupied has turned potential supporters against it. What is the point, they ask, of inviting the regime to bombard an area that cannot be held? There was particular resentment in Aleppo toward the rebel occupation of the souqs in late September. Before that, the vast, covered marketplaces were much as a former Australian ambassador to Syria, Ross Burns, described them in his definitive study of Syrian antiquities, *Monuments of Syria: An Historical Guide*:

Largely unchanged since the 16th century (some go back as far as the 13th), [the souqs] preserve superbly the atmosphere of the Arab/Turkish mercantile tradition. In summer, the vaulted roofs provide cool refuge; in winter, protection from the rain and cold. While many of the products on sale have been updated, there are still areas where the rope-maker, tent outfitter and sweetmeat seller ply their trade much as they have done for centuries.

The majestic lanes of markets and ateliers were the city's commercial hub, but also the embodiment of its spirit. Although the rebels accused the regime of starting the fires, most people, even the rebels' supporters, blame the rebels. The Free Army followed its assault on the souqs with two one-thousand- and one five-hundred-kilogram bombs in cars near an officers' club and the main post office in Saadallah Jabri Square, the city's central park, on the morning of October 3. A Syrian journalist who witnessed the explosions that killed more than 40 people and left another 125 injured told me, "There are divisions within the Free Army. If it had a few hundred people, they could have occupied city hall and proclaimed Aleppo a liberated city." That they didn't was as much a measure of rebel disunity as of tactics that strike blows here and there without capitalizing on them.

The battle for Aleppo is a war for Syria itself. Another Aleppin who asked me not to print his name said, "If Aleppo falls, the regime will falter." In political and military terms, Syria's commercial capital is vital to both sides. Yet both the regime and its armed opponents are alienating the people they are ostensibly trying to cultivate, as they jointly demolish Aleppo's economy, the historic monuments that give the city its unique charm and identity, the lives and safety of its citizens, and the social cohesion that had, until now, made it a model of inter-sectarian harmony. Another friend confided, "The revolution died in Aleppo. They thought they would win the battle of Aleppo. They thought the people of Aleppo would support them."

Outside the city, the rebels launched an all-out assault on the industries that kept Aleppo alive, burning and looting pharmaceutical plants, textile mills, and other factories.

While the urban unemployed had good reason to support a revolution that might improve their chances in life, the thousands who had jobs at the beginning of the revolution and lost them when the Free Army burned their workplaces are understandably resentful. There are stories of workers taking up arms to protect their factories and risking their lives to save their employers from kidnappers.

Aleppo is under siege. Transporting heating oil for people to survive the winter has become a dangerous task. The price of *mazout*, the cheap diesel that heats most Aleppo homes, is now double what it is in Damascus, when people can find it. In Aleppo's center, where the Syrian Army maintains control with fortified positions, roadblocks, and regular patrols, the only commodity that seems to arrive without hindrance is food. Plentiful produce from local farms is on display on the open sidewalks that have replaced the burned-out fruit and vegetable stalls in the old souqs.

The government's brutal suppression of the rebels, especially the aerial bombardment of densely populated urban areas, has pushed some regime supporters into the arms of the opposition. One young woman, who told me in April that she loved Bashar al-Assad, said that she wept when she saw his air force bombing Aleppo. A physician, whose anti-regime views were familiar to me, said, "The majority of the Syrian people don't want Bashar al-Assad because of what happened in the last ten years. We want change, but not like this." This is a topsy-turvy war in which loyalties and animosities can no longer be predicted.

Syria's war is anything its fighters want it to be. It is a class war of the suburban proletariat against a state army financed by the bourgeoisie. It is a sectarian war in which the Sunni Arab majority is fighting to displace an Alawi ruling class. It is a holy war of Sunni Muslims against all manifestations of Shiism, especially the Alawite variety. The social understandings on which Aleppo prided itself are unraveling. Muslim fundamentalists have targeted Christian churches and Shiite mosques. Arabs have fought Kurds. Iraqi Shiites and Sunnis have crossed the border to fight each other in Syria.

Emigration, a remote option last April, has become common among those with the money, languages, and education to make livings outside. A civil engineer who has served years in prison for criticizing the regime said, "Syrians are destroying each other. Education, how to live together, it's all being destroyed. You can see it in the official workplaces. The attitudes are different. People who were not religious, even Communists, are becoming more religious."

One's choice of armies depends on experience. Those who have been tortured by government security forces look to the Free Army for deliverance, while anyone whose son or father has been kidnapped by the Free Army demands government protection. During the six months since my previous visit to Aleppo, opinions shifted in unexpected ways. The Christians were for the most part in favor of the regime or neutral, hoping to avoid the attentions of either side. Aleppo was quiet, though conflicts in the rest of Syria were clear harbingers of the earthquake about to hit. At the time, Mar Gregorios was convinced that the regime and the opposition could resolve their differences: "If we solve our internal problem and sit down and talk, we can have a constructive dialogue. We can gradually rebuild our society." As bishop of a small community of about two hundred thousand in Syria, he accepted that the regime had protected Christians while avoiding a commitment to either side.

Now, however, his worry has turned to fear. On the night I saw him in the sheltered confines of his rectory in the middle of Aleppo, he had just received a shock. "I was optimistic for the last weeks, but I visited my school today. Out of 550 students, only fifty are left." Along with his discovery that every day about twenty of his local congregation were receiving visas for foreign countries, the collapse of the school had changed him from the jocular, relaxed prelate I met in October to a profoundly shaken man with little hope for his country's future. "The issue now," he said, "is how to convince the president to step down." This was the first time I had heard a Christian bishop call for Bashar al-Assad to end the war by leaving office.

Didn't Mar Gregorios fear the Muslim Brotherhood? "If there is democracy, there will be rights for all the minorities," he said. "I don't think fanatics and the Muslim Brotherhood are planning to control this country. They plan to be a part." Walking back to the Park Hotel at the edge of the public gardens that evening, I heard in the distance the steady beat of artillery and machine-gun fire that no one in Aleppo can ignore any longer. It comes closer at times, then seems to recede to the outskirts, but it is always there, day and night.

Aleppins display a studied nonchalance as the bombs fall nearby. It is bad form to mention the fact that, at dinner, explosions are shaking the table. Yet the conflict is forcing them to make political choices for the first time. A scientist from a government ministry told me:

Five or six friends at work were waiting for the regime to finish. They said they will celebrate in Saadallah Jabri Square. In the last month, they changed their minds. One has a Ph.D. in agriculture. He was totally against the regime. He said we'll celebrate its fall. Then he came to me and said the Free Army came to his area and destroyed his house. They kidnapped four of his cousins. He told me the whole story. Now we wish the *mukhabarat* had taken them and not the Free Army. That is the big change.

One of the few activists who gave permission for me to quote him by name was Zaidoun al-Zoabi, a professor at the Arab European University in Damascus until his dismissal for political reasons last February. He lamented, "Aleppo has been destroyed. It was a city with the regime. No more. Now the regime is losing, but we are losing too. The country is being destroyed." Zoabi struggled to keep the original and peaceful revolution alive and was superseded by the armed rebellion. The young Syrian businessman whose family has long been at odds with the regime blames the armed opposition for trying to bring down the regime by force: "You cannot just break a regime like this, it is built to last. The regime is built for this." The regime, which in its early days immunized itself against coups d'état with the arrest of suspected dissidents in the army and constant surveillance, made itself rebellion-proof in 1979 as a result of an uprising in Aleppo.

The 1979 revolt provides an instructive comparison with the present rebellion. A May 1982 US Defense Intelligence Agency (DIA) report, "Syria: Muslim Brotherhood Pressure Intensifies," analyzed that insurrection and Assad's response: "In early 1979, encouraged by the Islamic Revolution in Iran, the Syrian Muslim Brotherhood developed a plan to trigger a similar popular revolution in Syria to oust Assad." The Brotherhood's first salvo was a massacre of eighty-three Alawite cadets on June 16, 1979, at the artillery school in Aleppo. That led to widespread arrests and gunfights in Aleppo's streets. By the following June, in the opinion of the DIA, "President Assad had broken the back of the Muslim Brotherhood challenge."

The Muslim Brothers who escaped evolved a two-pronged plan for insurgency and a coup against Assad by their sympathizers in the army. The DIA report stated:

> In early 1982, however, Syrian security uncovered the coup plot and began to intensify their operations against dissidents within the country. As a result, the Muslim Brotherhood felt pressured into initiating the uprising in Hama which began on February 2, 1982.

The Brotherhood hoped Aleppo, Homs, and other large cities would imitate Hama and usher in a new era. The other cities did not rise, and the Defense Brigades of Hafez's ruthless brother Rifaat annihilated the Brothers in Hama. The DIA put the number of probable casualties at two thousand, although later Amnesty International concluded that as many as twenty-five thousand people died.

For the Iranian Revolution of 1979, read the Arab Spring of 2010 and 2011. If Syria was not Iran, it isn't Tunisia or Egypt either. The new rebellion is pitting Sunni against Alawi and other minorities, but more importantly it seethes with the class resentments that the displaced rural poor acquired when they confronted urban luxury. Droughts between 2007 and 2011 exacerbated the hardships of country life, driving many people into Aleppo.

This was not new. In 1987, I spent time among the peasants along the Euphrates east of Aleppo. Their village, called Yusuf Basha, was earmarked for evacuation under a scheme to build a hydroelectric dam. Driving west back into Aleppo, I saw peasants drying wheat on the sidewalks as they did in their villages. I wrote:

Before, I had seen the city of Aleppo growing along the hill-tops, as the suburbs ate into the countryside. Now, I realised that the village had come to the city, planting itself outside and growing in. The poor farmers were bringing their customs, their ways, to cosmopolitan Aleppo, as they were to Damascus and Beirut. They were turning their apartments into compact versions of their mud houses—the families sleeping together in one room, cooking in another, washing in another, each room like one of the little huts around their yards. It was not poverty, but tradition, that put a whole family into one room. This was the only security they had in a city that was at once unwelcoming and alien.

That return to Aleppo, when I saw the city as new arrivals from the village did, was an enlightening moment. If Aleppo had accommodated the peasants and slowly absorbed them into the city's economic and cultural life, as it had in centuries past, they might not have welcomed rebels from backgrounds similar to theirs. Instead, the neoliberal economic policies that Bashar al-As-sad introduced when he succeeded his father in 2000 exacerbated their plight. The beneficiaries of these policies were newly privatized bankers, Bashar's cousins who obtained licenses to sell mobile phones, middlemen and brokers with urban educations and customs—not the newly landless trying without money or education to adapt to metropolitan life. For them to react as they are now doing is part of an ancient pattern I noticed on that return to Aleppo twenty-five years ago:

> For the first time in all my years in the Levant, I saw how corrupting the peasant and the bedouin found the city. Arab tradition said that every other generation brought a wave of reformers, religious zealots, from the desert to purify the city. It had happened in Saudi Arabia many times, lasting until the luxury of city life corrupted that generation's sons. I wondered whether it would happen in Syria.

Twenty-five years later, it is happening. An estimated forty thousand Syrians have paid with their lives, and another two million are displaced, four hundred thousand of whom fled over the borders to wait out the war as refugees. The increasingly well-armed opposition recently declared in Qatar that it was uniting in a Western-sponsored coalition, a self-declared unity that is fragile at best. Soon after, a number of Islamist factions said they rejected the coalition and wanted to establish an Islamic state. On November 20, the head of the Kurdish Democratic Union Party (PYD) also refused to join the coalition. With the regime remaining obdurate, all sides seem primed for a long and destructive war.

CHAPTER FOUR
ARAB SPRING, SYRIAN WINTER

Damascus, Autumn 2013

A dog in Lebanon, an old joke goes, was so hungry, mangy, and tired of civil war that he escaped to Syria. To the surprise of the other dogs, he returned a few months later. Seeing him better groomed and fatter than before, they asked whether the Syrians had been good to him. "Very good." "Did they feed and wash you?" "Yes." "Then why did you come back?" "Because I want to bark."

It is impossible not to sympathize with Syrians' desire to be treated like adults. The Syrian regime is not alone, of course, among Middle East dictatorships in regarding its people as subjects rather than citizens. Under the portrait of the great dictator, little dictators grant some supplicants permits, demand bribes from others, and abuse the rest. Syrians can identify with what Italians under Mussolini used to say: "The problem is not the big dictator. It is all the little dictators." Little dictators, though, thrive under the big dictator.

But all dictators are at risk from changed international circumstances, a spark (like a self-immolation in Tunisia) or the sudden realization that the regime is vulnerable. People in Syria have reasons to demand change, as they have in the past. But history has not been kind to Syria's desire for reform. During the First World War, Arab nationalists in Damascus wanted to rid themselves of Ottoman rule.

Ottoman officials could be corrupt and arbitrary, but they kept the peace, allowed the Syrians representation in the Istanbul parliament, and put no restrictions on travel within the empire. The nationalists collaborated with Britain and France. They ended up with British and French colonialism, contrived borders, the expulsion of three quarters of Palestine's population, insurrections, and wars.

At independence in 1946, Syria had a parliamentary system, even if landlords, urban merchants, beys, and pashas dominated it. Into the mix came the Arabian American Oil Company (Aramco), which announced plans in 1945 to construct the Tapline oil conduit from Saudi Arabia to the Mediterranean. Three countries on the route—Saudi Arabia, Jordan, and Lebanon—granted immediate permission. Syria's parliament, seeking better terms, delayed. The project stalled further when the Arab governments launched a war for which their colonially-created armies (with the exception of Transjordan's) were unprepared. When they lost, demonstrations condemned the corruption that had deprived soldiers of adequate resources. In Damascus, the protesters forced the government to resign.

The United States embassy in Damascus seized the opportunity to win Syrian approval for Tapline. The Central Intelligence Agency's man, Stephen Meade, approached the army chief of staff, Col. Husni Za'im, to arrange a coup. The Kurdish former Ottoman soldier took embassy money to foment an insurrection that justified his seizure of power in 1949. The embassy reported to Washington that "over 400 Commies [in] all parts of Syria have been arrested." Syria signed an agreement with Aramco in May and an armistice with Israel in July. Colonel Za'im antagonized sectors of society by raising taxes and attempting to give women the vote. Although he did not kill anyone, another colonel overthrew and executed him a month later. That colonel was eliminated by a third colonel. Thus began Syria's instability, with military coups as regular as changes of season. In the meantime, Colonel Za'im's suppression of the Communist Party produced, in the last free vote held in Syria, the election of the Arab world's first Communist member of parliament. The United States made two more major attempts in the 1950s to decide Syria's future—with Operation Straggle and Operation Wappen. Both failed. The era of chronic coups ended with the last one, Hafez al-Assad's, in November 1970. Syria enjoyed continuity, if not freedom, until the latest uprising was launched in 2011.

Revolutions elsewhere in the Middle East have also gone wrong, among them the Lebanese, Palestinian, and Iranian. In 1975, young Lebanese, every bit as idealistic as their Syrian counterparts in 2011, began a revolution against corruption and pseudo-democracy. It produced a fifteen-year war, foreign occupation, and devastation. The Palestinian revolution sold out, making the lives of the people it claimed to represent more wretched in the Israeli occupied territories and in exile (most obviously, in Lebanon and Kuwait). The Iranian revolution, begun as a coalition of hope in 1978, led to a regime more brutal and corrupt than the one it replaced. Revolutions produce surprising outcomes, and those who start them must be prepared for the unintended consequences of success as much as for failure. Alas, the course of the rebellion in Syria over the past four years emphasizes the point.

§

In 1987, I travelled by land through what geographers called Greater Syria to write a book, *Tribes with Flags*. I began in Alexandretta, the seaside northern province that France ceded to Turkey in 1938, on my way south through modern Syria to Lebanon. From there, my intended route went through Israel and Jordan. My destination was

Aqaba, the first Turkish citadel of Greater Syria to surrender to the Arab revolt and Lawrence of Arabia in 1917. For various reasons, my journey was curtailed in Beirut in June 1987. (I returned in 2002 to complete the sequel, *The Tribes Triumphant.*)

The ramble on foot and by bus and taxi gave me time to savor Syria in a way I couldn't as a journalist confronting daily deadlines. People loved to talk, linger over coffee and tea, play cards, and complain. One of the more interesting critics of President Hafez al-Assad's then seventeen-year-old Baathist regime was Hafiz Jemalli. Dr. Jemalli, a distinguished statesman and diplomat then in his eighties, had been a founder of the Baath Party. By 1987, he belonged to Syria's silent opposition.

"Everyone is afraid," he told me then. "I accepted to be a minister. Why? Because, if not, they put me in prison. Nobody has the courage to tell our president there is something wrong. Our president believes he is an inspired person, with some special relationship with God. If he is inspired, nothing is wrong. If there is some crisis, it is a plot, of Israel or America, but nothing to do with him, because he is inspired."

Many of the civilian members of the Baath Party, whose founders claimed to believe in secularism and democracy, deserted its ranks when the party took power in 1963. They rejected the militarization of the party, which kept power not through elections but by force of the arms of its members within the army. Among them was the father of Roulla Rouqbi, whom I met in 2012 at the Firdoss Tower Hotel that she managed in Damascus. Faissal Rouqbi had died a month earlier, which explained why the attractive fifty-four-year-old was dressed in black. A vigorous supporter of the revolution that began in Syria the previous year, she believed it represented the same struggle her father waged against one-party military rule.

"I was questioned twice by the security forces," she told me in the hotel's coffee shop, whose picture window looks onto a busy downtown street. "They did it just to show me they know what I am doing and that they are here." Young dissidents gathered in her coffee shop with their computers. Although the police cut the hotel's Wi-Fi connection, I saw several young people there discussing the rebellion, much as their forefathers did in the old cafés of the souqs that the French destroyed to put down their revolts, over strong Turkish coffee or, now, newly fashionable espresso.

Ms. Rouqbi detected a generational split in the conflict: "A lot of people here, nationalists of the old generation, are with the regime because they think it's against imperialism and the Zionist project." There was also an economic divide: "In Damascus, only the poor class is taking part. In Homs, all classes, all sects. It's really a revolution."

That was before the Arab Spring became the Syrian winter; before an uprising against dictatorship sparked by demonstrations against torture in the desert border town of Dera'a in 2011 degenerated into civil war. Syria had narrowly avoided prolonged civil conflict in 1982 during the Muslim Brothers' rising and in 1983, when Rifaat al-Assad put his troops on the streets to overthrow his brother. Faced with an uprising of democrats in 2011, joined later by Sunni fundamentalists, Hafez's son and successor as president, Bashar, moved to crush unarmed demonstrators with the same ferocity. The violent suppression of peaceful dissent led some opponents to take up arms in defense of the protestors. The armed men were a minority among dissidents who recoiled from the despoliation of their country that would inevitably accompany a violent revolt, yet they gained the ascendancy by the force of their actions and the international support they gained for their choice of the rifle over the banner.

As casualties mounted, advocates of a military solution dominated both the regime and the opposition camps. The center, inevitably, could not hold. Battles that had been limited to border zones, where rebels were easily supplied from Turkey, Jordan, and Lebanon, spread to the rest of the country. Damascus and Aleppo, whose populations had for the most part either supported the regime or opposed it without resort to weapons, became theaters of bloody confrontation. The rebels, advised by intelligence officers from western countries working in Turkey and Lebanon, seized outlying neighborhoods of Damascus. The regime used all its means to drive the rebels out and retake those areas. The next target of the rebels' strategy was Aleppo, where the pattern repeated itself: the rebels established themselves in the suburbs, residents fled and the regime returned with infantry, armor, and air power to "restore" order.

Many of the country's approximately twenty-two million people had a vested interest in the continuation of the Assad regime, even as others demanded change. On Assad's side were the minorities who had done well under his and his father's rule since 1970, his own Alawite community, other Shiite groups, most of the Christians, and parts of the Sunni merchant class. Against them stood fundamentalists, Syrians from every community whose families had felt the rough heel of injustice, and the young who were sickened by ways of governing that do not permit peaceful power transfers. But after living through two and half years of violent war, many of the young idealists I met at the café of Roulla Rouqbi's hotel when I returned in September 2013 were exhausted and discouraged. The café itself was nearly empty. "Stop the war. Stop the blood. The Syrian people are tired now," said Khaled Khalifa, author of the acclaimed Syrian novel *In Praise of Hatred*. He is fed up with the revolution he once longed for. "You can play revolution for some time," he said. "But not for a long time."

Peaceful activists were arrested, including Professor Zaidoun al-Zoabi of the Arab European University and film festival director Orwa Nyarabia. Zoabi and Nyarabia were not tortured, although Zoabi says he heard the screams of torture victims in nearby cells. Interrogators may have spared them such abuse because they belonged to what Graham Greene in *Our Man in Havana* called the "non-torturable classes." From prominent families, they were released and went into exile. Others were not so fortunate. One former protester told me, "I spent three days in jail, three days of hell. I've gone back to my job and stay out of politics." He fears ISIS more than the security forces who arrested him, and he tries to avoid them both. "The demonstrations are finished," said a young woman whose activism has given way to resignation. "That was the good time." The good time ended almost as soon as it began.

If the revolutionaries are exhausted, so is the government; more tired still are the country's civilians, who have borne the brunt of the suffering. According to the UN nearly two hundred thousand people had been killed as of April 2014, a figure acknowledged to be an underestimate, while hundreds of thousands more have been injured and maimed. Atrocities by both sides have become routine. On August 4, 2013, ISIS and other Islamist militias launched an offensive against Alawite villages in the hills above Latakia. A Human Rights Watch (HRW) report, *You Can Still See Their Blood*, estimated that the rebels kidnapped more than two hundred Alawite women and children before they withdrew twelve days later. Kenneth Roth, the executive director of HRW, described how government forces indiscriminately attacked civilians with rockets, cluster bombs, and other heavy weapons and used guns and knives to execute 248 civilians in a

Sunni enclave that May. But he and his organization also condemned Islamists in the opposition for massacres and the ethnic cleansing of civilians "on a smaller scale":

> Human Rights Watch has collected the names of 190 civilians who were killed by opposition forces in their offensive on the villages, including 57 women and at least 18 children and 14 elderly men . . . The evidence collected strongly suggests they were killed on the first day of the operation, August 4.

The FSA, which distinguishes itself from the Islamists by claiming to represent Syrians of all sects, dissociated itself from the killings. Nonetheless, it has continued to cooperate with extreme Islamist jihadis in other operations against the government. Sectarian killings and hostage-taking—largely of Alawites and Christians—by the rebels terrify the minorities, but they do not threaten the regime. Instead, they force communities to turn to the regime for protection without bringing the war closer to a conclusion. The UN's Human Rights Council condemned all factions, including the government, for atrocities and concluded, "There is no military solution to this conflict."

While armed struggle has indeed failed to end the war through outright victory, international diplomacy has done no better. The UN-Arab League initiative, led first by Kofi Annan, then by former Algerian foreign minister Lakhdar Brahimi and later by Staffan de Mistura, failed to break the impasse. While diplomats pursued talks about talks, Syrians died in their tens of thousands.

"Children are paying the heaviest price in this war," reported United Nations Children's Fund (UNICEF) Syrian director Yusuf

ARAB SPRING, SYRIAN WINTER

Abou Jelil in 2013. "Within Syria, four million children are directly affected. Two million are displaced in Syria. One million are on the front lines. One million are refugees." The escalation of suffering has reduced a country that fed itself before the war to living on international charity. Syria's medical and educational services, once among the best in the region, have been crippled. Children are suffering from malnutrition, and those in rebel areas have had difficulties receiving vaccines for polio, mumps, measles, and rubella. At the end of October 2013, the World Health Organization (WHO) confirmed an outbreak of polio among children in northeastern Syria. Dr. Annie Sparrow, a professor of public health at New York's Mount Sinai Hospital, described her conclusions from nearly two hundred interviews with Syrian medical workers and civilians in the border regions of Lebanon and Turkey:

> Over the past two and a half years, doctors, nurses, dentists, and pharmacists who provide treatment to civilians in contested areas have been arrested and detained; paramedics have been tortured and used as human shields, ambulances have been targeted by snipers and missiles; medical facilities have been destroyed . . . Five public hospitals have been taken over by the military, and there are no longer any left at all in the rebel-dominated cities of Idlib and Deir ez-Zour. Fewer than forty ambulances in the country still function out of the original fleet of five hundred . . . Now, more than 16,000 doctors have fled, and many of those left are in hiding . . . At least thirty-six paramedics, in uniform on authorized missions, have been killed by Syrian military snipers or shot dead at checkpoints.

As of February 2014, more than 2.4 million Syrians were registered as refugees abroad, while Refugees International estimated that approximately 6.5 million have been internally displaced. Together, that's more than forty percent of Syria's population. For many refugees, the rallying cries of the regime and of the armed opposition ring equally hollow. Some have been sheltered in tented camps in Turkey and Jordan, while others have found lodging within Lebanon with friends or relations or in disused buildings. Syrians, who earned an average of three hundred dollars a month when they had jobs, are paying rents of one hundred dollars a month or more to sleep in Bekaa Valley car parks or five hundred dollars for space above a garage. Others sleep rough and beg for sustenance in the streets of Lebanese cities.

The exiled Syrians are learning what Palestinians have known since their expulsion by Israel: refugee existence is demeaning, cruel, and crippling. Palestinian refugees themselves, 486,000 of whom are registered with the United Nations Relief and Works Agency (UNRWA) in nine camps in Syria, have suffered more in the Syrian war than at any time in all their stateless years since 1948.

§

In mid-March 2011, the people of Dera'a protested against the torture of children arrested for writing anti-government graffiti. Their demands were not revolutionary: dismissal of Dera'a's governor and the trial of those responsible for torture. But for the people to demand, rather than beg, for anything from their government had violent consequences. The children's courage emboldened their elders to march through the streets of Damascus, Homs, Idlib, and other cities to voice discontent, as they never had before. This was not a violent insurrection by religious obscurantists as in 1982. Rather, this was a popular movement that was finding its way, learning from its mistakes, and winning support.

As the protests spread, the regime responded, predictably, with gunfire, arrests, and torture. But many of the demonstrators sought to continue peaceful opposition that would garner more and more public support, even at the risk of their lives. Other oppositionists believed that only weapons would bring change and found outsiders willing to subsidize their methods. Regimes that were anything but models of democracy, namely Saudi Arabia and Qatar, poured in weapons and money. Turkey opened its border to arms, rebels, and refugees. Clandestine training and logistical help came from the US, Britain, and France. Protests turned to civil war. As in post-2003 Iraq, whose monuments and museums were ravaged, Syria's historic souqs and castles were burnt. Alawites and Sunnis, whose villages had coexisted through ages, turned on one another with Balkan ferocity. Christians were caught in the middle. Those who could do so fled.

The mosaic of cultures that made for Syria's richness was being lost.

The rebels calculated that, as in Libya, NATO would ensure their swift victory. The US decided that the regime was so unpopular that the rebels would overthrow it without NATO help. Both were wrong. Yet neither took the obvious alternative to the failed policy of violence: a negotiated settlement. Hillary Clinton, when she was US secretary of state, repeatedly said, as she did when Kofi Annan urged discussions between President Assad and his armed opponents, "Assad will still have to go." Her successor, John Kerry, took a more nuanced stance but did nothing to bring it about, while Britain and France devoted their energies to promoting arms transfers to the rebels. Russia and Iran have contributed primarily by sending weapons to the regime, and at least a half-dozen countries are meddling on the other side. Does anyone have the Syrians' well-being in mind?

Thomas Hardy, in his novel *The Woodlanders*, wrote of the knowledge required of anyone interfering with the lives of the people in his fictional Hintock:

> He must know all about those invisible ones of the days gone by, whose feet have traversed the fields which look so grey from his windows; recall whose creaking plough has turned those sods from time to time; whose hands planted the trees that form a crest to the opposite hill; whose horses and hounds have torn through that underwood; what birds affect that particular brake; what bygone domestic dramas of love, jealousy, revenge or disappointment have been enacted in the cottages, the mansions, the street or on the green.

Who in Washington, Moscow, Tehran, Riyadh, or Doha had that knowledge of Syria? Who among them foresaw the consequences of escalating the Syrian conflict with more weapons and money?

Hardy had in mind an outsider ignorant of Hintock's "bygone domestic dramas," a doctor named Edred Fitzpiers. Fitzpiers was treating the aged John South for an unnamed malady that appeared to be related to his fear of a tree growing outside his window. The doctor ordered: "The tree must be cut down, or I won't answer for his life." South woke the next morning and, seeing the hated tree gone, died. Fitzpiers said only, "D—d if my remedy hasn't killed him!"

CHAPTER FIVE
A FRATERNAL BLOODBATH

Tadamon, Damascus, Winter 2013

The commander is thirty-six years old. A few strands of white in his dark, curly hair make him seem older, as do his words. He points to six young men, posed like football players in a team photograph on a wall of his forward command post, and says, "Two are martyrs, two are prisoners, and two are still working." By working, he means fighting. Those recruits under his command were friends in their twenties. Of the two who died, he explains, "He was twenty-two years old when he was killed. And this one was martyred in June this year here in Tadamon."

Tadamon is a ragged neighborhood of Sunnis, Druze, and Alawites on the southern outskirts of Damascus, bordering the Palestinian refugee camp of Al-Yarmouk and perched astride the road to Jordan. The commander's makeshift headquarters in a battered apartment building, where he fields calls on military radios and cell phones, is less than two hundred yards from other Syrians determined to bring down the regime he is defending. Although a regular army officer with a degree from the military academy in Aleppo, he commands paramilitary brigades of half-trained young men and former army conscripts of the year-old National Defense Forces (NDF). They protect their neighborhoods and, on rare occasions, take part in offensive operations. The NDF includes former members of the unpopular *shabihah*, mainly Alawite gangs whom the regime recruited at the beginning of the rebellion to add depth to the overstretched regular army. The commander provides his NDF troops with basic training, uniforms, weapons, ammunition, communications, and leadership.

"Most of the fighting is done by NDF fighters," he says, "because they are the inhabitants of the region and know the region well." On the other side are troops from the FSA and its erstwhile allies the Nusra Front, ISIS, and other extreme Salafist militias. Some rebels are as familiar with the terrain as the NDF, because they too come from Tadamon. The commander knows many of their names. "You cannot imagine that some of our neighbors from this street here are now fighting on the other side against us," he says. "During some clashes on the front, they called us by name." He tells me that the previous commander on the other side was Nabil al-Laqoud, who came from Dera'a. "He was killed last year in Abu Trabi Street." The commander asks me not to publish his own name, because he is speaking to me without authorization.

The commander and his opponents hole up in shattered buildings, fire small arms at each other, and wait. What they are waiting for is unclear, but it is not a military triumph. Neither side has achieved that in almost three years of fratricidal bloodletting. Instead, daily attrition decimates Tadamon and the rest of Syria without the decisive battles that would bring the war to a conclusion. The street fighting has begun to resemble the civil war in Lebanon, where opposing forces faced each other across a Green Line for fifteen years without either defeating the other.

The house where we drink coffee and discuss the war was in rebel hands a year ago, before the government recaptured most of the area. Part of Tadamon remains under rebel control, and the commander does not expect to conquer it soon. "There are more important fronts than Tadamon," he says, and then names three: "Jobar. Barzeh. Qaboun." Those contested districts in the north of the capital control access to Homs, Hama, Aleppo, and the ports of Tartous and Latakia. Rebel positions in Jobar are within mortar range of the city's largest Christian districts. The insurgents frequently hit churches, houses, and public squares in the districts of Kassa', Bab Sharqi, and Bab Touma. One afternoon in Kassa', the Syrian novelist Colette Khoury showed me a bullet hole in her study window as well as handfuls of cartridges and shrapnel that she clears each day from her balcony. "We will die," she says, "but we will stay." Rebel damage to Damascus is minor compared to the government's heavy artillery barrages on the rebel-held suburbs.

The commander says his sector has "been secure since last year," when a government offensive restored regime control over several outlying sections of Damascus. Areas that were inaccessible or under bombardment when I visited last year have become safer, and there are quarters where going out to restaurants for dinner is normal again. Government gains in Damascus were matched by rebel success in the north of the country, where short supply lines from Turkey helped them to hold or besiege large parts of Aleppo and to launch the ethnic cleansing of the Alawite heartland near Latakia.

A car bomb was detonated near the commander's office forty-eight hours before we met, ripping the façades from most of the buildings. Within hours, the little shops at street level were back in business. Tadamon's inhabitants adapt to an endless staccato of automatic rifles and mortar rounds, making their way from home to work, taking their children to school, and visiting hairdressers, bakers, and butchers. Old men sit outside, absorbed in backgammon or gossip, ready to seek shelter when a mortar falls or a sniper's bullet comes close. A Druze friend, who lives in Tadamon with his wife and children, told me he likes the area because it has a mixture of religious groups and it feels safe.

Tadamon is nonetheless a free-fire zone of checkpoints, kidnappings, and hostage exchanges that force adversaries to negotiate. To reclaim the body of a young fighter named Ribal, who had been a third-year English literature undergraduate at Damascus University, the commander engaged a local woman to act as a messenger to his opposite number, the local leader of the rebel FSA. The commander explains:

> We exchanged the body of Ribal for eight or nine prisoners. Later, what was happening, some of my men told me the wife of this same leader was outside [the rebel area]. So, I sent my men and they brought her here. I brought her very gently, for some days. She was treated well, and no one harmed her. I telephoned her husband and said, "Hello, your wife is here." . . . I told him, "She is well, but we need some things from you." "Like what?" There were five women hostages kidnapped since the invasion of Al-Yarmouk camp. There was an exchange. I sent him his wife, and I sent him some medicine, a gift from me to him. He sent me a gift, a pistol, to begin a new friendship. His wife told him she was well treated. Sometimes, I telephone him and his wife answers. She always asks, "How are you?" This war created new kinds of relations in Syria.

The commander later sent his adversary packages of cigarettes and bread, both difficult to find in rebel areas under government siege.

Dialogue with the FSA is desirable, he believes, because it is for the most part secular. I ask whether it is possible that the army and the FSA might one day unite against the Sunni Muslim extremists of the Nusra Front and ISIS. "I expect that," he answers. "Look at the paradox. Salim Idris, the commander of the FSA, was our teacher at the academy in Aleppo." He speaks of Idris with respect and affection, praising two books he wrote on electronics.

Idris, a Syrian Army general before he defected, has failed to find common ground with his Islamist allies. The FSA and the Islamists have fought one another for control of areas near the Turkish border. General Idris's assessment of his allies is candid: "They do not want to create a unified formation because, in all honesty, they have private goals: they all just want to be leaders themselves." In an interview with the Saudi-financed daily *Asharq Al-Awsat*, Idris accused the Islamists of playing the regime's game:

> The Syrian regime says [to the FSA] do not fight us, and that those fighting the regime are a set of extremist foreigners who want to slaughter minorities. But look at things objectively and honestly, when these groups, like ISIS, come and execute a child in a public square, what message does this send to the world? Exactly the message that Assad wants to send to the world.

The war has reached the stage at which neither side regards the other as human, let alone as citizens of a country in which all must coexist. The introduction of chemical weapons, allegedly used by the government and rebels, was only the most dramatic escalation by combatants who seek nothing short of the annihilation of the other side. As Islamist rebels pursue the ethnic-sectarian cleansing of Alawite villages in the northeast, the government batters the rebel-held, mostly Sunni Muslim suburbs of Damascus and the old city of Homs. The population that survives the violence is contending with famine, disease, and exposure to the extremes of Syria's summers and winters.

The deployment of poison gas in the eastern Ghouta on the edge of Damascus on August 21, 2013, unexpectedly led to hope for a way out. The Russians compelled President Bashar al-Assad to relinquish his chemical weapons to the United Nations, creating a diplomatic opening to revive the Geneva conference that the US and Russia promised the previous May. Russia had delivered President Assad, who agreed to attend without preconditions. The US, however, was slow to persuade the militias it funds or those armed by its Saudi, Qatari, and Turkish allies to attend. When the use of chemical weapons underscored the urgency of stopping the carnage, the US persuaded a few opposition leaders to negotiate at Geneva, albeit conditionally.

Veteran Moroccan diplomat Mokhtar Lamani, the UN-Arab League representative on the ground in Syria since September 2012, told me: "If there is no political solution, I would not be surprised to see a genocide." Lest I misunderstand him, I asked him to repeat what he said. In slightly different form, he stated: "The ingredients are there for a genocide in a few months." He did not say whether he meant a genocide by government or rebel forces or both.

Lamani's mission has taken him to rebel and government areas in all parts of the country. He is on first-name terms with Assad, Assad's senior advisers, cabinet ministers, and defense chiefs. He has had face-to-face encounters with rebel commanders in the field. His expeditions required crossing dangerous checkpoints through uncharted and fluid terrains of government and rebel forces. He somehow achieved guarantees from all parties not to fire on his convoys or to kidnap him. After he came to know the rebels, he continued his communications with them less intimately but more safely via Skype.

Lamani shared the view, asserted by Jane's Terrorism and Insurgency Center (JTIC) and other analysts, that the opposition comprises more than a thousand groups with at least one hundred thousand fighters. For Geneva negotiations to succeed, representatives of at least half the rebels and the non-violent opposition—consisting of the National Coordination Committee for Democratic Change and the Local Coordination Committees—must attend and be prepared to sign an agreement that few of them will find palatable. Lebanon's warring militia leaders were forced into such negotiations at Taif, in Saudi Arabia, in 1989, ending fifteen years of "no victor, no vanquished" warfare. The regional powers, backed by the US, forced the Lebanese warlords to amend the constitution and, except for Hezbollah, to surrender their weapons. No one was satisfied, but the war stopped. When I asked a Western diplomat who works with the Syrian opposition for his assessment of the preparations for Geneva, he answered in one word, "chaos." Lamani seemed almost as fearful of the state of diplomacy over Syria as of the military stalemate: "It's much better not to have a Geneva than to have a failed Geneva."

Comparing Syria to Iraq, where he served as Arab League representative from 2000 to 2007, Lamani said, "It's even worse here." Syria has become the venue of what he calls "a proxy war" or wars: the United States versus Russia; the Sunni theocracies of Saudi Arabia and Qatar against the Shiite theocrats of Iran; and Turkey versus Arab nationalists over the attempted restoration of Turkey's pre-World War I regional dominance. The peaceful protestors' original demands in

2011 for reform and justice are as forgotten as, two years and millions of deaths into the Great War, was Austria-Hungary's July 23, 1914, ultimatum to Serbia.

While Syrians do most of the fighting and dying, both sides have welcomed foreigners into their ranks. Iranians and Lebanese Shiites reinforce the government army, while Sunni jihadis from more than forty countries have become the revolt's shock troops. They are less concerned with majoritarian democracy than with deposing a president whose primary offenses they consider to be his membership in an Islamic sect, the Alawites, that they condemn as apostate, and his alliance with Shiite Iran. An International Committee of the Red Cross (ICRC) worker who, like Lamani, has worked on both sides of the barricades, said, "If there are secularist rebels, I haven't met them."

Nearly everyone wants intervention, but they disagree on its form. One view is that massive military force of the kind that the United States can provide will end the war by deposing the dictatorship. The other is that the United States must force mutually antagonistic rebel factions to meet at Geneva to discuss a transition to a freely elected government. Disbanding the army and abolishing government services, as the US occupation did in Iraq, would be anathema to most Syrians. Bashar al-Assad remains the sticking point for both sides. The opposition insists that he resign immediately, while he and his supporters claim that he is crucial to a successful transition.

If there were a genuine election, the opposition would divide its votes into so many rival candidates that they would hand the presidency back to Assad. Many fear that a victorious Assad would emulate his father's revanchism following his bloody repression of the Muslim Brotherhood's uprising at Hama. Hafez al-Assad's biographer, Patrick Seale, described the elder Assad's sudden appearance in the streets of Damascus on March 7, 1982: "That day it was a new Asad, brutal and vengeful, who roared: 'Brothers and sons, death to the criminal Muslim Brothers! Death to the hired Muslim Brothers who tried to play havoc with the homeland!'"

A few samples from my discussions over the past month in Damascus give the flavor of the debate about negotiations. A former political prisoner said, "Geneva will not happen. Nothing will be fixed until an external force comes to Syria. No one has control here, not the regime, not the Free Syrian Army, not America. He [Assad] will fight to the last Syrian." A normally conservative Sunni businessman echoes this view: "Geneva II is bullshit. There is no will to stop on either side."

By contrast, the acclaimed novelist and peaceful oppositionist Khaled Khalifa, who remained in Syria at that time rather than live a safer life in Europe, said, "All of the intelligentsia has left Syria. We need Geneva." The Greek Catholic Patriarch of Syria, Gregorios III Lahham, said, "Let's go all together to Geneva." For him, it is the only way to staunch the permanent flow of his congregation of 350,000 from the country. Minister of Information Omran Zoabi said, "The external opposition doesn't want to go to Geneva, because Geneva will produce a political solution. And they choose to fight." Yet fighting achieves only the country's unremitting destruction.

There are limits to what a Geneva meeting can achieve. Louay Hussein, one of the internal opposition leaders who is working with the government, said, "My ambition is that shortly after Geneva there will be a possibility for a real political life inside Syria and the emergence of leaders within Syria. This is a hope, not a certainty." At this time, for most Syrians, suffering the daily grind of this war of attrition, it is not even a hope.

As elsewhere in Syria, the war in the Tadamon quarter has reached stasis. Europe's Western Front must have been like this for long periods of World War I. Instead of trenches, shelter takes the form of two- and three-story apartment buildings. All that is missing is a Christmas truce of the kind that allowed British and German troops to play soccer with one another in 1914. For the most part, WWI was confined to uniformed troops, but Tadamon's battlefield mixes soldiers and half-trained militiamen with an estimated eighty thousand civilian men, women, and children. Before the war, they lived here peacefully, and those who survive will probably do the same when the armed groups leave. No one, however, dares to predict how many more will die before that comes to pass.

CHAPTER SIX
A SHATTERED MOSAIC

Aleppo and Damascus, September 2014

Sir Mark Sykes, in his *Dar Ul-Islam: A Record of a Journey through Ten of the Asiatic Provinces of Turkey* (1904), observed: "The population of Syria is so inharmonious a gathering of widely different races in blood, in creed, and in custom, that government is both difficult and dangerous."

Yet the history of Syria's fragile mosaic is one of surprising co-existence and tolerance. Take Ahmad Badreddine Hassoun, who recounted a drive he and his wife made from Montreal via Toronto to New York in 1994. Somewhere past Niagara Falls, they stopped at a McDonald's. All the seats were taken. "I was dressed like this," Hassoun said, pulling at the lapel of his robes, "and my wife was in *hijab*." An American man, aged about sixty-five, got up and offered them his table. When Hassoun declined, the man insisted, "I'm an American, and I can go home and eat. You are my guest."

The gesture impressed Hassoun, who became grand mufti, or chief Sunni Muslim religious scholar, of Syria eleven years later: "A good human being is a good human being. I don't know if that man was Jewish, Christian, or Muslim." Mufti Hassoun belies the stereotype of the Muslim clergyman. He has preached in the Christian churches of Aleppo, Syria's second city, and he has invited bishops to speak in his mosque. His official interpreter is an Armenian Christian. "I am the mufti for all of Syria, for Muslims, Christians, and non-believers," he says, an ecumenical sentiment placing him at odds with more fundamentalist colleagues among the religious scholars known as the *ulema*.

The contrast with many other Sunni Muslim clergymen is stark. Another Syrian mullah, Sheikh Adnan al-Arour, broadcasts regularly from Saudi Arabia with a different message:

> The problem is actually with some minorities and sects that support the regime...and I mention in particular the Alawite sect. We will never harm any one of them who stood neutral, but those who stood against us, I swear by Allah, we will grind them and feed them to the dogs.

Another Sunni preacher, the Egyptian Sheikh Mohammad al-Zughbey, went further: "Allah! Kill that dirty small sect [the Alawites]. Allah! Destroy them. Allah! They are the Jews' agents. Kill them all . . . It is a holy jihad."

"I don't believe in holy or sacred wars or places," Hassoun told me. "The human being is sacred, whether Muslim, Christian, Jewish, or non-believer. Defend his rights as if you are defending the holy books." His tolerance and acceptance of the secular state in Syria have earned the mufti condemnation as a mouthpiece for a repressive regime and threats from Salafist Muslims, whose interpretation of Islam excludes tolerance of atheists, Christians, and Shiites. Yet the mufti's views are not atypical in Syria, where Islam and Christianity have co-existed for fifteen centuries, and which the Greek poet Meleager of Gadara called, in the first century BC, "one country which is the whole world."

The world of communities dwelling in Syria includes its Sunni Muslim Arab majority alongside a multitude of minorities: Sunni Kurds; Armenian and Arab Christians of Catholic, Orthodox, and Protestant denominations; Assyrians; Circassians; Kurdish-speaking Yazidis, with their roots in the teachings of Zoroaster; and the quasi-Shiite Muslim sects of Druze, Ismailis, and Alawites. The Syrian population included a few thousand Jews, descendants of ancient communities, until 1992. The country is one of the few places where Aramaic, the regional lingua franca at the time of Christ, is still spoken. In the Aramaic-speaking village of Maaloula, it was not unusual for Muslim women to pray with Christians for the births of healthy children at the convent of Saint Takla.

During centuries of productive co-existence, there were only two outbreaks of sectarian conflict that resulted in massacres. Both took place in the mid-nineteenth century, when Christians were accumulating wealth thanks to their association with Christian businessmen from Europe. In the first, a minor incident in Aleppo in 1850 sparked a Muslim massacre of Christians and the burning of several churches. No more than a dozen Christians were killed, but many more lost property to looters and vandals. Ten years later, a similar incident in Damascus led to the massacre of eleven thousand Christians. Nineteenth-century Christians were close to the Europeans who came to dominate the country's economic life, and today's Christians and Alawites are seen as too close to a regime that many Sunni Muslims detest as much as their ancestors did the Europeans. Those who prospered under Assad family rule fear a revolution that might repeat that bloody history.

§

It took less than a year for the armed militias that coalesced into the nominally non-sectarian FSA and the Islamic Front to supersede the pro-democracy demonstrators of 2011. The FSA predicated the success of its rebellion on a repetition of the western air campaign that deposed Muammar Qaddafi in Libya. "When that failed to materialize," Patrick Cockburn wrote in his enlightening *The Jihadis Return: ISIS and the New Sunni Uprising*, "they had no plan B." Without the air support they demanded, the FSA-Islamic Front offensive ground to a stalemate. ISIS came along to supersede the FSA, as the FSA had replaced the protesters. ISIS was more combative, more ruthless, better financed, and more effective, using mobility across the desert in Syria and Iraq to launch surprise attacks. Suicide teams in bomb-laden trucks opened the way into regime strongholds that rival rebels had merely besieged. Moreover, ISIS achieved the one objective that eluded the FSA: it brought American airpower into the war, but not in the way the FSA wanted. Instead, the Syria war produced an opposition to Assad so repellent and so antagonistic to western allies in the region that when the air intervention came, it arrived in the guise of the regime's ally in all but name.

The unwillingness of both the regime and the armed opposition to compromise plunged the country ever deeper into war. The increasingly militarized and sectarian character of the opposition saw both sides murdering unarmed civilians—effectively, the Lebanization of the conflict. When I visited Damascus in September 2014, I met a young woman who brought out a smart phone from her handbag and asked, "May I show you something?" The phone's screen displayed a sequence of images. The first was a family photograph of a sparsely bearded young man in his twenties. Beside him were two boys, who appeared to be five and six, in T-shirts. The young man and his sons were smiling. Pointing at the father, the woman said,

"This is my cousin." The next picture, unlike the first, came from the Internet. It was the same young man, but his head was severed. Beside him lay five other men in their twenties whose bloody heads were similarly stacked on their chests. I looked away.

Her finger skimmed the screen, revealing another photo of her cousin that she insisted I see. His once happy face had been impaled on a metal spike. The spike was one of many in a fence enclosing a public park in Raqqa, a remote provincial capital on the Euphrates River in central Syria. Along the fence were other decapitated heads that children had to pass on their way to the playground. The woman's cousin and his five comrades were soldiers in the Syrian Army's 17th Reserve Division. ISIS had captured them when it overran the Tabqa military airfield, about twenty-five miles from ISIS headquarters in Raqqa, on August 24, 2014. The family's sole hope was that the young man was already dead when they cut off his head. There was no question of returning the body or holding a funeral. The woman explained that her cousin had recently turned down a chance to leave his unit for a safer post near his home. It would not be right, he reasoned, for him, as a member of Syrian president Assad's minority Alawite sect, to desert his fellow soldiers who were Sunni. He stayed with them, and he died with them.

The first victims of a war in Syria were always going to be the religious minorities. The Alawites and the Christians, who each comprise about ten percent of the population, have found security under the Assad regime. The Alawites—whose doctrines are related to those of Shia Islam, and whose rule is opposed on principle by many Sunnis—are concentrated in the west near the Mediterranean. The Syrian government does not publish casualty figures by sect, but martyrs' notices pasted on the walls in Jabal Alawia, the Alawite heartland in the hills east of the port of Latakia, indicate that the

Alawites have suffered a disproportionate share of deaths in the war to preserve the Alawite president. A myth promulgated by the Sunni Islamist opposition was that the Alawites have been the main beneficiaries of forty-four years of Assad family rule over Syria, but evidence of Alawite wealth outside the presidential clan and entourage is hard to find. The meager peasant landholdings that marked the pre-Assad era are still the rule in Jabal Alawia, where most families live on the fruits of a few acres. Some Alawite merchants have done better in the seaside cities of Latakia and Tartous, but so have Sunni, Druze, and Christian businessmen. This may explain in part why, from my observations, a considerable proportion of Syrian Sunnis, who comprise about seventy percent of the population, did not take up arms against the regime. If they had, the regime would not have survived.

The Alawite monopoly of the armed forces is, like much of Syria, a legacy of foreign intervention. As Dr. Hafiz Jemalli, a Baath Party founder, told me in 1987, "When we resisted the French, we had to act as a unified people. Now we are divided. We are Muslim. We are Alawi. We are Druze. We are Christian. How did it happen? Syria in the 1940s was liberated from sectarianism, but now we are divided into sects. The army is now composed of Alawi officers. A majority of our army is a minority of our people. It comes only by chance?" Alawi dominance of the armed forces began under French rule, when Sunni and Christian Arab nationalists refused to serve in the army of the occupier. The French recruited among the smaller minorities, especially the Alawis who had been persecuted by the Ottomans.

The rising number of Alawite young men killed or severely wounded while serving in the army and in regime-backed militias has led to resentment among people who have no choice other than to fight for President Assad and to keep their state's institutions intact. Their survival, as long as Sunni jihadis kill them wherever they find them, requires them to support a regime that many of them oppose and blame for forcing them into this predicament. After my friend's cousin and his comrades were decapitated at Tabqa and their corpses left on the streets of Raqqa, ISIS publicly executed another two hundred captured soldiers. It was then that someone, said to be an Alawite dissident, declared on Facebook, "Assad is in his palace and our sons are in their graves."

Many Christians view the opposition's driving force as Sunni fundamentalism battling secularism. The fundamentalists would deprive them, as well as secular Sunnis, of social freedoms. Gregorius III Lahham, the Melkite Catholic Patriarch of Antioch, warned early against the "criminals and even fundamentalist Muslims who cry for *jihad*. This is why we fear that giving way to violence will only lead to chaos." An Armenian high school teacher, whom I have known for many years, became uncharacteristically loquacious when explaining her support for the Assad regime. She told me in Aleppo in 2012, barely a year into the rebellion:

I'm free. I am safe. . . . "You're a *kafir* [unbeliever]": I have not heard that phrase for thirty years. At the school, some of my friends are Muslim Brothers. They respect me, and I respect them. Who is responsible for that? . . . Look at this terror. Is this what Obama wants? Is this what Sarkozy wants? Let them leave us alone. If we don't like our president, we won't elect him. From a woman who is sixty years old, and I've been free for thirty years. I should be afraid to go out? I should cover myself? Women should live like donkeys? . . . We are citizens. We are equal.

She, along with many other residents of Aleppo, installed a steel-reinforced front door to her house. Tales of the rape, kidnapping, and murder of Christians in Homs, the city halfway between Aleppo and Damascus that became the bastion of the revolution, created unease among their coreligionists throughout Syria. At the same time, cameras have recorded civilian deaths there from attacks by government forces. In Aleppo, bombs that damaged buildings occupied by the security forces took with them nearby Christian apartments, schools, and churches. The chaos led to large-scale emigration of the Christian communities who have lived in Syria for two millennia. "Many Christians have left," Dr. Samir Katerji, a fifty-eight-year-old architect and member of the Syrian Orthodox Church, told me in mid-2012. "Many Armenians have bought houses in Armenia. Even the Muslims are leaving." Katerji, who designed the amphitheater for outdoor films in the Aleppo Citadel, had "visited my aunt's house," a local euphemism for going to prison, several times. The security services arrested him for his outspoken criticism of the Assad regime and the Baath Party. "I feel the majority of the Syrian people is against this government," he told me over a drink in his office. "It's a very bad government. Governments and armies everywhere are dirty, even the Vatican."

Many opposition members of minority communities insist that their security is part of the historical nature of Syria rather than the gift of the regime that came to power with Hafez al-Assad's bloodless coup of November 1970. A Christian woman, who spent several months in prison for unspecified political crimes a few years ago, told me, "It's wrong to say the government was helping the minorities. They are using the minorities."

Fear forces people into the ostensible safety of sectarian or ethnic enclaves, repeating a pattern established during the civil war in Lebanon and the American occupation of Iraq. Mixed neighbor-hoods, so prominent a feature of Syrian life now and in the past, are making way for segregated ghettos where people feel safe among their own. Nabil al-Samman, an engineering professor in Damascus, wrote ominously in *Syria Today*, "The current crisis proves that you cannot depend on the government, but only on your immediate family, your tribe, and others' charity." Some Christians who fled from Homs following vicious fighting there between the army and the dissident FSA blamed Muslim fundamentalists for seizing their houses to use as firing positions. Others left because of the violence or the threat of kidnapping, rape, and murder. Alawites loyal to the regime in and around Homs are accused of killing Sunni men and raping Sunni women, while the rebels are blamed for committing the same crimes against Alawites. The effect has been the same: to drive each out of the other's areas and into tribal *laagers* that further divide the country into armed and hostile camps.

Mufti Hassoun's criticism of the opposition has been stronger than his criticism of the state. He has received death threats. "When I refused to leave Syria," he says, "they threatened me on my cell phone," referring to callers whose numbers were in Saudi Arabia. "They left messages." When he did not answer, his enemies took their revenge. On October 2, 2011, his twenty-two-year-old son, Sariya, was driving with one of his university professors from the country-side to Aleppo when armed men fired on their car and killed them both. The mufti recalled the murder in our conversation, wiping tears from his cheeks: "He was twenty-two years old, a student at the university. What did he do to be killed? At his funeral, I said I forgive you all. I expected them to show remorse. They said we don't need your forgiveness. We are going to kill you. They say this on televi-sion in Saudi Arabia, Egypt, and Britain. They say the mufti of Syria speaks of Christianity in a positive way. He believes in dialogue, even with Israelis and non-believers. He goes to churches. They say I do not represent Islam. When you say a mufti does not represent Islam, it's a *fatwa* to kill him. This is the Arab revolution."

While lamenting Syria's lack of basic political freedoms, including free speech and assembly, Samir Katerji acknowledged that "we have social freedom. We are free to declare our thoughts and beliefs and to practice our Christianity." He condemned murderers within the regime, but he had no faith in its armed opponents: "Inside the opposition are also murderers who will not allow stability." A year later, Katerji emigrated to the United States.

CHAPTER SEVEN
FRIENDS LIKE THESE

Damascus, Summer 2015

Syrians used to tell a joke about a survey that asked people of different nationalities, "What is your opinion of eating meat?" This was during the Cold War, so people in Poland answered, "What do you mean by 'meat'?" In Ethiopia, the response was, "What do you mean by 'eating'?" But in Syria, the universal response was, "What do you mean by 'what is your opinion'?"

Nothing much has changed, as Syrians confront the choice between a government they never voted for and a violent opposition dependent on foreign powers. Think back to when this mess began, which was a long time before young Mohamed Bouazizi burned himself to death in Tunisia. It was about the time the British and the French decided to save the Arabs from the Ottoman Empire's oppression. "A man may find Naples or Palermo merely pretty," James Elroy Flecker, poet and one-time British vice-consul in Beirut, wrote in October 1914, "but the deeper violet, the splendor and desolation of the Levant waters, is something that drives into the soul." A month later, Russia, Britain, and France declared war on the Ottoman Empire in response to the Turkish fleet's foolhardy bombardment of Odessa and Sevastopol. Throughout Ottoman lands, where they had for centuries exercised considerable influence, consular staff from the Allied states departed their posts. Flecker died of tuberculosis barely a year later, aged thirty, in the Swiss Alps, leaving behind a few dreamy letters and poems like "The Golden Journey to Samarkand." François Georges-Picot, a French consular officer in Beirut, also withdrew after war was declared. His legacy was a packet of letters implicating local notables in a conspiracy to detach Syria from the Ottoman Empire. Georges-Picot had lodged his papers at the American consulate and a dragoman there turned the evidence over to the new Turkish military governor, Jemal Pasha. Jemal had the twenty-five Christian and Muslim plotters tried for treason, found guilty, and hanged, some in Damascus and the rest in Beirut on the site of what would subsequently be called, in their honor, Martyrs' Square.

The sultan's subjects who conspired with the French consul were naive in colluding with a power that had no intention of granting them independence. Britain and France, with imperial Russian collusion, had been operating under a 1916 secret agreement to divide the Ottoman Empire into British and French zones. The secret treaty, negotiated by Georges-Picot and Sir Mark Sykes, carved borders across a region that had not known them before and whose people did not want them. The new borders fragmented the region without settling the contradictions among competing nationalisms, and in 1917 Britain's Balfour Declaration added the complication of European Zionism. Britain's paramount concern was not what the Syrians wanted or needed but what *The Times* of London on August 21, 1919, called "the traditional rights and interests of France in Syria."

The inhabitants' own conceptions of what constituted the nation and its frontiers varied. Some believed in a Lebanese nation made up of Mount Lebanon and, possibly, the coastal cities and the Bekaa Valley. Others were Syrian nationalists, whose patrimony was

Greater Syria, which meant all the territory south of Antioch as far as the Red Sea, including the future mini-states of Syria, Lebanon, Palestine, and Transjordan. Most of the rest were Pan-Arabists, who sought the unity and independence of Arabic-speaking peoples from Morocco to Iraq. Between 1914 and 1918 all these nationalists united against the Ottomans, in opposition to the majority of their fellow subjects, who were either loyal to the empire or indifferent to nationalism's appeal. These differences would play out in the decades following the Ottoman retreat. It's hard, however, to dispute the notion that the subjects of the empire were better off under the Ottomans than under the British, the French or the later regimes in Damascus, Beirut, and Tel Aviv.

On the rare occasions when Syrians have been asked their opinion, their preferences were ignored. The most famous instance was the King-Crane Commission of 1919, when more than eighty percent of the petitioners demanded full independence and the continued unity of Syria, which then comprised today's Syria, Lebanon, Jordan, and the areas that became Israel and Turkish Hatay (or Alexandretta). Most inhabitants favored a constitutional monarchy under the leader of the Arab Revolt, Emir Feisal. A year earlier, however, Feisal had learned from British General Edmund Allenby that his struggle, in which he raised a force of nearly thirty thousand men from all parts of Syria, had been futile.

T. E. Lawrence was present at the Feisal-Allenby meeting on October 3, 1918, in newly conquered Damascus and later wrote in *Seven Pillars of Wisdom*:

Allenby gave me a telegram from the Foreign Office, recognizing to the Arabs the status of belligerents; and told me to translate it to the Emir: but none of us knew what it meant in English, let alone in Arabic: and Feisal, smiling through the tears which the welcome of his people had forced from him, put it aside to thank the Commander-in-Chief for the trust which had made him and his movement.

More significantly, although Lawrence did not mention it in *Seven Pillars*, Allenby told Feisal that France would assume the government of Syria. The Arabs had risked their lives not for freedom, but for British and French domination.

On July 24, 1920, French troops crossed from Beirut over Mount Lebanon to the Maysaloun Pass, and defeated the cavalry of General Yusuf Al Azmeh. They expelled Feisal and imposed the so-called Mandate over little Syria and Greater Lebanon. Al Azmeh, the brave former Ottoman general who had been Feisal's minister of defense, gave his life to save the country from foreign domination, as did twelve hundred Arab fighters. It was too late. Damascus fell to France, although the "natives" rebelled continuously throughout the quarter-century of French rule.

Soon after the French conquest of Damascus, *The Times* admitted that Feisal had "maintained public security throughout 1919 and 1920, along the desert edge of Syria, to a degree never attained by the Turks." Of course, this standard is comparative only, and his government was emphatically run by Syrians for Syrians. But he was a ruler of a country broken by four years of war; deprived of customs duties (that had been more than half the revenue) by the terms of the Sykes-Picot Treaty; distracted by the activities of his Turkish, French, British, and Zionist neighbors; and deprived of all foreign advice and technical assistance.

On August 7, 1920, *The Times* reminded its readers that Feisal's army had been in effect an adjunct of the British army during the war:

The Arab army was equipped from the stores of the Egyptian Expeditionary Force in Cairo, and it was accompanied in the field by a small staff of British specialists in irregular war, who acted as advisers and as liaison between Feisal and Allenby.

As a British tool, Feisal's Arab army had to accept British occupation of Transjordan and Palestine, and French dominion in Syria and Lebanon. France, having seized Syria, proceeded to divide it into four mini-states. Most Sunnis and Christians were Arab nationalists opposed to French rule. They refused to serve in the *Troupes Speciales du Levant* that became the Syrian Army, so the French recruited impoverished Alawite peasants. The Alawite foothold in the armed forces was one legacy of that brutal twenty-five years of colonial rule, a legacy that lies at the root of Syria's present crisis. The Alawites, whose daughters were mistreated as household servants in Damascus until recently, helped the French to crush nationalist rebellions in the 1920s. When the CIA sponsored the army coup that destroyed Syria's parliamentary democracy in 1949, the way was open for Alawite officers (whose survival over centuries of religious intolerance had required them to be master conspirators) to come to the fore in 1966.

When Bashar al-Assad said that "Britain has played a famously unconstructive role in our region on different issues for decades," he was not, then, far off the mark. A country that, with France, imposed and modified the borders it drew across Ottoman Syria under the Sykes-Picot agreement carries historic baggage. A country that has done nothing since June 1967 to end Israel's occupation and annexation of Syria's Golan Heights has a way to go to prove its *bona fides* to a skeptical Syrian audience. And a country that, from the current rebellion's outset, predicted and sought the imminent downfall of the Damascus regime may find it hard to play the role of honest broker.

In 2012, a new armed force, calling itself the Free Syrian Army, seized many Syrian towns and parts of its main cities. Like Feisal's volunteers, its members were a mixture of idealists and opportunists. There were other similarities: they received weapons, training, and commands from outsiders; they had no idea what demands the foreign powers—among them the old imperialists Britain and France, as well as the United States, Turkey, Saudi Arabia, and Qatar—would make of them if they should seize power in Damascus; and they did not know where their insurrection would lead the country.

When the rebellion's foreign patrons discuss Syria's fate, their own interests will inevitably prevail—as Britain's and France's did in 1920—over the desires of a "native government."

§

Today Syrians are surrounded by more new-found friends than a lottery winner. Not since the old Soviet Union signed all those "treaties of friendship" with everyone from Bulgaria to Afghanistan has one country had so many new pals. On one side, Russia and Iran have supplied weapons, ammunition, and diplomatic cover for President Assad. On the other, there is the Group of Friends of the Syrian People, a collection of 107 countries and organizations modeled on the Friends of Libya who cheer-led NATO's air war in that country. Where, you might ask, have these friends been hiding for the past fifty years? What were they doing in 1967 when Israel seized the Syrian Golan? What support did they send to more than one hundred thousand Syrian citizens when Israel demolished their villages and expelled them from their homes? What was their reaction to

Israel's illegal annexation of the Golan in 1981? Have they taken a stand against the thirty settlements that Israel planted on property stolen from Syrians? Are they calling for sanctions against Israel until it withdraws from Syrian territory, dismantles its settlements, and permits Syria's Golan citizens to return home?

Would it be churlish to suggest that Syria's friends want something from Syria for themselves? You know the answers. So do the Syrians.

George W. Bush was eyeing Syria when he left the White House, and, as in so much else, the Obama administration has taken the policy further. On March 5, 2007, Seymour Hersh, whose American intelligence sources are second to none, wrote in *The New Yorker*:

> To undermine Iran, which is predominantly Shiite, the Bush administration has decided, in effect, to reconfigure its priorities in the Middle East. In Lebanon, the administration has co-operated with Saudi Arabia's government, which is Sunni, in clandestine operations that are intended to weaken Hizbollah, the Shiite organization that is backed by Iran. The US has also taken part in clandestine operations aimed at Iran and its ally Syria. A by-product of these activities has been the bolstering of Sunni extremist groups that espouse a militant vision of Islam and are hostile to America and sympathetic to Al Qaeda.

When Syria erupted in 2011, the US and Russia turned up with flame-throwers. Four years after the firing of the first shots, a conflict which screamed from the outset for a diplomatic settlement was perpetuating itself with outside help, for outside interests. External

support has not merely escalated the killing but, mirroring fratricidal struggles from Spain in 1936 to Yugoslavia in 1992, made it
ever more personal and vicious. No hands are clean. No one, apart
from the undertaker, is winning. Yet it goes on and on with each side
certain of the justice of its cause.

The CIA has been arming and guiding gunmen near the
Turkish border, as it once did anti-Sandinista Contras along the
Honduran-Nicaraguan frontier. To avoid Congressional scrutiny
as it did in Nicaragua, the US turned to Saudi Arabia. The British
have run anti-Syrian government operations from Lebanon. France
has played a similar role from both Turkey and Lebanon. Russia
and Turkey still vie for influence in a country whose citizens hate
them both. If Syria's friends set out to destroy the country, they have
done well.

For outsiders, whose own countries are not the chessboard on
which this game is played, war makes more political capital than the
more subtle and difficult route of negotiation and compromise. Yet
which is more likely to preserve Syria, its secularism, its economy
and the healthy relations among its communities—civil war, as in
Spain, Lebanon, and Yugoslavia, or the example of Nelson Mandela
meeting the enforcers of apartheid? When the British government
and the Irish Republican Army swallowed pride and distaste to
negotiate seriously, rather than win outright, the war in Northern
Ireland ended.

The record of foreign military intervention is, to put it mildly,
less impressive. Dissidents, journalists, and mullahs who call for foreign forces to fight in Syria have only to look next door to Lebanon.
During its long war, every foreign power that got involved burnt
its fingers and escalated violence for the Lebanese. The Palestine
Liberation Organization (PLO) ostensibly responded to an appeal

from Lebanon's Sunni Muslims for help in obtaining equality with the Christians. When the PLO left in 1982, their movement was badly wounded and even the Sunnis were glad to see it go. Syria intervened at various stages of the war on behalf of the Christians, the Palestinians, and the Shiites. Its departure in April 2005 was welcomed by the vast majority of Lebanese. Israel came in 1982 promising to help the Christians. When it left in 2000, not even the Christians had a good word for them. As for the US's brief encounter with Lebanon in 1982–83, the less said, the better. Do the families of the 241 American service personnel killed in the suicide bombings of October 23, 1983, believe the price was worth paying?

§

In October 2014, ISIS militants murdered another western captive, Alan Henning. Henning, like his fellow humanitarian worker David Haines, had gone to Syria out of compassion for its people in the midst of a vicious civil war. His sympathy and bravery did not matter to ISIS any more than the pleas for mercy by the Henning and Haines families. ISIS beheaded both men as it did the American journalists James Foley and David Sotloff and more recently American aid worker Abdul-Rahman Kassig. The western world appears to be powerless to protect any of these captives.

No one can be sure how many of the journalists and aid workers who have gone missing in rebel-held areas of Syria are in ISIS hands, but it is a fair bet that the group will threaten many more executions in the months and years ahead. ISIS has not hesitated to behead Syrian, Iraqi, and Lebanese civilians and captured soldiers, and it uses the public murders as propaganda to recruit jihadis rather than as a negotiating ploy. It has also enslaved, sold, and raped hundreds, perhaps thousands, of Kurdish-speaking

Yazidi women, as the United Nations Assistance Mission for Iraq (UNAMI) and the Office of the UN High Commissioner for Human Rights (OHCHR) have reported.

There is no magic formula to bring the hostages home, but Turkey has demonstrated that it can persuade ISIS to release captives. In September, ISIS set free the 49 Turkish hostages it kidnapped in Mosul on June, 11, 2014. Turkey denied that it paid ransom, which may or may not be true. While it attributed the release to a "rescue operation," there was no evidence of a struggle, which means the "rescue" was more likely diplomatic than military. Turkey's past support for Islamic fundamentalists in Syria has given it leverage that made ransom irrelevant, because Turkey holds the power to deny ISIS access to arms, fighters, and equipment from its territory.

When I was in northern Syria in September 2014, Armenian villagers told me they had seen Turkish military vehicles bringing Islamist fighters to the border to conquer Armenian villages in the area of Kessab the previous March. Turkey is not the only enabler of the Islamist fundamentalists who have kidnapped and murdered Syrians, Iraqis, and westerners for the past four years. Two other Middle East allies of the United States and Britain, namely Qatar and Saudi Arabia, funded the groups that became ISIS throughout the Syria rebellion against President Assad.

American Vice President Joe Biden admitted as much to Harvard University's John F. Kennedy Forum:

> And what my constant cry was that our biggest problem is our allies—our allies in the region were our largest problem in Syria. The Turks were great friends—and I have the

greatest relationship with [Turkish president Recep Tayyip] Erdoğan, which I just spent a lot of time with—the Saudis, the Emiratis, etc. What were they doing? They were so determined to take down Assad and essentially have a proxy Sunni-Shia war, what did they do? They poured hundreds of millions of dollars and tens, thousands of tons of weapons into anyone who would fight against Assad except that the people who were being supplied were al-Nusra and Al Qaeda and the extremist elements of jihadis coming from other parts of the world.

What Biden neglected to say was that US allies conducted that policy with the knowledge of the Obama administration, which did nothing to stop it. The weapons supplied to the fanatics were manufactured in the US. American intelligence in Turkey knew which rebels Turkey, Qatar, and Saudi Arabia were assisting. Moreover, the moving forces within ISIS, including its mercurial leader Abu Bakr al Baghdadi, were graduates of the American prison system in Iraq, where previously non-political Sunni Muslims became radicals.

ISIS's brutal rise has complicated the alignment of foreign forces in Syria. In 2014, the United States reversed its policy from threatening to bomb the Syrian regime to bombing its enemies. This gave the regime hope. It saw that not only would it survive, but that it would become, however covertly, a partner of the nations that had worked most assiduously to remove it. Although I left Syria just before the US began bombing ISIS-held towns, with the predictable civilian casualties and targets that turned out to be grain silos and private houses, Syrian officials were anticipating American involvement with satisfaction.

Contacts with the US had been underway at least since June 20, 2013, when Syrian presidential adviser Bouthaina Shaaban met former US president Jimmy Carter and former assistant secretary of state for Near Eastern affairs Jeffrey Feltman in Oslo. Feltman was attending a conference as a newly appointed UN official, but he still had his State Department connections. Officials present at his meeting with Dr. Shaaban recounted a conversation in which Feltman told her, "We know President Assad is going to stay, but you know what President Obama said. So, how can we solve the problem?" Having said for four years that Assad must go, Obama had yet to explain why Assad can, for the time being, stay. This change would not be unusual for an American president, since the recurring theme in US-Syria relations throughout the Assad era has been one of hostility followed by cooperation—that is, cooperation when both sides needed it.

During the early years of Hafez al-Assad's rule, which began in 1970, Richard Nixon and Henry Kissinger refused all dealings with the ostensibly pro-Soviet ruler. The October 1973 war, launched by Egypt and Syria to regain territories Israel occupied in 1967, put an end to that. Kissinger flew to Damascus in December 1973 and wrote later:

> Withal, I developed a high regard for Assad. In the Syrian context he was moderate indeed. He leaned toward the Soviets as the source of his military equipment. But he was far from being a Soviet stooge. He had a first-class mind allied to a wicked sense of humor.

The US opened an embassy in Damascus in 1974 and enjoyed a brief honeymoon with Assad *père*, until his meddling in Lebanon

made him persona non grata again in Washington. A near victory
by Palestinian commandos in Lebanon's civil war in 1976 prompted
Kissinger to ask Assad to send his army into Lebanon to control the
PLO and save Lebanon's Christians.

By 1982, the US was again fed up with Assad for giving aid
to Yasser Arafat. That turned out to be disastrous for Arafat.
Syrian tolerance of his actions only worsened his situation and
that of his people as Palestinian commandos had a part in dividing and ruining Lebanon. Ronald Reagan let the Israelis expel
the PLO and Assad's army from most of Lebanon. A few years
later, when Hezbollah was making life unbearable in West Beirut
and Westerners were easy pickings for kidnappers, the first Bush
administration invited Syria back into the areas that its army had
evacuated in 1982. This was followed by another freeze in relations that ended when Bush and his secretary of state, James Baker,
asked Syria to take part in the war to expel Iraq from Kuwait.
Assad obliged, making him a temporary hero at the White House
if something of a pariah to those of his citizens who were Arab
nationalists.

After September 11, 2001, the US rendered terrorism suspects
to Syria for torture. That relationship ended with the assassination
of former Lebanese prime minister Rafic Hariri in 2005 and Syria's
humiliating withdrawal from Lebanon after it was accused of conspiring against Hariri. If his father survived the ups and downs of
that seesaw, young Bashar, who succeeded him in 2000, has a good
chance of riding out a rebellion that has become, as he had prema-
turely claimed at its inception, an uprising of fanatics and terrorists
who wanted to take Syria into a dark age.

As Bashar's prospects improve with each American sortie against
his enemies in the east of the country, Damascus and the populous

towns to the north have been enjoying a respite of sorts from war. The Syrian Ministry of Education reported that, of the twenty-two thousand schools in the country, more than seventeen thousand reopened on time in the middle of September 2014. Needless to say, almost all of the functioning schools are in government-held areas. The souqs in the old city of Damascus, unlike their more extensive and now destroyed counterparts in Aleppo, have remained open. Shops selling meat, vegetables, spices, and other basic items to the local population have thrived, although the tourist boutiques in and around the famous Souq Hamadieh had no customers apart from UN workers and a few diplomats. At night, restaurants in most neighborhoods are, if not full, nearly so. Everything from wine to grilled chicken is plentiful, albeit at prices higher than before the war. Traffic remains heavy, although somewhat less obstructed since June 2014, when the government felt confident enough to remove many of its checkpoints. Electricity has been intermittent, and those who can afford private generators relied on them in the off-hours.

In September 2014, I stayed in an Ottoman palace converted into a hotel in the old city of Damascus. Every morning I would hear the roar of Syrian warplanes. They ran bombing missions on the suburb of Jobar, not more than a few hundred yards from the old city's walls. Most of Jobar's inhabitants fled long ago, and its buildings have dissolved to rubble under relentless shelling. The rebels are said to be safe underground in tunnels that they or their prisoners have dug over the past two years. They fire the occasional mortar, which the Damascenes ignore. People in the city refuse to see and hear the violence in their suburbs, much as Beverly Hills ignored riots in Watts in 1965 and 1992. It becomes easy to pretend there is no war, unless a bomb falls too close or kills someone you know. One morning as I was driving through the upscale Abu Roummaneh quarter, a rebel mortar shell whistled overhead, hit a fuel storage tank, sending black smoke soaring into the sky. Yet the shoppers around the corner went on as if nothing happened.

Jobar was one of the few outlying areas of the capital still in rebel hands in late 2014—the government having subdued the rest. It has recaptured some, like Mleiha on August 14. In others, a UN official said, the strategy has been subtler. Commanders from the warring sides make local agreements not to fight one another. "Local agreements for them are just stages of their military strategy," said a United Nations official involved in talks between the two sides. "Fragment areas. Isolate them. Besiege them, until the people understand that they are not going to win the war and are going to negotiate. The opposition calls this a policy of kneel or starve . . . The government uses the term 'reconciliation.' We call it 'surrender.'"

A young Druze friend, who like the rest of his community has struggled not to take sides, said, "People are exhausted. Even those who fought the regime are moving toward reconciliation." It is hard to blame them when two hundred thousand Syrians have died and another nine million have become refugees inside and outside their country in a war that has, to date, achieved nothing except death and destruction.

"It's a lot quieter in Damascus," admitted a UN aid worker, "but there are other places that are on fire." Yet the fire is burning far to the north and east of Damascus, many miles from the heartland of populated Syria. The roads west to Lebanon and north from Damascus to Homs look as if central Damascus has become a green zone that is contiguous with the regions the regime considers vital to its survival. The first sight as I drove on the highway north out of the capital was the district of Harasta, destroyed and mostly deserted. Then came Adra, an industrial town that was brutally

captured last year by Islamists who massacred its Alawite inhabitants. Shortly after I drove past, the government took it back and
invited its industrial workers to return.

Further north, the highway crosses open land of farms and
peasant hamlets. In 2013, the route there was not safe. Bandits and
rebels alike set up flying checkpoints to steal money or cars and to
kidnap those who looked prosperous enough to afford ransom. It
was a no-go zone for minority sects like the Alawites, Ismailis, and
Christians, as well as for visiting Westerners. A year later, the atmosphere has changed. The rebels in Homs, said in 2011 to be the cradle of the revolution, surrendered their positions to the government
and left with their light weapons in May 2014. Only the district of
Al Wa'er, about a mile from the old city, remains in rebel hands and
under regime siege. There is a tense and regularly violated truce, but
the city is mostly quiet. Some civilians are returning home, even to
houses that must be rebuilt after four years of fighting. Christians
fleeing from areas taken by ISIS and the Islamic Front groups have
found temporary refuge in an Armenian church in the city, and the
local aid organizations help people of all sects.

By mid-2014, rhe road west from Homs toward the sea was safe
for anyone not allied to the rebels. The famed Krak des Chevaliers
Crusader fortress, from which rebels shelled the highway and nearby
villages, had returned to government hands. So had the towns of
Qosair and Qalamoun, which the rebels used to keep their lines of
supply open to Lebanon. The road runs through fields where the
apple harvest has begun and the olives would soon be collected. The
coastal city of Tartous is buzzing with life, as if there had never been
a war. The ferry to Arwad Island, where families go for lunch, runs
every twenty minutes. Farther north, the port of Latakia has suffered
shelling only on the rare occasions that rebels took positions in the

Alawite hills above it until the army quickly pushed them back. It may sound odd to anyone outside Syria who has followed the conflict, but the beach in front of my hotel in Latakia was filled with families swimming and not a few women in bikinis.

There was fear, however, that a major onslaught by ISIS and similar jihadi groups would put an end to these pockets of ordinary life. It is hard for Syrians to accept that the countries in the Gulf and elsewhere that supported ISIS with arms, financing, and fighters are now signing up to an American coalition to bring it down. Yet ISIS may have gone too far, even for its backers. The caliphate that it declared in parts of Syria and Iraq struck a strong chord with Islamist fanatics in Saudi Arabia, Qatar, Turkey, and other states that had facilitated the group's rapid and rabid expansion. These states must fear that the movement they brought to Syria will haunt them. "It's like the lion tamer," an Arab diplomat in Damascus told me. "He feeds and trains the lion, but the lion might kill him at the right moment."

CHAPTER EIGHT
WAR DRUMS' SAD RHYTHM

Damascus, Autumn 2015

Folk memories endure, mothers' and grandmothers' sagas trumping documents in neglected archives. What will Syria's youth, when they are old, tell their children? All will have stories of cowering in flimsy houses while bombs fell, of deadening existence in refugee camps or of escapes through treacherous seas and perilous highways to uncertain lives in strange lands. My maternal grandmother left Mount Lebanon, then part of Syria, as a child in the late nineteenth century during a confrontation between the Christians of her village and their Ottoman rulers. Although her father was killed a few months before she was born, she told me many times how he faced Turkish troops on horseback as if she had witnessed it. I don't know what really happened; but her stories, including of a river that was so cold it could crack a watermelon in two, remain undeniable truths to her descendants.

Syrians have endured a brutal, unending ordeal replicating the drama of their ancestors during a prior war exactly one century ago that their families, novelists, and poets preserved for them. What we know as World War I was to Syrians, *Seferberlik*, which roughly translates to "travel across the land," when in only four years, military conscription, forced labor battalions, machine-age weaponry, arbitrary punishment, pestilence, and famine undid all that the Ottomans had achieved over the previous four centuries. The Palestinian sociologist Salim Tamari saw that period as

> four miserable years of tyranny symbolized by the military dictatorship of Ahmad Cemal [or Jemal] Pasha in Syria, *seferberlik* (forced conscription and exile), and the collective hanging of Arab patriots in Beirut's Burj Square on August 15, 1916.

Turkey's institutionalized sadism added to the woes of Syrians, who grew hungrier each year due to the Anglo-French blockade that kept out, as American and European Union sanctions did after 2011, many of the basic staples needed for survival. No part of Greater Syria from the Red Sea north to Turkey avoided the cataclysm. An economics professor at Beirut's Syrian Protestant College wrote at the time, "You never saw a starving person, did you? May the Almighty preserve you from this sight!!!" Rafael de Nogales, a freebooting Venezuelan officer in the Ottoman army, recorded that

> Aleppo kept on filling up with mendicant and pest-stricken deportees who died in the streets by the hundreds, and infected the rest of the population to such an extent that on some days the funeral carts were insufficient to carry the dead to the cemeteries.

The locust infestation of 1915 and hoarding by Beirut's grain merchants aggravated a famine so severe that there were tales of cannibalism. Hana Mina, a Syrian novelist born just after the war, wrote in his novel *Fragments of Memory*, "During the *Safar Barlik*,

WAR DRUMS' SAD RHYTHM

mothers . . . became like cats and ate their children." A half-million out of four million inhabitants in Greater Syria perished from starvation, disease, and violence.

The events since March 2011 have recreated the suffering of a century earlier: malnutrition, starvation, epidemics, the exodus of most of the population to other parts of Syria or to foreign lands, the brutality of the combatants, the traumatization of children, and Great Power preference for victory over the inhabitants' well-being. An anonymous Syrian poet, in words his twenty-first-century countrymen might echo, wrote:

The Drums of War are beating their sad rhythm
And the living people, wrapped in their shroud
Believing the war will not last a year. . . .
Dear God, may this fifth year be the end of it.

That fifth year, 1918, was the end of it, but this century's Syria war continued unendingly year after year with the battles transferred to the northwest corner of the country occupied by the Turkish Army and jihadi militias and under attack by the Syrian Army of President Bashar al-Assad.*

I have covered the Syria war off and on since the beginning, driving across the border from Lebanon whenever a suspicious Ministry of Information approved my visa request. In 2014, the regime seemed to be gaining the upper hand. The rebels had evacuated Homs, the first city they conquered. Jihadis had withdrawn from the Armenian village of Kessab near the Turkish border in the northwest, and

---

*In early March of 2020, Russia and Turkey hashed out an unstable ceasefire that involved joint Russian-Turkish military patrols and a disengagement corridor seven miles deep, running the length of Syria from west to east. The war reached another of its many phases, and peace remained elusive.

Assad's army was encroaching into the rebel-held Damascus suburbs. The rise of ISIS, which was soon to rebrand itself the Islamic State (IS), was causing the foreign supporters of the rebellion to recalibrate and consider Assad less villainous than the fanatics who threatened to export the war to the West itself. Popular complaints focused on electricity shortages, loss of wages, the hazards of sporadic rebel shelling and other mundane hardships.

By the time of my September 2015 visit, all had changed. The regime was in retreat. It lost Idlib province in the north. Jihadi forces backed by Turkey surrounded the vital commercial entrepôt and cosmopolitan center of Aleppo. The jewel of the desert, the ancient Roman and Arab city of Palmyra, was in the hands of IS militants who tortured and beheaded an eighty-two-year-old antiquities scholar and destroyed one ancient monument after another. Young men emigrated to avoid being drafted to fight for any side in what seemed to them an eternal and inconclusive war.

The few who remained were sons without brothers, who cannot be conscripted under Syrian law, which recognizes the loss of an only son as the end of a family. As in World War I, conscription led to a surfeit of women supporting their families by any means necessary. Inflation was around forty percent. Estimates of territory held by regime opponents ran from the United Nations' sixty-five percent to the *Jane's* report of eighty-three percent, while the UN estimated that anywhere between sixty and eighty percent of the population still within the country lived in areas held by the government. Migration from rebel-held areas into the capital had, as measured by the company that collected city waste, multiplied Damascus's population five times, from about two million before the war to ten million in 2015. Elizabeth Hoff, WHO director in Syria, said, "Nine out of ten people in Damascus hospitals are not from Damascus. They come from Raqqa and elsewhere." Raqqa was then held by IS.

Supporters of the original uprising of 2011 imagined a quick victory over the dictator along the lines of what happened in Tunisia, Egypt, and Libya. A Syrian friend of mine, living in exile, told me that American Ambassador Robert Ford tried to recruit him to take part in a government that he promised would shortly replace Assad's. When the French ambassador to Syria, Eric Chevallier, left Damascus on March 6, 2012, barely one year into the war, he told friends that he would be back when a post-Assad government was installed "in two months." The government-in-waiting that Ford and other Western diplomats had hoped to install in Damascus collapsed amid internal squabbling and a lack of committed fighters.

The only forces fighting with success against the Assad regime were Sunni Muslim holy warriors who destroyed all that was best in Syria: its mosaic of different sects and ethnic communities—including Christians, Druze, Turkmen, Yazidis, and Kurds, along with Alawites and Sunni Arabs—its heritage of ancient monuments, its manuscripts and Sumerian tablets, its industrial and social infrastructure and its tolerance of differing social customs. "The worst thing is not the violence," the Armenian Orthodox primate of Syria, Bishop Armash Nalbandian, told me. "It is this new hatred."

More than eight years of war left little of pre-war Syrian society intact, forcing everyone to ask, in one form or another, how did we get here and where are we going? What is the reason for the savagery from all sides in this apocalyptic struggle for dominance and survival? Why, back in 2011, did the regime shoot at demonstrators who were not shooting at the government, and why did the uprising come to depend on a contest by weapons, in which the regime would hold the upper hand?

The United States encouraged the opposition from the beginning. *The Guardian* reported on October 24, 2011:

The US vice-president, Joe Biden, last week triggered speculation by saying that the military model used in Libya—US air power in support of rebels on the ground backed by French and British special forces—could be used elsewhere.

It did not happen, although the CIA trained rebels in Jordan and Turkey, Saudi Arabia and Qatar provided arms, and Turkey opened its borders to jihadis from around the world to wreak havoc in Syria. Western predictions of the regime's quick death were not realized.

A consensus among the US, Britain, France, Saudi Arabia, Qatar, Turkey, and Israel held that Assad's strategic alliance with Iran was detrimental to their interests. These powers perceived an expansionist Iran, using indigenous Shiites in Bahrain, Yemen, and Lebanon along with the quasi-Shiite Alawite minority in Syria. They sought to eclipse the "Shiite Crescent" on the battlefields of Syria. Rather than eliminate Iranian influence in Syria, however, they multiplied it. The Syrian military, once an independent secular force that looked to Iran and Hezbollah solely for men and weapons, came to rely on Iran to determine strategy in a war of survival that placed the Iranians in a stronger position than they were before the war.

Major military decisions came not from Syria's discredited officer class so much as from Iranian General Qassem Soleimani, the astute commander of the Iranian Revolutionary Guards' elite Quds force who would be assassinated by American drones in January 2020. In Aleppo, residents told me about an Iranian officer called Jawal commanding Shiite militia forces from Iran, Iraq,

Afghanistan, and Lebanon against the Sunni jihadis who surrounded the city in 2016.

"Most people feel we are under Iranian occupation," a Sunni businessman told me, expressing a widespread perception in government-held areas. A Sunni shopkeeper in Damascus's old city pointed to some bearded militiamen at a checkpoint near his front door and complained that Shiites from outside Syria were taking over his neighborhood. This disquiet was not restricted to the Sunnis. "I'm thinking of leaving," a friend in Damascus told me. "I'm Alawite, and I'm secular, but I don't like this Islamicization that came with Hezbollah."

The spread of Iranian influence in Syria pitted two theocratic ideologies, the late Ayatollah Khomeini's *wali al faqih*, or "rule of (Islamic) jurists," against the Saudi-inspired Wahhabi fundamentalism of IS as well as the Turkish-backed, Al Qaeda-affiliated Jabhat an-Nusra that changed its name later to Hayat Tahrir al-Sham. This led many Syrians who rejected Sunni and Shiite fundamentalist ideology to welcome Russian military engagement. Russia, however corrupt and self-interested, was secular.

The West and its local allies suffered the unintended consequences of their policies, as the Ottomans did when they declared war on the Allies in 1914. Turkey's goals then were to take Egypt back from the British and expand its empire into the Turkish-speaking Muslim lands of the Russian Empire. To say that the Young Turk triumvirate guiding Sultan Mehmed V's policies miscalculated is a historic understatement: rather than achieve either objective, they lost all of their empire outside Anatolia, disgraced themselves for all time by their genocide of the Armenian population, and suffered the indignity of Allied occupation of their capital, Istanbul. When Sultan Mehmed V proclaimed a jihad against the British in 1914, most Muslims ignored it. Similarly, calls for jihad since 2011 against the

Alawite usurper, Bashar al-Assad, failed to rouse the Sunni masses of
Syria's main population centers, Damascus and Aleppo. Assad made
his own error from the day he allowed his security services to fire on
unarmed demonstrators in the belief that, as in the past, fear would
send them home. They did not go home. They went to war.

Elia Samman, a member of the Syrian Socialist Nationalist Party
(SSNP) that seeks to unite all the states of Greater Syria, participated
in the early demonstrations against the regime in 2011. Within a
month of the first rallies in the southern desert town of Dera'a, he
detected a significant change: On April 18, at the demonstrations in
Homs, the biggest banner said, "No to Iran. No to Hezbollah. We
need a Muslim leader who feels God."

"A Muslim leader who feels God" was code for a strict Sunni
Muslim to replace Assad as leader of Syria, in which seventy percent
of the population are Sunni. When street demonstrations began chal-
lenging the system in 2011, Iran and Hezbollah did not concern most
dissidents, who regarded Assad's alliances with the two Shiite powers
as less important than their demands for genuine elections, multi-
party democracy, a free press, an independent judiciary, and the end
of elite corruption that was crippling the economy. Samman recalled:
"A couple of months later, we observed weapons [being distributed]
under the guise of 'protecting the demonstrators.' When the violence
became predominant, we told our members not to participate."

Within the year, the government's use of force and the rise of
armed groups in the opposition made public protest both impossible and irrelevant. Jihadis dominated the opposition, and democrats had no place on either side of the barricades. The population
of Syria hemorrhaged to the four corners of the world. Europe's
leaders, who had resisted wave after wave of Syrian refugees until a
drowned Syrian Kurdish child's photograph embarrassed them into

action in early September 2015, again spoke of a diplomatic solution that required the agreement of the US, Russia, Iran, Saudi Arabia, Qatar, and Turkey. There was much shuttling by Syrian oppositionists, Syrian intelligence chiefs, Russian and American diplomats, and Saudi princes. It recalled the so-called "peace process" that had failed to break the Israeli-Palestinian impasse over the previous quarter century. A senior Syrian official, who asked me not to publish his name, said, "We are at the threshold of a joint American-Russian effort with the UN to get the Syrian government and opposition into a collective effort against terrorism."

This was an illusion, given the US refusal to coordinate with the Assad regime to defeat IS and the other jihadis. Moreover, neither the US nor Russia budged from their initial positions about Bashar al-Assad. The Russians insisted he stay. The Americans demanded he go. Although they spoke about negotiations, which were made more urgent when IS gained territory in Syria and Iraq, they did not negotiate. Instead, they supported the combatants' efforts to kill one another and turn more Syrians into refugees. A prominent Syrian oppositionist in exile told me that he explained to Russian Foreign Minister Sergei Lavrov that for the opposition to fight against "terrorism" along with the Syrian Army, "you would have to restructure the army." When I said that Assad would refuse to restructure the army, the oppositionist conceded, "Okay. That's why the war would never end."

Turkey, which had the most influence among the rebels in northern Syria, used its professed war against IS as a smokescreen to attack Kurds, the most effective fighters opposing IS in Syria and Iraq. Egypt's president, General Abdel Fattah el-Sisi, suddenly threw his hand in with Assad against the same sort of fundamentalists he deposed and was imprisoning at home. He and Assad shared what Assad called "a joint vision" on security issues. The Syria war became a free-for-all in which outsiders pursued their own interests to the detriment of Syrians.

At the end of *Seferberlik* in 1918, Britain and France occupied Syria and partitioned it into the statelets that have failed their populations ever since. What will today's children pass on to the next generation? During the conflict of a century ago, the exiled poet Kahlil Gibran watched from Boston, and wrote in "Dead Are My People":

> My people and your people, my Syrian
> Brother, are dead. . . . What can be
> Done for those who are dying? Our
> Lamentations will not satisfy their
> Hunger, and our tears will not quench
> Their thirst; what can we do to save
> Them from between the iron paws of Hunger?

The United Nations' 2015 "Report of the Independent International Commission of Inquiry on the Syrian Arab Republic" painted a depressing portrait of the population's unimaginable torment at the hands of government and opposition forces alike. The regime dropped barrel bombs in Aleppo, and the rebels responded with gas canisters of explosives and shrapnel. IS raped and brutalized Yazidi women whom it declared slaves to be bought and sold. The regime's security services practiced wholesale torture. Both sides besieged villages, and both sides committed massacres. The UN report's forty-four pages of horrific war crimes should have been sufficient for the outside powers to budge and call a halt to the war. What were they waiting for?

§

The Syrian story is a tapestry of tales, woven together from pain and courage, love and hate, innocence suffocated and cruelty ascendant that remains undeciphered by those who are determining the fate of that ancient land. Wendy Pearlman wrote in *We Crossed a Bridge and It Trembled*, "One wonders what might have been different had we listened to Syrian voices earlier."

Disregarding Syria's people has been a constant theme since the creation of modern Syria in 1920. Had anyone listened to them, the multiple tragedies of the past century might have been avoided. France and Britain, after expelling the Ottomans from their Arab empire during World War I, excelled at denying Syrians a voice in their destiny. With the notorious Sykes-Picot Agreement that split the Ottoman Empire into British- and French-controlled segments, they severed what became Syria from its historic peripheries in Lebanon and Palestine. Retired Syrian diplomat Ghayth Armanazi, in *The Story of Syria*, a sympathetic history of his homeland, called the Anglo-French accord "an iconic example of imperial deceit and duplicity." After dividing Syria, the British and French imposed colonial rule on the inhabitants, who had made clear their unanimous desire for independence in multiple petitions to the King-Crane Commission that US president Woodrow Wilson had sent to the region to gauge public opinion. The British and French armed forces crushed rebellions and uprisings to enforce their rule throughout their tenure in the Levant.

When independence came in the aftermath of World War II, the CIA took no more account of Syria's "voices" than the British and French had. It engineered a military coup that overthrew the parliamentary government in 1949, setting a precedent for the army, a construct of French rule, to govern without consulting the populace any more than the imperialists had. Repeated wars with Israel led to a loss of face and territory, as well as the displacement of hundreds of thousands of Palestinians, in addition to the Syrians driven from their villages in the Golan Heights in 1967. An experiment in Arab unity—the United Arab Republic that cleaved Syria to Egypt from 1958 to 1961—was another failure of governance. The Syrian military occupation of Lebanon that began in 1976 ended in ignominy in 2005, with a forced withdrawal amid sharp hostility from the Sunni Muslim community that had once seen their country as part of historic Syria.

Armanazi, whose ancestors took part in the struggle for independence and civilian governance, provided a brief and reliable account of Syria from Neolithic times to the present. His book explained how the country went from the optimism of 1920, when it established an independent monarchy for a few months, to 2011, when it devoured itself in fratricidal bloodletting encouraged and financed by outsiders. Damascus had been the capital of the first Arab empire, the Omayyad. Syrian, as well as Lebanese, writers and politicians had led the drive for Arab independence from Turkey. Syrian schools taught that the country was a significant part of a larger Arab nation.

Arab nationalism, accommodating all sects of Muslims, Christians, Jews, and Yazidis, clashed head-on with Islamism's narrow focus on orthodox Sunni ascendancy. This became one of many themes—alongside democracy vs. dictatorship, Saudi vs. Iranian, Turk vs. Kurd, America vs. Russia—that played out during the war that began in 2011. For every young idealist in the streets of Dera'a, Damascus, and Homs calling for free speech and an end to torture, there was a Muslim Brother seeking to replace a secular dictator with a theocratic one. This was as fraudulent, but as real, a choice as that between British and French colonial masters in 1920.

The Syrian refugees that Pearlman interviewed in Jordan, Turkey, Lebanon, Europe, and the US emerged as intelligent, perceptive, and deserving of our attention. A few examples:

Miriam, a young woman from Aleppo: "If Bashar had only come out in his first speech and said, 'I am with you, my people. I want to help you and be with you step by step,' I can guarantee you 1 million percent that he would have been the greatest leader in the Arab world."

Jamal, a physician from Hama: "It became painfully clear: This person should not be ruling us. He is too stupid to deserve to be our president."

Waddah, a medical school graduate from Latakia: "I started yelling in a loud voice, 'Dignity!' What did we want after dignity? We didn't know."

Aziza, a school principal from Hama: "I asked them [the rebels], 'Do you have tanks or planes? They have an army created to fight Israel. You don't stand a chance.'"

Yousef, a former medical student from Hasaka Governorate: "No one supported us. Instead, the US-led coalition bombed . . . Its airstrikes have destroyed the country."

Kareem, a physician from Homs: "The truth is that Syria has no friends. It is just a chessboard for the great powers to settle their accounts."

Syria made one serious attempt at Arab unity by entering the union with Egypt in 1958. Yet Egypt's greater size and Nasser's overwhelming popularity reduced the Syrian half of the United Arab Republic to what it had been in the early nineteenth century: a short-lived colony of the Egyptians. One year after the union's dissolution in 1961, a rebellion seeking to restore it erupted in Aleppo and other parts of Syria. The uprising's leaders called on Egypt to intervene.

Ghayth Armanazi observed, "Nasser, however, calculated that any such intervention would be fraught with risk." The army quickly crushed the rebels, sparing the country a civil war. Those who responded to the rebels' plea for weapons and funding from 2011 onward showed no such restraint.

CHAPTER NINE
THE BATTLE FOR KESSAB

Kessab, northern Syria, Autumn 2015

Garo Manjikian is a strongly built farmer with a degree in chemistry and a flourishing moustache like those in sepia photographs of Armenian gentlemen from the late Ottoman era. On the evening of March 20, 2014, he was having dinner at George's Restaurant in the woods where Syria's Mediterranean shore adjoins Turkey's. At his restaurant table, he told me, were five of his friends and their families. Their discussion turned to the conflict, entering its fourth year, to unseat Syrian president Bashar al-Assad. "The mayor of Kessab was with us. We asked him about the situation," Manjikian recalled. "He was very quiet."

Kessab is the only Armenian town in Syria, although other Syrian villages and cities have Armenian minorities. Perched on a hillside within sight of the Turkish frontier, its two thousand-plus inhabitants also include about five hundred Alawite Muslims and Arab Christians. In the summer, tens of thousands of tourists used to fill its hotels and guest houses to bursting. The beaches, pine forests, and fruit orchards hosted camps for Armenian Boy Scouts, as well as hikers, picnickers, and Saudis seeking respite from stifling desert heat. In addition to the three churches for the Armenian Orthodox, Catholic, and Protestant congregations, a large, modern mosque occupies a prominent position.

The conflict was killing tourism in Kessab. Incomes were down, hotels empty. Family visits to Aleppo, with its large Armenian population, became impossible after rebels occupied parts of the city in July 2012. Yet until now the conflict had left the region relatively unscathed. The greatest calamity to hit the town in 2013, apart from the decline in tourism, was not the war between Assad's supporters and opponents but unseasonal hailstorms that destroyed the peach and apple crops.

However, events elsewhere in Syria were conspiring to engulf Kessab. On March 16, 2014, the Syrian Army with its Hezbollah allies expelled opposition forces from the town of Yabroud near the Lebanese border. This cut the opposition's supply line from Lebanon and left the government dominant in most of western Syria. When the rebel leadership organised a response to threaten the regime's coastal bastion of Latakia, their line of march led directly through Kessab.

Throughout March, one portent after another had made the Armenians of north-west Syria apprehensive. First, smugglers tipped off inhabitants that militant jihadis were gathering nearby in parts of southwest Turkey that had not seen them before. Then, Syrian farmers living beside the international frontier noticed gunmen mustering on the Turkish side.

By March 18, regular Turkish Army units were disappearing from the forts guarding the twenty-five-mile border between Turkish Hatay and Syrian Kessab. Bearded paramilitaries in assorted non-Turkish uniforms were replacing them. A United Nations source confirmed what Manjikian told me. "Large numbers of fighters in minivans were going up the mountain. A Turkish Army convoy was coming down." The UN and the Syrian military received reports on March 19, 2014, that guerrillas in Turkey were moving dangerously close to Kessab. It seemed that the Turkish Army was relinquishing control of the border to ragged units of the Syrian opposition, although no one in Syria knew why.

On March 20, 2014, while Garo Manjikian and Kessab's mayor Vazgen Chaparyan discussed politics over spicy *sujuk* sausages and Syrian wine, a fellow Armenian from Kessab telephoned the Syrian Army's central command thirty miles to the south in Latakia. He relayed widespread fears of imminent rebel infiltration from Turkey. The commander dismissed the man's worries on the grounds that an old agreement making the Turkish Army responsible for security north and east of Kessab was still in force. The Armenians were not reassured.

At four o'clock the next morning, March 21, residents of the village of Gözlekçiler in Turkey observed paramilitary units driving through border checkpoints toward Kessab. They later told *The Economist*'s veteran Turkey correspondent, Amberin Zaman, that the Turkish military had evacuated civilians from Gözlekçiler and prohibited journalists from entering the area.

A half-hour later in Kessab, an artillery bombardment woke the Catholic pastor of St Michael the Archangel Church, Father Nareg Louisian. "The sounds became louder. The Turkish Army attacked our village," the forty-three-year-old priest told me. "Everybody felt it was a dangerous situation. We ran away. At the beginning, we thought it would be for some hours and it will finish."

Residents of Sakhra, one of a dozen scattered hamlets and villages near Kessab, watched guerrilla fighters massing over the border in Turkey. They summoned Syrian border police. "The rebels shot at them at 5:30," a United Nations official said. "The Syrian border police shot back." Minutes later, assisted by mortar fire from Turkey, other rebels assaulted the Syrian police post at Qommeh. The battle for Kessab had begun.

Garo Manjikian woke as usual at 5:30 a.m. to start work in his family's apple orchards between Kessab and Sakhra. "I heard voices from the Syrian police station," he told me when we met in Kessab six months later. "Then I heard guns. Then, after half an hour, explosions. Missiles. At 6:30, I saw with my eyes the Sakhra police station." By then, he recalled, it had become "a column of fire." He woke his father and mother. As he struggled to move his mother, who was dying of cancer, the telephone rang. An Arab Christian woman from Sakhra begged Manjikian for help. She worked at Latakia's university, where his children had studied. He drove to her house beside the border to rescue her, with her mother and son. Two mortars barely missed them, and he made it back home. Both families, including Manjikian's three children, crammed into his light pickup truck. "There was not time to take my documents or my diploma," he said. A barrage of mortar fire hastened their departure. It was nine when they reached the village of Nab'ain, about five miles south. "When we saw the mortars hit Nab'ain, I knew this was going to be longer than we imagined." They fled again, this time all the way down to Latakia.

That evening, Syrian television broadcast the arrival of most of Kessab's inhabitants at Saint Mary's Armenian Orthodox Church in Latakia. Many of the two thousand men, women, and children who fled Kessab crowded into the nave, the adjoining school, and the church hall. Some had not had time to put on their day clothes, and most lacked basic provisions.

In Damascus, Armenian scholar Dr. Nora Arissian watched her compatriots on television. "I saw them in their pyjamas," she said, "and it was 1915 again."

Armenians do not forget April 24, 1915, the day they commemorate the beginning of a slaughter that in fact started earlier. By the time the genocide ended, the Ottoman Empire had killed between 650,000 and 1.5 million Armenians in their homes, on death marches, and in concentration camps. Some were murdered outright, while others died from starvation, disease, frost in the mountains or dehydration on the plain.

The Armenian genocide had historical roots. In the late nineteenth century, rebels in Bulgaria and Serbia, with Russian, British, and French encouragement, massacred Muslims and caused the flight of hundreds of thousands of Muslim refugees to Turkish Anatolia. Turkish rulers, who had lost almost all their European lands in the Balkans, feared that leaving Christian, non-Turkish majorities in their eastern provinces would lead to further partition. That belief lay behind the removal of Armenians from areas where they predominated, while leaving small Armenian minorities elsewhere. Removal, however, meant murder. Talat Pasha, one of the triumvirate of Young Turks who ruled the empire from behind the sultan's throne during the First World War, told a German consul in June 1915: "What we are dealing with here . . . is the annihilation of the Armenians."

When Turkey joined the German war against the Allies, in 1914, its leaders had dreams of expanding the empire through Russian territory to include the Turkish-speaking regions of Central Asia. Their attempt to invade the Russian Empire collapsed in January 1915, when the Russians smashed the advancing Turkish Third Army at Sarikamish in the mountains of eastern Turkey. Between sixty thousand and ninety thousand Ottoman soldiers died in battle or froze to death. Turkey's leaders blamed Armenians as the ostensible "enemy within," although Armenian soldiers lay among the Ottoman dead. From then on, the Armenians were doomed. Armenian men between the ages of twenty and forty-five, all of whom had been conscripted into the army, were disarmed. Commanders forced them into labor battalions, digging trenches, paving roads, and cutting trees. Those who did not die of overwork, disease, and starvation were taken out in small groups and executed. Armenian women, children, and elderly men were left without protectors.

The Turks gave some of them a few days to pack their things and sell their property at a fraction of its value. Others were driven from their houses in their pyjamas with no time to gather any possessions. Turkish police and troops deported the defenseless civilians on what were in effect death marches to the desert in Syria. En route to Deir ez-Zour, more than two hundred miles through the desert from Aleppo, they were robbed, raped, kidnapped, starved and tortured.

The remnant who made it to the concentration camps were enslaved, butchered or burned to death. A few brave Turkish, Kurdish, and Arab civilians provided refuge to Armenians, sometimes adopting the children in order to save them. Thousands of Armenian women were forced into marriage with Muslim men, while others suffered rape by soldiers or tribesmen.

Following the armistice between Turkey and the Allies on October 30, 1918, the killing stopped, leaving traumatized survivors, along with the Armenians of Istanbul and a few other large cities who were not deported. Some tried to go back to Turkish Armenia, but the Turks drove them out. A few hundred remained in the village of Vakifli on the Turkish side of the border north of Kessab, but most emigrated to the Americas or settled in Lebanon and Syria. A country called Armenia, in the eastern portion of the ancient nation that had little connection to Ottoman western Armenia, rose out of the war as a socialist republic of the Soviet Union. Like Syria and Lebanon, it gave shelter to refugees from Turkey.

Many Turks and Kurds today have Armenian grandmothers, a fact some deny and others have come to embrace. One day, a Kurdish waiter at a riverside restaurant outside Damascus interrupted my conversation with Missak Baghboudarian, the musical director and chief conductor of Syria's National Symphony Orchestra, to ask Missak whether he was Armenian. When Missak responded in the affirmative, the waiter said that his grandmother was Armenian. He looked proud of the fact. When the waiter left, Missak compared the Kurds, who participated in the genocide, to the Turks: "The Kurds admit they made a mistake. That is the difference."

Dr. Nora Arissian, the young history professor at Damascus University, speaks in a gentle voice that belies her determination to bring attention to the Armenian tragedy. I met with her during my visit to Syria in autumn 2014. "The Syrian press was the first to use the word 'genocide' about the Armenians, in 1917," she told me over espresso at Il Caffè di Roma in the Christian Kassa' neighborhood near Damascus's ancient walled city. She discovered during her research that Syrian Arabic newspapers like *Al Asima*, *Alef Baa*, and *Al Muktabas* reported on the mass deportations of Armenians as they took place. Despite Ottoman censorship, the papers published stories with the terms "extermination," "annihilation," "uprooting the race."

The Arabic word for genocide, she said, was *ibada*, which appeared often in the Syrian press during the First World War. The immediacy with which Dr. Arissian spoke of Armenian genocide was new. Most of the Armenians who spoke to me in Damascus before I drove to Kessab talked about genocide, past and possibly future, when in years past their conversation had been about food, drink, love affairs, and Mid-East politics. Something changed in March 2014 to make the only topic of conversation genocide, and fear of genocide.

Despite their apprehensions, most of them had no desire to leave Syria. Dr. Arissian said, "The Armenian genocide made the Armenians in Syria grateful to Syria." In Syria, they had built churches, schools, social clubs, sports centers, and businesses. There were no restrictions on speaking or publishing in Armenian. Armenians constituted a separate, respected community, whose honesty and industry were acknowledged by Syria's Arabs and Kurds. "In Aleppo, any Arab who wants to repair his watch or his shoes goes to an Armenian," she said. "They know the Armenians are straight. You never find an Armenian thief." True or not, this is the popular perception in Syria among Armenians and non-Armenians alike.

"Once, I did not do my homework," Missak Baghboudarian recalled of his Damascus childhood. "My teacher told me that, until now, we Armenians have a good reputation. 'You must keep that reputation.'" Armenian leaders in the refugee shanty towns of the 1920s forbade criminal activity and prostitution that would shame their community. Memories of rape and forced marriages were strong. The refugees had neither property nor money, but they worked hard to create businesses and move out of the camps. In Damascus and Aleppo, they joined a middle-class community of Armenians who had lived in Syria since at least the sixteenth century. The communities melded and ensured their survival by staying out of politics.

Their acceptance in Syrian society became evident when the people of Kessab fled to Latakia in 2014. One Kessab Armenian told me, "We must be proud to be Syrian, because all the ethnic mosaic of Latakia—the Alawis, the Sunnis, and the Christians—helped us." Dr. Arissian believed that the war was bringing Armenians closer to their fellow Syrians: "Before the war, I said we are not integrated in the Syrian community. But I was wrong."

Decades of instability, tyranny, and intermittent threats from Islamic exclusivists seeking a pure Sunni Muslim Syria had always made the temptation to emigrate strong. In 1960, there were about 150,000 Armenians in Syria. The numbers steadily declined to 115,000 in 1996. Bishop Armash Nalbandian, the primate of the Armenian Orthodox Church in Damascus, told me that about thirty thousand Syrian Armenians had left since the war began. "Nobody has sold his property or his house," he added. "They are waiting to come back." This may be optimistic, but Armenians who remain in Syria fear the fate of their more numerous brethren in Paris and Los Angeles: assimilation into Western culture leading to loss of language and faith. It is within Islamic Syria, paradoxically, that they feel most Armenian. "We like Armenia," Kessab farmer Garo Manjikian said, "but we love Syria. This is my country. We can keep our originality here. We can keep our identity in this Muslim environment more than in the West." Speaking in his office next to the Armenian school in Damascus, Bishop Nalbandian echoed Manjikian. "We witnessed a new kind of Islam. We were persecuted in Turkey, because we were not Muslim. My grandparents came as refugees. We were welcomed."

An Armenian house decorator named Samir Mikho told me over coffee in his modest flat in Dweila, a mixed Damascus neighborhood of Muslims, Christian Arabs, and Armenians, that Syria would always be his home. "A century ago, my parents left their country," he said. "Their church became a stable. We don't want that to happen here." Mikho's resolve to stay was unexpected in light of the fact that, a year earlier, a mortar shell hit the Armenian school's bus stop and killed his ten-year-old daughter, Vanessa.

Every April, Armenians mark the anniversary of the massacres. It may have been no more than a coincidence that German officers, whose empire was allied to the Ottomans, participated in some of the bloodletting. During the First World War, the Allies declared

Turkey's deeds "crimes against humanity," originating a term they would later apply to Nazi actions. British prime minister David Lloyd George called what befell the Armenians then a "holocaust." After 1945, Germany recognized its guilt and made some restitution. Turkey never did.

A new generation of Turkish historians, notably Taner Akçam in his epic *A Shameful Act: The Armenian Genocide and the Question of Turkish Responsibility*, has taken the risk of using the word, with its implications of moral culpability and the obligation to redress wrongs. The expulsions and murders of the Ottoman Empire's Armenian subjects continued until Turkey lost the war and the Allies occupied Istanbul. It resumed for a time under the nationalist government of Mustafa Kemal Atatürk. Atatürk himself later conceded that it was "a shameful act," subsequently the title of Akçam's powerful book.

To this day, however, Turkey's official position is that the Armenians brought disaster on themselves by supporting the empire's enemies. The government has forbidden its citizens to utter the word "genocide." Article 301 of the Turkish Penal Code makes it an offence to "insult Turkishness," and those convicted can be sentenced to ten years in prison. Armenian writer Hrant Dink, who was assassinated in 2011, novelist Elif Shafak and Nobel Laureate Orhan Pamuk have all been prosecuted under Article 301.

Turkey's continuing denial made Armenians around the world particularly sensitive to the occupation of Kessab in 2014. It was as if modern Germany, while refusing to acknowledge its genocide of Jews, had unleashed bands of neo-Nazi skinheads on a Jewish town over the border with Holland. As Dutch Jews would discern a German hand in their victimization, Armenians understandably saw Turkey's. Moreover, Kessab was a last corner of the medieval Armenian

Kingdom of Cilicia that fell in 1375. The oldest Armenian church in the region, St Stephen's, built in the tenth century, is located there. Turkey had ethnically cleansed Kessab twice, during the pogroms of 1909, when it also killed thirty thousand Armenians in Adana, and in 1915. Both times, the people returned and rebuilt. Thus the attack on Kessab resonated more with the Armenian diaspora than the rebel attacks on Armenian quarters in other Syrian towns.

The 2014 conquest of Kessab was not a repetition of 1915. There was no massacre, possibly because most of the inhabitants fled. The first casualty was twenty-four-year-old Gevorg Juryan, whom, Catholic Father Louisian conceded, rebels might have mistaken for a soldier because he wore military-style boots. "They left his body in front of his house," he said. "The family begged to be allowed to bury him, but they allowed it only after three days." Fighting between army and rebels killed another Armenian civilian, but two deaths do not constitute genocide. The jihadis spared twenty or so aged villagers who were too infirm to escape. They were escorted to the border, and the Turkish Army drove them to the Armenian village in Turkey, Vakifli, about twenty-five miles north. Syria, which by then had suffered more than 150,000 deaths in its increasingly savage war, had witnessed far worse.

Yet the jihadis called their offensive in Kessab *al-Anfal*, "the Spoils," from a chapter in the Quran:

And know that whatever ye take as spoils of war, lo! a
fifth thereof is for Allah, and for the messenger and for
the kinsman (who hath need) and orphans and the needy
and the wayfarer, if ye believe in Allah . . .

Al-Anfal was a provocative term. The last military campaign to take the name *al-Anfal* was Saddam Hussein's 1988 slaughter of more than one hundred thousand Kurds in northern Iraq, belatedly condemned around the world as genocide. In 1915, the Ottoman state distributed the spoils seized from deported Armenians—land, houses, furniture, books, jewelry, and clothing—to its Muslim subjects. In Kessab in 2014, similarly, the jihadis looted houses, churches, hotels, and shops, trucking much of the booty to Turkey.

A minority of the rebels were from the American-supported Syrian National Coalition, but most belonged to Sunni fundamentalist factions, like the Islamic Front, Ansar ash-Sham, and Al Qaeda's official wing in Syria, the Nusra Front. They transformed Kessab into a barracks, commandeering abandoned houses and hotels. They posted their destruction of church crucifixes on social media, but did little other damage in the first week.

A day later, rebels moved south to the region's highest summit, Observatory 45, where a television transmission tower overlooked most of Latakia Province. The hilltops changed hands several times, as the opposition and the Syrian Army fought bitter battles for the high ground. On March 23, a Turkish warplane downed a Syrian jet attempting to bomb the Nusra Front rebels near Kessab. Recep Tayyip Erdoğan, who was elevated from prime minister to president of Turkey in 2014, praised the pilot. Meanwhile, opposition artillery exploded near the Armenians' refuge inside Saint Mary's Church in Latakia. They felt they had nowhere to hide from forces they viewed as nothing more than Turkey's mercenaries.

By the end of March 2014, rebels with Turkish air cover and artillery support controlled most of the Kessab region. On April 1, the head of the Syrian National Coalition, Ahmad Asi Al-Jarba, came to Observatory 45 to be photographed with his men and their Islamist allies. Other rebels posted video pictures of themselves in the sea below George's Restaurant, where Garo Manjikian and Mayor

Vazgen Chaparyan had dined the night before they fled. There were now two wars: one for territory, the other for public opinion. Rival propaganda machines manufactured evidence for the Internet, television, and the press. Accounts by jihadis, the Turkish government, and Turkish media on the one hand and the Syrian government and media as well as overseas Armenian lobbies on the other conflicted in every detail. It became almost impossible, especially with no journalists able to enter Kessab without risking rebel kidnapping, to sift truth from fiction.

The Turkish press peddled an image of benevolent jihadis in Kessab. One article stated that two octogenarian sisters, Sirpuhi and Satenik Titizyan, were grateful to the fundamentalists for rescuing them and bringing them to "paradise" in Turkey. However, in a subsequent interview with Istanbul's Armenian newspaper, *Agos*, the sisters said, "The bearded men came to our home. They spoke Turkish. They rifled through our belongings and asked if we had guns." The paper added, "The two women reported that they were deported to the Turkish border, even though they told the men that they wanted to leave for the Syrian port city of Latakia."

One Armenian paper, *Asbarez* of Los Angeles, claimed that Turks and rebels had murdered eighty Armenians in Kessab. Other overseas Armenians disseminated reports of mass killings and posted photos and videos that included the bloody corpse of a woman with a crucifix rammed into her mouth. It later transpired that the photo was from *Inner Depravity*, a 2005 Canadian horror film. Armenians worldwide mobilized behind the #SaveKessab social-media campaign. Armenian-American television celebrity Kim Kardashian, whose public persona would previously have offended Syria's conservative Armenians, tweeted: "Please let's not let history repeat itself!!!!!! Let's get this trending!!!! #SaveKessab

#ArmenianGenocide." Mayor Chaparyan tried to set the record straight, declaring, "Armenians [have not been] killed. I do not know where these rumors are being created."

Nonetheless, the Armenian disinformation campaign was having an effect. Four members of the US Congress wrote to President Barack Obama on March 28: "With the Christian Armenian community being uprooted from its homeland, yet again, we strongly urge you to take all necessary measures without delay to safeguard the Christian Armenian community of Kessab." On April 2, California Congressman Adam Schiff questioned American UN ambassador Samantha Power, a vocal supporter of anti-Assad rebels, about Kessab's Armenians. Schiff stated that "there is a particular poignancy to their being targeted in this manner." One week later, six members of Congress denounced Turkey at a news conference in Washington. The Armenian National Committee urged the president and Congress to compel Turkey to cease its support for another genocide of Armenians. An online petition demanded that the US stop "history repeating itself." Despite the Armenian lobby's exaggerations and distortions, the onslaught was forcing Turkey to weigh its patronage of the rebels in Kessab against the harm to its relationship with the West.

On June 3, for the first time, Turkey branded the Nusra Front that had led the assault on Kessab a "terrorist organization." Turkish support for al-Nusra and its allies gradually dried up in the Kessab region, easing the way for a Syrian Army offensive. Although Turkey continued to allow jihadis to enter Syria along the rest of the five-hundred-mile border, Kessab became a no-go area for the jihadis. Syrian government forces took the town on June 15, ending a three-month occupation. The people began returning the next day.

Garo Manjikian told me that he returned within hours of Kessab's liberation. He reopened his grocery store, but his tractors and other farm equipment had been stolen. He and some friends founded the Syrian Armenian Committee for Urgent Relief and Rehabilitation of Kessab to oversee reconstruction. Strangely, I did not see Syrian soldiers in the town. Apart from a few check-points on the roads outside, there was no military presence to defend the area from a second rebel invasion. And there was little if any fear of it. "The Turks will not do the same thing again," Manjikian said with confidence, placing his trust in the Armenian lobby in the US.

Although the rebels damaged the town, they did not destroy it. Most buildings were intact, but windows were smashed, doors removed, and furniture looted. The rebels were not alone in the pillaging—one house that I visited had been looted by "liberators" from the Syrian Army. The jihadi occupiers took a special interest in pianos, destroying every single one. The Armenian Cultural Center, whose music school had been teaching piano to twenty-seven students, had been burned along with its books and pictures.

The pastors of the three Christian denominations took me on a tour of their churches. They were pleased that so many members of their respective flocks had returned, although about 20 percent stayed in Latakia or left Syria. "We cannot stop people emigrating," Pastor Sevag Trashian said, "but the majority of our community wants to stay here. We want to return Kessab to its good days. We have our own contribution as Christians and as Armenians to this mosaic."

The three clerics showed me the damage to their churches, the desecration, the burned books, the slashed paintings. Artisans laboring to restore the church buildings had yet to remove the jihadis' Arabic graffiti:

Soldiers of the Only One were here. God willing, we will
crush the Christians, Armenians, and Alawis.
We will go after you wherever you go, God willing.
Do not rejoice, Christians. We will step on you.
It is a matter of time before we get you, worshippers of
the cross.

In Deir ez-Zour, where a century ago thousands of Armenians had
been herded into camps, starved, and killed, jihadis blew up the
Armenian Genocide Memorial Church. They then scattered the
bones of the victims who perished between 1915 and 1918.

The first time I visited Kessab was in 1987. My friend Armen
Mazloumian, whose grandfather founded the famous Baron's Hotel
in Aleppo, escorted me to the Evangelical Protestant church. It was
as austere as any Presbyterian kirk in Scotland, devoid of Eastern
Christianity's icons, incense, and statues. The only decoration was a
childlike painting that I described at the time:

It showed Jesus Christ, the Good Shepherd, holding in
His arms the body of a slain boy, the boy's head and arms
dangling like Christ's own in Michelangelo's Pietà. Behind
Him were the mountains of Armenia, and at His feet was a
mound of skulls and bones with the date "1915" written on
them. The caption was in Armenian, which Armen trans-
lated: "So much blood. Let our grandchildren forgive you."

The painting, like everything else in all of Kessab's churches, had
been burned to ash.

CHAPTER TEN

CAMP OF THE DEFEATED

Damascus, Winter 2016–2017

In Damascus people call it the "million-dollar checkpoint," although it is not one but two face-to-face roadblocks, barely a rifle shot apart. On a suburban road between government and opposition zones of control in Damascus, President Bashar al-Assad's soldiers and their rebel enemies inspect cars, vans, and pedestrians. Their shared objective is extortion, exacting tolls on medicine, food, water, and cigarettes, as well as people, that are moving in and out of the besieged orchards and homesteads about ten miles from the center of Damascus in an area known as the eastern Ghouta.

This devastated region, where a half-million people lived before the Syrian civil war, was the scene of the chemical weapons attacks, blamed on the regime, in August 2013 that nearly drew American air power into the conflict. Partly as a result of a deal with Vladimir Putin, United Nations inspectors arrived instead, and removed or destroyed most of the government's poison gas stocks. Since then, the frontier between the state and its opponents has provided profits to both. Such cooperation between enemies surprises those unfamiliar with Syria's political and economic landscape, although neither side has concealed its recurrent contacts with the other.

The fierce game between the government and its adversaries is not confined to eastern Ghouta. Wherever the warring sides want peace, there is peace. Where they contest territory, as they did until recently in the eastern quarters of Aleppo, there is war. Where they want profits, they collaborate. Hence, the "million-dollar checkpoint" and lesser checkpoints throughout the country that sustain the business of war. Paltry exactions from beleaguered citizens add up to large fortunes, giving the fighters incentives to mute the conflict in certain areas and marshal their forces elsewhere.

No one denies that the regime is winning the war. It owes its ascendancy as much to its opponents' disunity and incompetence as to its own effectiveness. Rebel policy, whichever group was involved, was to seize and hold terrain for as long as possible in violation of every tenet of guerrilla warfare. The local people welcomed the rebels in some places and tolerated them in others.

In both cases, opposition fighters failed to shield people from the regime's sieges and assaults as well as the misbehavior of their own "rogue elements." Rather than wage a mobile guerrilla war and build a solid coalition within the population, they occupied land they could not defend. This alienated many Syrians whom the rebels could not govern and risked the lives of those they could not hold. The rebels failed to create effective alliances among their more than a thousand armed bands. Their reliance for arms and other support on rival outside powers—Turkey, Saudi Arabia, and Qatar, with the United States, Britain, and France in the wings—left the rebel groups vulnerable to the antagonistic and variable priorities of their sponsors. In sum, the opposition had no more chance against the Syrian regime than the similarly fractured Palestine Liberation Organization had in the 1970s and 1980s against Israel's superior military and intelligence apparatus.

From the outset, forces loyal to President Assad held the main population centers, notably central Damascus, most of Aleppo, and the coastal cities of Tartous and Latakia. Throughout 2016, the government, with Russian and Iranian assistance, recovered plots of lost territory. While the battle for eastern Aleppo raged last autumn, parts of suburban Damascus were coming back under Assad's control. Discussions with the rebels were followed by capitulation.

The government, with its known record of harsh human rights abuses including torture, demonstrated more flexibility than its opponents. The state security system, armed with intelligence files amassed over generations, knew its enemies and their vulnerabilities. Discovering that no tactic worked everywhere, the regime's negotiators dangled offers of a deal with some rebel fighters and civilians while dropping barrel bombs on others. In some neighborhoods, the government allowed the wounded out and medicine in. In others, it tightened the siege.

The means varied, but the objective was the same: pacification and restoration of control. Among the negotiators for the government were army and intelligence officers as well as pro-regime residents of contested areas. They talked with militiamen from a variety of groups, as well as Muslim clergy, local mayors, and community leaders. The government promised to end its assaults if the rebel forces departed. To obtain food, water, electricity, and a respite from bombardment, the local people put pressure on their self-proclaimed defenders to leave. The process of trial and error that the government called "reconciliation" may have reconciled hardly anyone, but it brought more relief to more people than did its badly divided opponents.

"Reconciliations are doing very well now," President Assad's political and media adviser, Dr. Bouthaina Shaaban, told me. "And there are many areas in the pipeline. We feel that this is the best way to end the war." Bitter fighting and expansion goes on, but there is some truth to what she said.

The government established a Ministry of National Reconciliation at the beginning of the conflict in 2011, but its brief did not involve discussion with armed militias officially designated "terrorists." Ziad Haidar, a Syrian journalist who covered the war for the Lebanese daily *As-Safir* until the paper closed at the end of 2016, said that negotiations with so-called terrorists began almost by accident two years after the ministry was established. "The governor of Homs, Ahmad Munir, started the reconciliation in Tal Khalak on the border with Lebanon in 2013," he recalled. "He discussed it with the head of the militias in Tal Khalak. This was the first reconciliation process. It triggered others in Homs."

"Reconciliation, Reward and Revenge," a ten-month study by the Berlin-based Berghof Foundation, stated: "By 2014, local ceasefires formed a clear part of the Syrian government's strategy in managing the insurgency as well as appeasing the strong international interests [i.e., US, Russian, and European] for a de-escalation of violence for humanitarian and political purposes."

Ahmad Munir moved to the Reconciliation Ministry to initiate discussions with other rebels. His successor as Homs governor, Talal al-Barazi, continued the policy locally and negotiated the surrender of the old city of Homs in December 2015. By that time, most of the rebel-held portions of the city had been destroyed.

In February 2016, a day after the US and Russia declared another cease-fire that the combatants ignored, the Russians inserted themselves into the reconciliation scheme. Major General Igor Konashenkov, the spokesman of the Russian Defense Ministry, declared on February 23, "Representatives of the opposition groups in Syria, who decided to stop the hostilities and start peace talks, will be able to call the Coordination Center round-the-clock on the common phone number." Russia invited anyone interested in resolving local conflicts to contact its Coordination Center for Reconciliation at its Hmeimim air base. By November last year, the center claimed, "the number of settlements joining the reconciliation process has reached 971." The United Nations estimated that seven hundred thousand people remained under siege in fifteen main areas as of January 16, 2017. A small number were speaking with the Russians, while by this time some four hundred thousand people had been killed and eleven million made homeless.

Surrounded, cut off from supplies, and losing ground, rebels near Damascus were receptive to offers that guaranteed their lives. "They need to have the sense of losing," Ziad Haidar said. "Why reconcile with the government if you are winning?" Damascus and its environs were too remote from rebel supply lines along the five-hundred-mile border with Turkey for fighters to hold out for long periods. But nearer Turkey in the northern province of Idlib, insurgents had the upper hand and were besieging regime forces in the Shiite villages of Fu'ah and Kefriya. They had no reason to give up.

On the southwestern periphery of Damascus, the adjoining neighborhoods of Moadimiya and Daraya illustrate the regime's tactics and the opposition's limitations. At the outset of the conflict in March 2011, both relatively poor quarters depended for their livelihoods on farming, light industry, and small businesses. Their Sunni Arab majorities believed rebel promises of a brighter future when Assad left. In 2012, parts of both areas became what the media called "rebel strongholds."

Artillery, sniper fire, and barrel bombs ground the rebels down. Most of the residents fled to safer places in and out of Syria. Civilians and combatants dwindled to an estimated four thousand in each area from pre-war populations of about one hundred thousand in Daraya and sixty thousand in Moadimiya. When the government encircled each of the neighborhoods by seizing the land bridge between them in February 2016, its stranglehold intensified the pressure to capitulate. An activist in Moadimiya, Qusai Zakarya, told the website *Syria Direct*:

> The Fourth [Armored] Division was responsible for negotiations in Moadimiya and the truce as well. They sent the External Committee, which contains people from Moadimiya who live outside the town, some of whom have good relationships with the Assad regime.

By September 2014, the government was in a position to dictate terms: civilians and rebels with small arms could leave for another part of Syria, which in practice meant traveling about two hundred miles from Damascus to Idlib; or they could go without weapons to government-supervised camps for the displaced. The town of Moadimiya, but not Daraya, was given a third alternative: its people, even rebels who had given up their arms, could remain in their homes. The anti-regime Syrian Observatory for Human Rights estimated that eight hundred rebels and 2,400 civilians went to Idlib from Daraya and 1,500 rebels and only two hundred civilians from Moadimiya. Most of Moadimiya's inhabitants stayed to repair their houses, and some exiled residents came back. In Daraya, no one remained and no one returned.

"When we went in, people were given one hour to evacuate," a United Nations official said of Daraya. "They took nothing with them." Regime soldiers looted everything the residents left. A Syrian friend, who has avoided taking sides in the war, told me,

"When soldiers conquer an area, they regard everything as theirs." Soon furniture, crockery, linens, televisions, refrigerators, and electrical cables turned up in the *ta'afish* (market for stolen goods) of Damascus.

With the pillage came destruction. The government forces were "razing Daraya to the ground," a UN official told me. This was obvious when I drove along the highway beside Daraya and saw, beyond earth barricades, a devastated territory of demolished houses, mountains of rubble, and untilled fields.

"Moadimiya did not attack outside," said a Syrian aid worker. "Daraya was attacking." More importantly, Daraya was close enough to the government's Mezzeh military airport for rebels to hit it with mortars. Rami Abdulrahman, who runs the Syrian Observatory for Human Rights, told Reuters, "The Islamist groups which control Daraya have been launching rockets into the military airport zone." The government is trying to ensure that Daraya never threatens the airfield again, although a missile attack on it on January 13, 2017— blamed on Israel by the Assad government—indicates that it remains vulnerable.

I found some of Daraya's rebels and residents in a new camp ten miles south of Damascus near Harjallah. Harjallah is a Sunni Arab village beside the sprawling base of Syria's Fourth Armored Division, whose presence deters the defeated fighters from taking up arms again. The government's detention of several hundred Daraya and Moadimiya residents, whom it releases in stages, provides another source of control. According to government figures, the people of Harjallah, like their compatriots in the rest of Syria, welcomed refugees from Daraya and took in about seventeen thousand of them. The government installed others in new single-story concrete houses that give the impression of permanence. The camp stretches along three main avenues, in contrast to the jumbled streets of the semirural village they left behind.

When I arrived, boys were kicking a soccer ball up and down a paved road in the middle of the camp. A young man, one trouser leg pinned up where his lower leg had been, leaned on crutches and watched. The camp director, a sixty-six-year-old retired charity worker from Harjallah named Mohammed Dib Karawan, introduced himself and invited me into his spartan office. He said that a week earlier the camp housed nine hundred people. When I asked how many remained, he consulted a sheaf of typed white pages that listed 285 men, 303 women, and 64 infants. Where did the others go? He produced another list, this one of the families and their destinations: Harjallah village, Tartous, Suwaida, and other places in Syria where they had relatives or friends. "If you want to leave, you can leave," he said. "If you want to stay, you can stay." The advantages of staying are free food, water, electricity, medical care, and education with help from the Red Cross, Red Crescent, and several UN agencies. The government was not releasing comprehensive figures for those participating in the reconciliation program.

The camp, which the regime must regard as a "Potemkin village" to attract other rebels to accept amnesties, was achieving a kind of normality in an abnormal environment. The children attend school in Harjallah, and they receive remedial lessons in mathematics, Arabic, and English to make up for four years of lost education. "Fifteen women are giving birth," Dib said. "There will be a wedding for five couples in two days."

I left Dib's office to walk through the camp. Four women sitting on the doorstep of a house invited me inside for coffee, as they would have done with a stranger in any Syrian village. My hostess was Ghousoum al-Ghazi, the thirty-three-year-old wife of a farmer whose two children followed us in. Her friend, fifty-four-year-old Ruweida Abdel Majid Naccache, came as well and offered me a cushion to sit on. The house had one bedroom, a bathroom, and a modest front room with a kitchen built into the far wall. Paper-thin mats marked "UNHCR" for the UN's High Commissioner for Refugees covered the freshly washed floor. Mrs. al-Ghazi told me she had moved into the house on August 26, 2016, weeks before the final surrender, when civilians were fleeing Daraya. "We were very hungry," she said. "There was fighting every day. The children were afraid at first. Then they got used to it."

Mrs. Naccache recalled life in Daraya: "When there was an airplane, we fled to a shelter. It was just a hole in the ground. We stayed like that for five years. I was there when they besieged the town. I lost a lot of weight. There was no food. Here we are living in heaven."

Two men removed their shoes, entered the house, and sat down. One of them, who preferred not to give his name, said, "I thought all Syria was like Daraya. We thought it [the war] was everywhere. When we were in Daraya, there was no electricity, no television. The destruction was everywhere." His companion, a forty-six-year-old electrician who called himself Abu Anis, said: "When we were in Daraya, we didn't care who was going to win. We thought it would end in fifteen days. That was before the siege. On the road between Daraya and Moadimiya, we could pay the soldiers to let us leave." Was he a fighter? "I never carried a weapon, but I worked with the rebels. If they needed anything, I helped."

The other man admitted using weapons against the government. Unlike other regions of the country, he said, most of the rebels in Darya were Syrian. As defeat loomed, he had considered going to Idlib with his comrades: "We were given a choice. Even when I came here, it was not an easy choice. Everyone said the regime would take me to prison."

Why did he take the risk? "Because I know that here is better than there. Going there means continuing the fight." The government was encouraging men like him to call their former comrades in Idlib and tell them they would not be arrested if they accepted an amnesty. I asked people in the room, "Will you go back to Daraya?" They all said, "Yes," but the disarmed fighter added, "*Insha'Allah*"— God willing.

The government has made their return extremely unlikely. "They looted my house," Mrs. Naccache said. "Then they burned it." "They" are the government. Is there anywhere to return to? She said, "No."

The war seems unending. Armed militants from many rival Sunni groups, including Faylaq al-Sham, Jaish al-Fustat, and Jaysh al-Islam in eastern Ghouta on the fringe of Damascus, have yet to give up, but their front line is static and mostly quiet. "Furthermore," the Berghof Foundation's report noted:

> The extremely lucrative checkpoints between Ghouta and Damascus—and the inflated prices of smuggled goods within Ghouta—provided numerous military and political actors on both sides with strong financial incentives to keep the siege firmly in place.

The Damascus suburbs of Jobar, Barzeh, Harasta al-Qantra, Hawsh Nasri, Arbin, and Hawsh Haraba remain redoubts for numerous, mainly indigenous rebel factions, who fire occasional defiant barrages while enduring government artillery and air strikes. Syrian rebels and foreign jihadis retain control of Idlib province. The most extreme jihadi groups move freely in large parts of eastern Syria. IS was holding Raqqa, capital of its self-declared caliphate on the banks of the Euphrates in the eastern desert. In December, it reconquered the Roman ruins at Palmyra and the adjoining town of Tadmor that it lost to government and Russian forces the previous March, and in January it cut off an important government supply route in the eastern province of Deir ez-Zour. Jabha Fateh al-Sham, the Al Qaeda branch that previously called itself Jabhat an-Nusra, attacked government troops near Hama in January. Both remain resourceful, resilient, and immune to civilian pleas for an end to the ordeal.

The two jihadi groups are not part of the discussion about ending the war. Russia did not invite them to its peace conference in Astana, Kazakhstan, in January—already the scene of bitter quarreling—and they would not have attended if it had. They will not go quietly.

Such was the state of play as the war moved into 2017.

CHAPTER ELEVEN
MORNING CHORUS

Damascus and Aleppo, Spring 2017

> For what can War, but Acts of War still breed,
> Till injur'd Truth from Violence be freed . . .
> —John Milton

It is March 2017, and I am back in Syria after four months away. Dawn breaks to a daily chorus of artillery and mortar fire in two of humanity's most ancient settlements that today are Syria's two largest cities, Damascus and Aleppo. Projectiles rain on their rural peripheries, where opposition groups fighting the regime of President Bashar al-Assad shelter in tunnels below mountains of rubble.

Muezzins wake the faithful to pray, and warplanes deliver the day's first payloads just after 5:00 a.m. The rebels respond with desultory mortar rounds fired at cities they once dreamed of ruling. In Damascus, their shells explode in the Christian neighborhoods closest to the eastern front lines. In Aleppo, artillery batters opposition bases along the western frontier with Idlib province. Both cities' exhausted citizens have cause to fear for their country's uncertain future.

I happened to arrive in Damascus on March 19, a few hours after insurgents launched a large-scale assault to break into the city from the eastern suburbs. They emerged out of underground caves; smashed through army checkpoints with suicide bomb vehicles;

and seized buildings between two besieged districts, Jobar and Qaboun. This happened within sight of the Christian neighborhoods surrounding Abaseen Square. It took the army more than a day to drive them back. Some Damascenes doubted their government's ability to defend them, and many feared a massacre of minorities. When the battle ended, the lines were back where they had been. The regular pattern of artillery exchanges and aerial sorties resumed. Citizens continued what passed for normal life in wartime, going to work and school to the sounds of violence on the outskirts.

Inside the walls of the old city, the narrow streets around my Ottoman-era hotel sounded like a steel mill. First came the heavy presses, pounding up and down, metal smashing metal, shaking the ground: outgoing artillery from the border separating the old city from Jobar. Then the rumble of turbines, furnace doors screeching open, and flames gushing forth: Syrian air force planes soaring low over No Man's Land, between the old city and Jobar to strike tunnels and mortar launchers. Finally, the staccato of jackhammers breaking ground with relentless fury: jeep-mounted .45-caliber heavy machine guns and old Dushka 12.7-millimeter antiaircraft weapons. Occasionally, something like a compressor rumbled the houses of the old city and splattered shards into the walls: mortar rounds from Jobar, the response of weakened warriors repaying their enemies for keeping them down.

At breakfast one morning, the hotel roof rattled as if a ton of lead had fallen on it. I was about to seek cover, when I looked up. Two cats were fighting on the roof, whose clear plastic sheeting amplified their footsteps. The war seemed to affect even stray animals.

A friend of mine, who has longed for a change of regime since the March 2011 protests in Dera'a sparked the conflict, finally abandoned hope. "I don't care how they end it," he said, "just so they end it." Ending it was already difficult, but the early April chemical attack that killed more than eighty civilians in Khan Shaykhun, a rebel-held village in Idlib province in the country's northwest, and the American missile strike on Syria's Shayrat airfield in retaliation were rendering the difficult impossible.

Over eight years of war, millions of Syrians have suffered. Each time I return, there are more dead, more injured, more homeless. By now, at least five hundred thousand have been killed and many more paralyzed, disfigured, blinded, traumatized, and uprooted from their homes and communities. The demolished neighborhoods of eastern Aleppo served as testaments to the brutality of the forever war. More than half of Aleppo's pre-war population lived there, until opposition fighters began seizing the area in 2012. Although measures of population movement are guesses at best, international aid agencies reported that at least fifty thousand eastern Aleppins fled to the western part of the city to avoid regime shelling or chaotic jihadi rule. Thousands more made their way to the government-controlled, war-free coastal cities of Latakia and Tartous. Others went to Lebanon, where they were not welcomed. Those who climbed the mountains into Turkey received visa-free entry, work permits, and, for many months in 2015, a blind eye to any who dared the perilous sea route to Europe.

In December 2016, the Syrian Army, with decisive Russian support, conquered the last insurgent strongholds in Aleppo's east. UNHCR officials estimated that about thirty-six thousand people, rebels and their families, departed by bus under Russian protection for the opposition redoubt in Idlib province. What they left behind conjured memories of Dresden, Coventry, and Tokyo in the aftermath of World War II. The multiple forms of destruction testified to the ingenuity of the world's arms makers. Bombs transformed Aleppo into an Escher-like vision of six-foot-thick concrete slabs twisted into braids; five-story apartment buildings compressed into piles ten feet high; and collapsed façades of entire streets exposing rooms with ceiling fans eerily intact and revolving in the wind.

This was the horrorscape to which many residents were returning, only to find themselves still homeless. They camped in makeshift tents beside the remains of their homes, to deter thieves from seizing unclaimed land at a time when many deeds have been lost or destroyed. Some slept inside buildings exposed to the elements and subject to collapse at any moment. Children died when balconies crumbled or when they found shiny objects that turned out to be unexploded bombs.

UNHCR reckoned that 150,000 of eastern Aleppo's former residents came back within the first three months of the area's return to government control. Eastern Aleppo lacked the basic services it enjoyed before the war: running water, electricity, garbage collection, sewage, television, Internet. Water pipes and electricity cables were ruptured, and mounds of debris made the streets impassable for public transportation and private cars. The rebuilding began in the ancient souqs, the center of commercial and social life in the city, with help from the Aga Khan Foundation.

Aleppo had always been known as the workshop of Syria, the place where artisans made the finest furniture and household utensils, a metropolis of stone fashioned by generations of master masons. Many of its residents did not wait for the state or international humanitarian agencies to restore their dwellings, install electric generators, replace broken windows, and bore holes into the ground for water. "Reconstruction will take decades," one foreign aid worker told me during my visit to the city in late March 2017. Yet the process was underway. "In east Aleppo," a United Nations official observed, "there has been a huge change in one month."

Most Aleppin industrialists in Beirut waited for the war to end before committing themselves to the reconstruction of the textile, pharmaceutical, and food-processing plants on which the population would depend for jobs. A few reopened factories, mainly for Aleppo's famed olive oil soap. In the meantime, city dwellers could not grow food in concrete. As of May 2017, World Food Programme (WFP) officials estimated that two hundred thousand eastern Aleppo residents were dependent on its food aid. Including the eastern Aleppins who were still displaced in western Aleppo and elsewhere, the number receiving WFP parcels of bread and other basics was six hundred thousand. Despite this, many children were suffering from malnutrition as well as years of missed schooling.

Some eastern Aleppo residents have lost all their belongings. Those who left during the Syrian Army's offensive in December 2016 said the government ordered them to leave their possessions behind and flee to safety. When they returned, those whose homes were standing found them looted. International aid agencies blamed Syrian Army troops. "They do not care how the population reacts," one aid official said. "If you liberate an area, the only thing that works is fear." Yet many Aleppins said that government control relieved them of the jihadis' obsession with requiring men to grow beards and women to cover themselves, banning cigarettes, forcing them to pray, and other intrusions into their private lives.

Western Aleppo, which remained under government control throughout the war, suffered less than the eastern side, a measure of the relative strengths of state and opposition forces. Each wreaked havoc within the limits of its firepower. Jihadi mortars demolished some westside apartments, but not entire buildings. Bullet scars were a common sight west of the former front, and the venerable Baron's Hotel lost its windows and part of its roof. In areas where the jihadis penetrated for short times, churches were dynamited and government buildings were gutted and robbed. Yet on the surface, life in the western half of the city appeared to go on much as it did before the war moved to rural Aleppo and Idlib provinces.

On both sides of Aleppo, there has been extensive damage to the city's social fabric. As we were sitting in a busy westside restaurant, a representative of the Armenian patriarch in Aleppo told me that of the city's pre-war Armenian population of forty-five thousand, only a third—fifteen thousand—remained. "Those in Lebanon may return," he said. "From Montreal, no." The Armenians were Aleppo's largest Christian community. Their decline portended the disappearance of the rest—and the waning of an essential part of the city's cosmopolitan character. Protestant pastor Reverend Ibrahim Nseir said that his Presbyterian congregation was down to fifty families in 2017 from five hundred before the war. His church continued to administer two schools, where, he said, "99.9 percent of our students are Muslim." (I know many Muslim families in Syria, as well as in Lebanon, who send their children to Christian schools that they believe provide a more modern curriculum than either the state schools or the madrasas attached to mosques.)

Some of the Christians who lived through the fighting seemed determined to remain, despite the declining size of their community. "Now I stay to support the Christian presence here," one woman told me. "I stay to support my government here." Relations between most Christians and their Muslim neighbors in Aleppo continue to be peaceful. However, the disappearance of two archbishops, Syriac Orthodox Mar Gregorios Yohanna Ibrahim and Greek Orthodox

Boulos Yazigi, who were kidnapped by antigovernment Islamists in April 2013, deterred many Christians who left from coming home. (As of 2025, their fate remained unknown.)

When I interviewed Mar Gregorios at Easter in 2012, he thought that Aleppo, because its citizens remained quiet while other Syrian cities were rising up, could avoid being drawn into the war. He said he was not afraid. At the end of that year, I saw the bishop again and wrote that he was "a profoundly shaken man with little hope for his country's future." He became the only prominent Christian prelate to call for President Assad to resign in order to end the war. His outspoken stance did not save him from capture by jihadis whom he met a few months later in the vain hope of obtaining the liberty of hostages.

Though the support of Iranian and Hezbollah forces has been crucial to the regime, the government kept most of them out of Aleppo. The city's Sunni Arab majority remained as hostile to them as the Sunnis of Mosul were to their Iraqi Shiite "liberators," who led the battle against IS. Russia, far more than Iran or Hezbollah, backed the Syrian Army in Aleppo. The Russian government also negotiated and oversaw the evacuation of opposition fighters and civilians in those areas. "If not for the Russians," one Western aid official said, "many more people would have died." He recalled that Russian soldiers stood guard every five hundred meters along the twenty-kilometer evacuation route from Aleppo to Idlib.

Russians, along with Muslim troops from the Russian Federation, became a common sight in Aleppo for several months after the jihadis' defeat. I had drinks with some affable Russian officers in an Aleppo bar, although they were not forthcoming about their operations. People in the streets, who in the past might have inquired whether I was American or British, stopped me to ask in friendly voices, "*Russki*?" This would have been unimaginable a few years before. The Russians had not been visible in Syria well into the war, and committing troops to the Middle East had long been unacceptable to Russia after its disastrous experience in Afghanistan.

"In March 2015, the government lost Idlib," said a Russian diplomat. "In autumn 2015, it was clear Damascus could fall." The fall of Damascus was another "red line," he said—something Russia could not abide. Choosing between unpalatable options, it increased air support and sent ground forces to guarantee the survival of Syria's government, army, and institutions. Its action saved Damascus from an insurgent onslaught and gave the Syrian Army the upper hand in the long seesaw war.

Another Russian I met said, "We want to cooperate with the Americans. The priority is IS, not Idlib." The priority for the Syrian government, in order to secure all of western Syria, has been to expel jihadi forces from Idlib. One senior Syrian official told me, "Daesh [IS] is shrinking, while [the other major Islamist group fighting in Syria, Jabhat al-]Nusra is trying to show muscle." The Nusra Front, under its new name of Hayat Tahrir al-Sham (Front for the Liberation of Syria), launched attacks on Syrian Army units in Hama province and near Damascus that forced the government to concentrate on protecting its rear before moving east toward IS in Raqqa. But the Russians had been seeking an accord with the US to defeat IS rather than Nusra.

In late March 2017, statements by President Donald Trump, as well as his secretary of state Rex Tillerson and UN ambassador Nikki Haley, gave the Russians hope that they could put Assad's future status aside while coordinating with US forces in northeast Syria to defeat IS. Russian troops had begun to emulate the American tactic of training young men who had lost family members in IS massacres. Russians called them *Saadoun Daesh*, IS Hunters. Primarily Christian and Alawite, these men were motivated above all by revenge. But with the April 4 chemical attack on Khan Shaykhun, the prospect of US-Russia cooperation receded.

The incident led to a surge in US public support for the war against Assad and for confrontation with Russia, with the National Security Council accusing Moscow of trying to cover up the regime's involvement. And it brought about a sudden volte-face by the Trump administration, which threatened deeper sanctions on Russia, questioned Russia's air defense umbrella over Syria and, on April 24, imposed sanctions on 271 Syrian scientists and other officials working for the Syrian government.

An analyst in Damascus blamed the chemical assault on the recent endorsements Assad had received from the Trump administration as recently as the end of March:

It seems that the initial US backing from six days ago has led to a growing sense of hubris among the leadership here which led them to act with impunity. Some say that Russia gave the green light for this to happen as a way of testing or showing to what degree US commitment to leaving the lion [the Arabic for lion is "Assad"] alone was serious. As for why the government would attack Idlib [province], it seems that they thought chemical weapons were the best way to kill as many Nusra Front fighters in Idlib as possible.

Others close to the regime insisted that Assad had little reason to use poison gas in a remote corner of Idlib where his forces were not threatened (in contrast, for example, to the jihadis' breach of Damascus's

SYRIA

defenses from the eastern suburb of Jobar). The Organization for the Prohibition of Chemical Weapons (OPCW) sent a Fact Finding Mission to Syria that confirmed a sarin attack, but it said its mandate "does not include identifying who is responsible for alleged attacks." A UN-OPCW Investigative Mechanism, which had not visited the site because of the danger of contamination but inspected some of the victims, concluded that Syrian government aircraft had most likely dropped chemical warheads on Khan Shaykhun. At the same time, it blamed IS for deploying mustard gas in 2016 on the village of Umm Hawsh.

In early 2017, the Syrian government claimed strategic victories with the conquest of eastern Aleppo, the surrender of Damascus's western suburbs to the army, and the departure of the last insurgents from the strategically important city of Homs. Yet government forces remained vulnerable on the edges of all its territories to jihadis and other insurgents, whose supply lines from Turkey and Jordan remained open.

The risk of a new Sarajevo of 1914 in Syria underlined the urgency of ending the conflict, but the war's sponsors continued to use the anguish of dying children to score propaganda points. Rather than negotiate a peace accord, they doubled their commitment to local warriors who would massacre, maim, humiliate, and torment many thousands more people before this pointless war ran its course.

My heretical view, based on my observation of the Syrian tragedy since it began, is that the chemical gas attack in Khan Shaykhun should not be the primary concern. Postwar tribunals, as at Nuremberg and Wuppertal, can deal with war crimes. More pressing was for the war to end. The chief British prosecutor at Nuremberg, Hartley Shawcross, wrote: "It is the crime of war which is at once the

154

object and the parent of the other crimes: the crimes against human-ity, the war crimes, the common murders."

What mattered was giving the Syrian people a viable future. No party to the conflict—not the United States, Saudi Arabia, Qatar, Turkey, Israel, and hundreds of jihadi militias on one side, or Russia, Iran, Hezbollah, and the Syrian Army on the other—cared how many Syrians died. While the conflict endured, all sought power at the expense of ordinary Syrians. Militarists in the White House, Congress, and the US media demanded escalation against Assad and Vladimir Putin, but they might have served Syria's beleaguered pop-ulation better by seeking an accord with the Russians and Iranians. Without that, there would be more war. And more war crimes.

§

Blue cloth, stretched like the fabric in which Christo enfolded Berlin's Reichstag, swaddled a six-story building in central Damascus. Inside, the shell of an old hotel awaited its rebirth. When the Hotel Semiramis opened in 1952, its owners advertised it as "the newest hotel in the world's oldest city." Sixty-five years later, within earshot of artillery and mortar fire on Damascus' outskirts, new owners bet on a prosperous future. The project to restore the Semiramis, just down the hill from the Ottoman Hejaz Railway Station, was one of many striking anomalies in 2017, the seventh year of Syria's civil war. Armies and militias battled one another across the face of the country. Jihadi fanatics destroyed ancient temples in Palmyra. The national army or its opponents, depending on whose story one believed, dropped chemical weap-ons on civilians in a northwestern province. And rivalry between the United States and Russia, both of which committed air and ground forces, threatened world war.

Yet somehow, business went on. Syrian entrepreneur Mazher Nazha explained why his family was refurbishing the Semiramis and a second hotel to be called Hayat (the Arabic word for life, not the Hyatt international hotel chain), despite a war that exacted a heavy toll on Syrian society: "There are fourteen five- or four-star hotels in Damascus. A total of two thousand rooms. If the war stops, you'll need more than two thousand rooms." His family, Christian merchants who owned a travel agency and freight company, had committed ten million dollars to the Semiramis project in the belief that businesspeople and tourists would fill its rooms in post-war Syria.

I met the Nazha brothers, Mazher and Mounzer, for reasons that had nothing to do with hotels. Early in the Syrian war, a UN worker told me that the United Nations was delivering tons of food, containers of medicine, and truckloads of schoolbooks to all parts of the country. I asked how it managed to get the aid where it was needed, despite the risks to drivers of violent death and kidnapping. He answered, "DHL."

I've sent books, documents, and small packages by the German logistics company, but thousands of tons of supplies to a war zone? I tracked down the owners of the local DHL franchise, who turned out to be the Nazha brothers. Their offices were in an old building near the ultra-modern Four Seasons Hotel.

Mazher Nazha told me his family's branch of DHL had delivered aid to Iraq in the wake of the 2003 American invasion. "Two billion tons of humanitarian food aid with World Food Program and other agencies went to Iraq," he said. "1.2 billion tons of it came through Syria, and most of that was through us." When Syria's own war erupted in 2011, DHL's rivals closed. The Nazhas had the field to themselves: "We had a ninety-five percent share for UN agencies." When other firms resumed trading a few years into the war, DHL's share dropped to twenty-five percent. In the meantime, the Nazhas built up capital that they needed to invest in Syria while American sanctions made spending the money outside the country problematic.

Nazha showed me his plans for the new Semiramis, a space-age luxury palace better suited to Dubai than to old Damascus: "116 rooms and suites, two executive floors, a ballroom, meeting facilities, business services, restaurants, a rooftop pool, and a huge sky bar." He said three hundred people could eat, drink, and enjoy the view of Damascus from the rooftop terrace.

Resurrecting the Semiramis required a makeover in public relations as much as engineering. The Armenian Yacoubian engineering firm, which the Nazhas contracted to undertake the reconstruction, built the hotel in 1952. Its modern luxuries, unusual in the Middle East in those days, included radios and telephones in every room, four elevators, and an orchestra playing in the Swiss-run dining room. Things began well, as tourists arrived to visit Syria's legendary antiquities and souqs. Then the hotel, like Syria itself, fell on hard times amid one military coup after another in the 1950s and 1960s, wars with Israel, and economic indolence. The hotel was already rickety in 1973 and 1974, when I stayed there with the rest of the foreign press covering Henry Kissinger's Damascus-Tel Aviv diplomatic shuttle. It was there that I first heard the old saw, uttered by Jeremiah O'Leary of the *Washington Star*, "Don't tell my mother I'm a reporter. She thinks I'm a piano player in a brothel."

Barely two years later, in September 1976, terrorists working for the renegade Palestinian assassin Abu Nidal attacked the hotel and took its guests hostage. Syrian special forces captured the hotel, killing one of the four terrorists. The authorities hanged the other three the next day in front of the hotel. Swift justice may have deterred others from staging terrorist attacks in Syria, but it didn't help business.

Newer hotels, such as the French Le Meridien and American Sheraton, opened and took the high-end trade. In 1979, Iran's Islamic Revolution brought poor religious pilgrims whom the government lodged in the deteriorating confines of the now-passé Semiramis. I visited a few times in the 1980s out of nostalgia, and the hotel staff lamented its establishment's reduced circumstances.

The hotel closed and stayed empty during the war that began in March 2011. Then, suddenly, the scaffold went up and the building disappeared behind its curtain. When it reemerges, most of its potential guests will be too young to remember the hangings and the Iranian pilgrims. If there is peace, the Nazhas will recoup their investment. If not, their only option may be to compete for the hundreds of UN staff members residing at exorbitant rates in the Four Seasons

"To rebuild Syria, you need people willing to invest and to work," Mazher Nazha said.

"You don't have to wait until the end." The last time we spoke, he said the hotel would open by the end of 2020. (As of 2023, it had yet to reopen.)

§

American policy since 1949, when the CIA instigated a coup d'état that overthrew an elected government in Damascus, has not been kind to Syria. In that long, sad story, no one emerges with less credit than President Richard Nixon's vainglorious secretary of state, Henry Kissinger. Even the harshest critics of the late Syrian president Hafez al-Assad appreciate him for his treatment of Kissinger, when he flew into Damascus on the evening of February 26, 1974. Assad made him wait for hours while he hosted dinner for Romanian dictator Nicolae Ceausescu. Only after midnight did he grant the

American an audience. Throughout the meeting, Kissinger was seated opposite "a massive canvas of the Battle of Hattin, where the Muslim Sultan Saladin defeated the Crusaders, and marched to capture Jerusalem," wrote Bouthaina Shaaban in *The Edge of the Precipice: Hafez al-Assad, Henry Kissinger, and the Remaking of the Modern Middle East.*

Assad lodged the Kissinger entourage in the Diyafa Palace, a modest dwelling where in 1958 America's nemesis Gamal Abdel Nasser had proclaimed the United Arab Republic, a union of Syria and Egypt. Thirty minutes into his slumber, Kissinger woke to the morning's call to prayer from the mosque next door. Shaaban wrote that none of the assaults on Kissinger's self-esteem—the dinnertime delay, the Saladin painting, Diyafa's link to Arab nationalism, and the early wake-up—was accidental. Shaaban, a former professor of English literature who became media and political adviser to Assad's son, Bashar al-Assad, provided for the first time a Syrian perspective on the famed Assad-Kissinger negotiations. Their final agreement framed relations between Syria and Israel, as well as Syria and the US, for nearly forty years. Kissinger, other Americans, and Israelis have written about the talks, but hers was the first Syrian account. Shaaban had unique access to the Syrian Presidential Archives with "the minutes of all their meetings and the messages they exchanged either through diplomatic channels through the US ambassador in Damascus or via [other] diplomatic channels." The archives contain transcripts from a tape recorder that turned in full view of the participants throughout Kissinger's twenty-eight visits to Damascus in 1973 and 1974. Her book was not, nor did it purport to be, the definitive story. Like the concealed microphones in Nixon's White House, it provided a corrective to the legend Kissinger fostered of himself as latter-day Metternich.

Kissinger intended the second volume of his memoirs, *Years of Upheaval*, to be the final word on his haggling with Assad. Fortunately, it was not. Edward Sheehan's masterful *The Arabs, Israelis, and Kissinger*, although written with Kissinger's cooperation, earned its subject's wrath. Kissinger said he "was 'thunderstruck' to see some of his conversations with foreign chiefs of state in print." If Shaaban's book, published in Beirut in 2013, reaches American readers, the thunder should strike again.

Kissinger came late to Mideast diplomacy. As Nixon's national security adviser from 1969 to 1973, he obstructed negotiations to resolve the Arab-Israeli conflict. Coveting William Rogers's job as Nixon's secretary of state, he discouraged moving beyond the ceasefire that Israel, Jordan, Egypt, and Syria had accepted under the Rogers Plan to end the "war of attrition" that was bankrupting Israel. The region was changing in September 1970, the month that King Hussein crushed the Palestine Liberation Organization in Jordan and Nasser died. Nasser's successor was his vice-president, Anwar Sadat. Two months later, a bloodless coup put Syria's minister of defense, Hafez al-Assad, in the top job. The door to diplomacy opened, but Kissinger slammed it shut.

Sadat approached Nixon and Kissinger through a variety of emissaries, including the former child actress Shirley Temple who was then a US delegate at the UN, to offer peace for territory. Kissinger ignored Sadat, believing the Israelis could defend the Sinai Peninsula from behind their "impregnable" Bar Lev Line on the east bank of the Suez Canal. Again and again, Sadat threatened war if the Americans failed to budge the Israelis. Kissinger believed Sadat was bluffing. When Sadat expelled all of the Soviet Union's fifteen thousand military advisers from Egypt in 1972, Kissinger refused to acknowledge the Egyptian's strategic shift.

Despite warnings from King Hussein of Jordan and various intelligence agencies, the Syrian and Egyptian armies took Israel and the US unawares when they attacked on October 6, 1973. The Egyptians reduced the Bar Lev sandbanks with water cannon, threw down pontoon bridges, and crossed into the Sinai. Syrian tanks and infantry poured into the occupied Golan Heights. Only American emergency supplies, the call-up of reservists, and a lighting run to the west side of the canal saved Israel's gains of 1967.

Kissinger, who had replaced Rogers two weeks before the war, stepped in to clean up the mess for which he was largely responsible. He flew to the Mideast with a twofold purpose: to exclude the Soviets from peace negotiations and to protect Israel. Sadat threw himself into Kissinger's arms, offering to go along with his diplomacy wherever it led. Assad was a tougher nut to crack, as much due to his country's position as what Nasser called the "beating heart of Arabism" as to his innate stubbornness.

Kissinger pioneered what would be called "shuttle diplomacy," carrying messages between the Israelis and their Arab antagonists in Cairo and Damascus while making his own suggestions. There were arguments over prisoners of war, how much territory Israel would concede, where to place lines of disengagement, how many weapons would be allowed on both sides, and the status of United Nations observers. Reporters like myself on the ground in Damascus had no idea what Kissinger was promising behind the palace doors. He briefed the press corps that accompanied him on the plane from Washington, whom we called his "trained seals," with whatever spin, true or false, he wanted to read in the morning newspapers.

Kissinger's first meeting with Assad on December 15, 1973, lasted six and a half hours. Assad astounded his guest, the first US secretary of state in his capital since 1953, by agreeing to exclude his Soviet patrons from the discussions on the understanding that the US alone could influence Israel. Kissinger surprised Assad with the claim that his major obstacle emanated from those who control "the financial capital and means of communications" in the US, not so subtle code for the Zionist lobby that had yet to achieve the influence it would wield in later years. The Syrian transcripts contain Kissinger's numerous disparaging remarks about the lobby, but, in Shaaban's words, "The US record makes no mention of him citing 'financial capital' or 'means of communication.'"

Kissinger had negotiated the Israeli-Egyptian disengagement in eight days in January 1974. "Unlike the relatively short negotiations that led to the Egyptian-Israeli disengagement agreement," the State Department website history notes with considerable understatement, "negotiations for a Syrian-Israeli disengagement proved far more arduous and took much longer." Unlike the Sinai, the Golan had hundreds of villages, thousands of displaced inhabitants who longed to return home and proximity to the country's capital. From the Israeli point of view, the Syrian lines threatened their illegal settlements in the occupied Golan as well as parts of Israel itself. And Assad, unlike Sadat, was no pushover.

Kissinger cajoled, lied, and manipulated. In the end, he got what he wanted: a deal that gave Israel its most peaceful border until the Syrian civil war changed the game. He also achieved an American monopoly on Arab-Israeli negotiations that abandoned comprehensive peacemaking in favor of what he called "step-by-step" diplomacy. The steps led to the Lebanese civil war, Israel's many invasions of Lebanon, the creation of Hezbollah and the expulsion of Israel from Lebanon, unrestricted Israeli colonization of the West Bank, the Palestinians' intifada uprisings, and the continuing degradation of Palestinian life. Indeed, the situation became worse than it was when Kissinger left Harvard for government service in 1969.

The Middle East may seem a minor infraction compared to Kissinger's crimes in Vietnam, Cambodia, Laos, Bangladesh, Chile, Cyprus, and East Timor. The man who advised Nixon to deploy "anything that flies on anything that moves" in Cambodia was photographed in May of 2017 sitting beside another American president, Donald Trump, whose policies were dangerous enough without advice from the old desperado. My late friend Christopher Hitchens, whose book *The Trial of Henry Kissinger* presents sufficient evidence for an indictment, wrote in 2010:

> Henry Kissinger should have the door shut in his face by every decent person and should be shamed, ostracized, and excluded. No more dinners in his honor; no more respectful audiences for his absurdly overpriced public appearances; no more smirking photographs with hostesses and celebrities; no more soliciting of his worthless opinions by sycophantic editors and producers.

Nothing in *The Edge of the Precipice*, despite its portrayal of Kissinger as a shrewd mendacious mediator, invalidates Hitchens's sage advice.

§

It may have been another American whose career inspired Assad's son and heir, Bashar. Chicago Mayor Richard J. Daley was the master of political survival, running his city for twenty-two consecutive years until his death in 1976. In 1968, though, his future looked grim.

When Chicago police beat and abused young anti-war demonstrators during the Democratic National Convention of that year, the party establishment turned against him, just as in 2011 much of the world condemned Assad's treatment of anti-government protesters. Liberals called Daley a fascist then; later, US politicians labeled Assad a tyrant.

Many Democrats called for Daley's resignation in 1968, but Chicago voters gave "Hizzoner" an unprecedented fifth term in April 1971 with a seventy percent majority. At a press conference the next day, a journalist reminded Daley about the leading Democrats who had condemned him in 1968—Ted Kennedy, George McGovern, Hubert Humphrey, and Edmund Muskie, among others. The reporter then asked, as legendary Chicago newspaperman Mike Royko wrote in his biography of Daley, "Have any of them telephoned with congratulations?" Daley smiled and answered, "All of them did."

By the eighth year of Syria's war, Assad's enemies were scurrying back to him. Insurgents with the combined backing of the United States, the United Kingdom, France, Turkey, Saudi Arabia, Qatar, and lesser powers had failed to dislodge him. Nothing succeeds like success, and Assad's tenacity forced his enemies to recognize that he was not going away. Washington stopped demanding regime change, reversing the policy of President Barack Obama and Secretary of State Hillary Clinton. CIA director Mike Pompeo telephoned Assad's military intelligence chief, Ali Mamlouk, in January 2017, to seek help in finding missing American journalist Austin Tice, but also to obtain information on Assad's jihadi enemies who might threaten the United States. The British sent diplomatic feelers to Damascus, and European states that withdrew their ambassadors in 2012 sent them back on regular missions.

"No one is able to say, 'Sorry, I was wrong,'" explained a Western source close to secret discussions between Assad and the West.

"French diplomats ask me how to get out of this." The Egyptians, who initially supported the rebellion against the Syrian president, came over to him. The Iraqis, America's allies in the war against IS, sent him military aid. The United Arab Emirates, which had funded some of the rebels, would reopen its embassy in Damascus in December 2018. Even neighboring Jordan, which permitted the CIA to train Syrian insurgents on its territory, admitted relations with its occasional adversary are "likely to take a positive turn." So they did. Jordan would reopen a border crossing in 2018 and upgrade its diplomatic relations with Damascus in 2019.

Saudi Arabia and Turkey, two of the most prominent enablers of jihadis in Syria, moved closer to Assad's Russian allies. Russian president Vladimir Putin visited Turkish president Recep Tayyip Erdoğan in September 2017 and, a month later, welcomed Saudi King Salman with notable ceremony in Moscow. Turkey broke with NATO policy for the first time by purchasing Russian arms in the form of the S-400 missile defense system, and it stopped mentioning regime change in Syria. It also sent troops into northern Syria with Russia's agreement, ostensibly to combat extremist militants but in reality to pressure US-backed Kurdish militias and expel Kurds from their homes in Afrin province. Then, with American approval, it drove Kurdish forces out of Kurdish-inhabited zones to the east.

By 2018, signs that the war had been decided were everywhere in Damascus. Unlike Beirut, whose war ended in 1990, and Baghdad, which endured the US invasion in 2003, the Syrian capital restored electricity for twenty-four hours a day. The private generators that used to hum outside my favorite Damascene cafés went into storage. The biggest demonstration I've seen in Syria since 2012 was a gathering of thousands of people on October 10, 2017, to watch the Syria-Australia soccer match on a giant screen in Umayyad Square. Two weeks later, Assad received the soccer players, including two who had defected to the opposition but changed sides. Schools were open, displaced people no longer slept outside in the parks, and traffic was incessant. New nightclubs opened, and young people flocked to cinemas and restaurants.

Conflict nonetheless persisted, as the deaths of two civilians killed by mortar fire near my hotel in the old city attested. About 60 percent of the country's territory and 80 percent of its population were by then under government control. The rest of the nation was separated from Damascus. The Kurds continued to govern the northeast, but they permitted civilian government institutions to function and state employees to receive their salaries from Damascus. Small rebel groups in the south near the Israeli border fought on. Rival rebel factions, entrenched under a Turkish umbrella in the northwestern provinces of Idlib and Afrin, battled one another. Some engaged in criminal activities like extortion, kidnapping, and smuggling that did not endear them to local residents. The future of these areas remained unclear and depended on whether the insurgents' foreign sponsors chose to use them as perpetual irritants against Assad or to abandon them altogether.

"They [the insurgents] failed to bring down the regime," explained one Syrian security expert. "There is a consequence for that. They cannot go home. They cannot stay here. What do you do when the garbage begins to stink? You burn it." He predicted the Turks would end up destroying the jihadi groups they helped to create rather than permit them to leave Syria to pursue their holy war in Europe, Russia, the United States, the Muslim regions of China, or Turkey itself. Others suspected that Erdoğan, despite his rapprochement with Putin, would maintain Idlib as a base from which to harass Assad and prevent him from enjoying his victory. With Russian air cover, the Syrian Army chipped away at areas of western Aleppo province and parts of Idlib, much to the annoyance of Turkey. The combat forced hundreds of thousands more Syrians into internal or external exile.

So far, Assad had won. But the war did not end.

CHAPTER TWELVE
ZENOBIA'S THRONE

Palmyra, October 2017

If you ask the stars to choose a place instead of the sky
They will say Palmyra.
—Yaseen al-Farjani

The young man betrayed no emotion as he told the story: "They asked him to kneel. He refused. He said, 'If you are going to kill me, it will be while I am standing. I will die like the date palms, upright.' Because he refused to kneel, they hit him behind the knees." The man's legs collapsed, and he fell. A sword swept through his neck, severing his head.

The young man, Tarek Assa'ad, hesitated. This was not a distant memory, and the murdered man was no stranger. It was his father, Khaled Assa'ad. The eighty-one-year-old archaeologist died on August 18, 2015, within sight of the house where he was born on New Year's Day in 1934. The Islamic State (IS), then at the summit of its conquests, decapitated him with the same destructive fury that characterized its demolition of the Hellenic and Roman treasures that Khaled Assa'ad had dedicated his life to protecting. In the burning summer of 2015, the guardian and his city, called Palmyra for its stately palm trees, were dying together.

Tarek resumed his account, going back in time to his father's childhood playing amid Palmyra's classical temples, marketplace, and sunlit theatre in the waning days of French rule over Syria. "He was so much in love with these artefacts," Tarek said. "When you wake up every day and see the Temple of Bel, you have to fall in love, don't you?" The temple dedicated to the Mesopotamian god Bel, or Baal, was Palmyra's most distinctive structure. Its sacred enclosure, surrounded by porticos and columns, has fascinated scholars and travelers since its completion in 32 AD. It intrigued no one more than the elder Assa'ad. He taught himself the Palmyrene dialect of Aramaic, the region's lingua franca during the Roman era, in order to understand Palmyra's elaborate inscriptions and the people who etched them in stone. After taking a degree in history from the University of Damascus, he stayed in the Syrian capital during its turbulent years of multiple military coups d'état to work for the Directorate-General of Antiquities and Museums (DGAM). In 1963, DGAM sent him back to Palmyra to oversee excavations and curate the new museum that had opened beside the ruins.

The energetic director uncovered hidden tombs, located the marble fort of the Emperor Diocletian's garrison, dug up hundreds of coins that had lain undiscovered for nearly two thousand years, and found memorials to ancient Palmyra's notable citizens. His discoveries and publications filled gaps in the elusive history of Palmyra's rise from desert oasis a thousand years before Christ to thriving center of world trade between Rome and India in the early Christian era. Thanks in part to his efforts, UNESCO declared Palmyra a World Heritage Site in 1980. It was no coincidence that Khaled Assa'ad named his first daughter for Palmyra's fabled queen, Zenobia, who is forever associated with the city that she led to its greatest triumphs and defeats in the third century after Christ. He retired in 2003, when his oldest son among eleven children, Walid, succeeded him as antiquities director. Retirement did not prevent him from persevering with his digging, researching, writing, and educating visitors about his beloved ruins.

In May 2015, more than four years into Syria's civil war, everyone knew that IS militants were headed to Palmyra. They had just invaded Raqqa on the Euphrates River about 130 miles to the north and declared it capital of their new caliphate. With the Syrian Army preoccupied to the west in the more populous provinces of Idlib and Aleppo, nothing but desert and a few undefended villages stood between Raqqa and the "pearl of the desert," Palmyra. Although strategically insignificant, it symbolized everything that the religious fanatics detested: Syria's pre-Islamic history, beautiful artworks celebrating pagan gods and ancient funerary monuments. Palmyra as a repository of Syria's historic cultures was to them anathema. Riding American armored vehicles captured from the demoralized Iraqi Army, IS advanced south in mid-May. Its militants, led by suicide bombers in exploding trucks, opened the way through army checkpoints. Within a week, they had seized Palmyra.

By the time Dr. Maamoun Abdul Karim, DGAM's director-general from 2012 until September 2018, learned of IS's intentions, it was too late to save Palmyra. The zealots had already demolished other historic sites, including Nineveh and Nimrud, in Syria and Iraq. Palmyra's Doric columns and temples were too large to move, but Dr. Abdul Karim ordered the transfer of as many valuables as a small fleet of trucks could carry from Palmyra to Damascus. "Three hours before the occupation by Da'esh," he said, using IS's Arabic acronym, "the Syrian official police in Palmyra sent twenty policemen to support my colleagues to move the artifacts. We decided to do it in the middle of the night." While the battle for Palmyra raged between IS and a rearguard of Syrian troops, museum staff and twenty police commandos loaded four hundred statues, along with hundreds of glass jars, ceramics, and medals, onto hastily assembled trucks outside the Palmyra Museum. They worked throughout the night of May 20. At dawn, the trucks moved out. IS rolled in ten minutes later.

Dr. Abdul Karim told me the story in a café near Damascus University, where he taught archaeology before, during and after his tenure as DGAM director. An archetypal Syrian gentleman of a bygone age, he smoked a water pipe and drank Turkish coffee. All that was missing was a red tarbush. Although aged fifty, he said, "After the last five years, I feel more than seventy. I've had no sleep for five years." The Syrian war saw him struggle to save antiquities all over Syria from jihadi vandals, who defaced what they called "idols," and criminal looters, who sold their country's heritage for huge profits overseas. His efforts earned him prizes from archaeological institutes in Italy, China, Algeria, and elsewhere, but at home his university would not even grant him a sabbatical to rest from his hard labors.

Dr. Abdul Karim's passion for the country's past had its roots in his background, which, while not Arab, was pure Syrian in its fascinating variety. "My father was Armenian, Bidros Krikor Eskidjian," he said. "In 1915, he was eight years old. His mother and father were killed." That was at the height of Turkey's genocide of Armenians during the First World War, when thousands of Armenian orphans were roaming the Syrian countryside unaccompanied. "He was saved by the Abdul Karim family. They are Kurdish." His father adopted his Kurdish benefactors' name and religion, Sunni Islam. "My mother is Syriac," he added. Her Syriac Orthodox Christian community, like the Armenians, had suffered massacres by Turks in the early twentieth century and more recent assaults by IS, including kidnappings and a suicide bombing attempt to kill the Syriac patriarch in Syria on the 101st anniversary of the Ottomans' campaign against them. He summed up without a trace of self-pity, "I am from three genocides: Armenian, Kurdish, and Syriac."

Like Khaled Assa'ad, Dr. Abdul Karim studied at Damascus University, but he went to France for his archaeology PhD. The Syrian civil war was entering its second year in 2012 when he became director-general. Responsibility for all of Syria's archaeological museums and locales, six of which were UNESCO World Heritage Sites, was placed in his hands. His greatest support came from private citizens in both rebel and government areas, who hid antiquities from looters and jihadis before delivering them to DGAM. This was a grassroots movement of Syrians—Arabs, Kurds, Armenians, Muslims, Druze, Ismailis, Alawis, and Christians—to preserve their shared patrimony. "In Aleppo," he said, "twenty-four thousand objects were moved to Damascus in one night." When IS was massing in April 2014 to assault the riverside city of Deir ez-Zour, Dr. Abdul Karim's volunteers packed up thirty thousand pieces and shipped them to Damascus. The basement of the National Museum of Damascus overflowed with Syria's most valuable historical relics.

Meanwhile, the trade in looted artifacts from Palmyra and elsewhere was flourishing. Stolen statues, manuscripts, jewelry, and ceramics turned up in Europe via Turkey, Lebanon, and Jordan. It was not as bad, however, as Dr. Abdul Karim had feared: "We found that more than seventy percent of the traffic outside Syria is fake." Many genuine items, when their provenance was revealed, went back to Syria with the help of Interpol and other police agencies. "It's not just our culture," Dr. Abdul Karim said. "It is a universal heritage."

Shortly after conquering Palmyra, on May 27, IS released an eighty-seven-second video promising to preserve the Roman ruins.

That did not inhibit IS a month later from initiating the systematic destruction of the graceful colonnades that stretched into the desert for nearly a mile along the ancient Roman road. Militants smashed the famed Lion of al-Lāt, a beautiful stone statue of a lion god protecting a gazelle that Polish archaeologist Michał Gawlikowski discovered only in 1977. Subsequent reports from Palmyra were vague about what was happening. Then, in late August, satellite photographs confirmed that IS had razed the site's most impressive structures, the Roman-era Temples of Baalshamin and Bel. UNESCO head Irina Bokova called IS's vandalism a "war crime" and an "intolerable crime against civilization." IS followed those outrages with the destruction of Palmyra's distinctive funeral towers that had stood for centuries at the fringe of the old city. If the jihadis stayed much longer, archaeologists feared, nothing would remain.

History may not be, as Henry Ford called it, "bunk," but it can be contentious and usually serves rival masters. Myth surrounds the IS occupation of Palmyra from 2015 to 2017 as much as it clouds the tale of Queen Zenobia seventeen centuries ago. Zenobia inherited the Palmyrene throne from her husband, Rome's ally and vassal Odaenathus, when he was assassinated in 267 AD. Zenobia, said by contemporaries to have been both beautiful and so chaste that she made love to her husband only in order to have children, claimed kinship with antiquity's other great queen, Cleopatra. Historian Yasmine Zahra wrote, "Zenobia was a Roman to the Romans, a PanHellene to the Greeks, but in fact she was a Hellenised Arab." Zenobia came to power when the trading center of Palmyra enjoyed its greatest revenues and the Roman Empire was suffering what historians call "the crisis of the third century" with rebellions east and west threatening its unity. Zenobia took advantage of Roman weakness to conquer all of Syria, Egypt, and part of Anatolia. When the

Emperor Aurelian consolidated Rome's control of the west, he led his army against her in 272.

Some chroniclers wrote that Aurelian killed her in battle, while others, like sixth-century Byzantine historian Zosimus, claimed that the emperor carried her as war booty to Rome, gave her a house in Tivoli, and let her mature from exotic beauty into respectable Roman matron. In our time, observers differ on what transpired in Palmyra when IS conquered the city in May 2015, withdrew under Syrian and Russian assault in March 2016, returned nine months later, and fled for the final time in March 2017.

Bashar al-Assad's defenders maintain that the United States sent IS into Syria, while his opponents blame him. In Palmyra, several civilians swore to me that they had seen American warplanes flying in support of IS. Others said the Syrian Army assisted IS's conquest of Palmyra.

In October 2017, I went to Palmyra for the first time since 1987. Syria thirty years earlier was an island of peace between Iraq, then in its fifth year of war with Iran, and Lebanon, whose civil war had another three years to run. Palmyra's ruins stretched over acres of a tranquil, isolated plain. Its allure owed as much to its position as to the structures left by the ancient Palmyrenes. "The beauty of Palmyra is its silence," Dr. Abdul Karim told me. In this, he shared the view of Sir Mark Sykes. Sykes, whose famous 1915 accord with French diplomat François Georges-Picot is not blameless in the Syrian tragedy, had written in his 1904 travelogue, *Dar-ul-Islam*, "The real attraction of Palmyra is its solitude; the great noisy money-proud city overturned, shaken, and deserted, the sand-worn colonnades, the crumbling temples, the ruined tombs, unprepossessing in themselves, have been beautified by decay, and rendered pathetic by their forlornness and silence." Nothing had changed when I saw it more than eighty years after Sykes. Palmyra was an exquisite diadem at the eastern edge of what had been the Roman world, its grandeur enhanced rather than diminished by millennia of neglect.

Until the 1930s, semi-settled nomads had lived in mud hovels within the ruins. The French Mandate authorities moved them into Tadmor, the town that was expanding on the northern and eastern outskirts of Palmyra. The French had already built a prison there to hold (and torture) Syrians who fought for independence in the uprising of 1925. Syria's post-independence governments kept the prison. It became the scene of the bloody murder of hundreds of political prisoners by Rifaat al-Assad in reprisal for the attempted assassination of his brother, President Hafez al-Assad, in 1980. I wrote about Tadmor in *Tribes with Flags: A Journey Curtailed*:

> Few buildings in Tadmor seemed over two stories high, but every roof had steel rods sticking out ready for a new floor to be added when a son married. The only building materials used in the last twenty-five years were those which cursed the whole Levant: grey breezeblocks and concrete of numbing uniformity. The old, simple houses of mud or stone were beautiful by comparison, but few remained.

At that time, Tadmor town was as squalid as Palmyra's ruins were majestic, but it was intact, and its people were hospitable. The IS occupations and the government's battles to retake it have ravaged it.

When photographer Don McCullin and I returned to Palmyra and Tadmor in 2017, we nurtured memories of them as they were before IS. Don ran to the Temple of Bel, which he had photographed for his 2010 book *Southern Frontiers*. Little was left of the monument he had painstakingly recorded. The empty horizon loomed over shattered stones. "Don't photograph the Russians," a Ministry of Information official warned him as he climbed atop a massive hunk of limestone.

I went into the town to see streets clogged with war detritus, water and sewage pipes crumbled, and buildings collapsed with their innards exposed to the elements. Barely a hundred people out of an estimated pre-war population of seventy thousand had returned. Among them were the al-Khateeb family, who had reopened their "supermarket," a small room on the ground floor of the building where they lived. Twenty-six-year-old Ghaith al-Khateeb was running the shop for his father, Issa. The young man offered me coffee and talked about life in Tadmor while Russian soldiers loitered outside.

He shed light on one point of contention: whether the army had aided civilians to evacuate or abandoned them in its hasty retreat in May 2015. He said, "The army facilitated the flow of the civilians. Some stayed, about 300 people." He had fled with his father, mother, two brothers, and two sisters to relatives in Homs. They came back after the Syrian Army expelled IS in March 2016 and reopened the shop.

The Russians celebrated victory in Palmyra with a concert in the ancient theatre. On May 5, Valery Gergiev conducted the Mariinsky Theatre Orchestra in performances of Prokofiev and Bach to an audience of Russian and Syrian military personnel. "We protest against barbarians who destroyed wonderful monuments of world culture," Gergiev declared. "We protest against the execution of people here on this great stage." Russian president Vladimir Putin appeared on a video screen to praise his troops for their "fight against terrorism without sparing their own lives." The ceremony proved both premature and vainglorious. The following December, IS returned.

IS's second conquest of Palmyra astonished everyone, feeding the belief in a Syrian government conspiracy to assist IS. Russian and American satellites should have spotted IS fighters speeding across the barren landscape and given US-backed rebels or the Syrian Army time to defend the city. Colonel Sami Ibrahim of Syria's Military Media Department, sitting in a shaded bunker beside the T4 oil pumping station about forty miles west of Palmyra, said it did not happen that way. "The second time, they made use of some of the enclaves that were not liberated," he said. He showed me photographs of tunnels that the IS fighters dug into rock outside Palmyra, when they fled from the city in March 2016. The deep tunnels were covered in gravel as camouflage from aerial reconnaissance. IS did not come all the way across the desert from Raqqa, he insisted, but infiltrated from positions nearby. That December, the Syrian Army, with Russian air cover, was concentrating on the expulsion of rebels from eastern Aleppo. Aleppo became the decisive battle of the war, initiating the steady restoration of territory to government control and undermining international support for the rebels.

On its return, IS accelerated the destruction of ancient monuments and the execution of anyone it labelled *kafir*, non-believer, until the army drove them out again in March 2017. The Khateeb family, which had again taken refuge in Homs, returned to Palmyra with the Syrian Army to reopen their shop. Khateeb led me from the modest grocery to a souvenir emporium below selling trinkets, small carpets, handmade mother-of-pearl boxes, and plaster replicas of the Roman temples. "At first, we opened a supermarket," he explained. "We saw that souvenirs were in demand, so we concentrated on such items." The souvenir buyers were the Russian troops who patrolled Tadmor's streets on foot, lodged in dispersed barracks, including one inside the Roman ruins, and appeared to act as a guarantee against a third IS invasion. One Russian soldier tested his few words of Arabic to negotiate the price of postcards and mementos to send home. Another soldier examined several items under the glass counter without buying any, much to Khateeb's amusement.

Khateeb pointed to a huge opening gouged in the wall. He explained, "They put holes in the walls and linked all the basements." His basement had been an IS field hospital, which he cleaned to install the shop. "Business is okay," he said. The only customers were Russian and Syrian soldiers. Most of the inhabitants of Tadmor were waiting for the restoration of electricity and running water. Khateeb kept the lights on with a small generator that vibrated outside. "I'm happy and unhappy at the same time," he said. "All my friends have left. Will they return? *Insha'Allah*."

A few streets away, Mohammed Khalid Allawi was grilling meat on a wood fire in the street in front of a shabby restaurant that was little more than a concrete box with a few tables. Beside him, his wife, Daline, and Aunt Fouda were washing and chopping vegetables. "The army helped us get out," he said, "or we would have been executed." Although he was a practicing Muslim and both women wore scarves over their hair, he said of IS, "They think of me as a *kafir*. They believe they are the custodians of religion. What kind of religion do they believe in?" He said that Christians had lived among Muslims in Tadmor, until IS drove them out. No one knew whether they would return.

Turning meat on the fire, Allawi continued, "This is our home. This is my work. I hope all the residents will be back. Thank God, it's safe all around. We fled twice." Did he think he would flee again? "No. It's finished. It's only a matter of one month or two and they will be driven out of all Syria." He directed me to a Christian church nearby. IS had burned it to a husk. The only signs of worship were the torn pages of charred hymnals.

Everyone in Tadmor had a story, none happy. A fifty-one-year-old man slouching in a chair inside his tiny sandwich shop stared at a vacant lot opposite. He invited me to sit and gave me Turkish coffee in a plastic cup. He introduced himself as Mohammed Saleh Ali Mahmoud. "I used to be a wealthy man in Tadmor," he said. "Take a look. See what I'm left with." It wasn't much. A few shelves of biscuits and tinned milk, loaves of Arabic bread in plastic wrap, a desk. Before IS occupied Tadmor the first time, Mohammed ran a building firm and a lucrative business leasing heavy construction equipment. His main customer was the Syrian Army, whose engineers were involved in various building projects in the region. "When Da'esh came, I left after two days," he recalled. "My son Adnan stayed." Adnan was twenty-six and unmarried. He worked for his father. His father advised him to leave, but he stayed to protect the company assets. IS looted the family's house and seized the heavy equipment. Mohammed said, "They said I'm a *kafir* and distributed my property to people they knew, to Da'esh people." Adnan hid in a friend's house, while IS hunted down everyone it suspected had connections to the Syrian regime. "Someone told them he was hiding there," the father said. "One of our relatives, who had come to Homs, phoned me and told me about it."

IS put scores of people on trial, including Adnan. Mohammed told me that they sentenced him to death and beheaded him. Later in our conversation he said they shot him. When IS retreated the second time, they took some of his equipment with them and detonated the rest. "I lost everything," he said, "but I wish they had taken everything and left my son." Unable to find Adnan's body, the family could not hold a funeral or bury him. IS had anyway despoiled graves of those whose bodies were found. "They even destroyed the tombs," Mohammed said, looking at the empty land in front of us, formerly a burial ground the size of a football field. Its elaborate tombstones were now pummeled to dust. "According to the Wahhabis," Mohammed said, referring to IS's Saudi Wahhabi ideology, "tombs should not be more than six inches above ground." I walked across the street to the cemetery. The graves were no longer discernible in the rubble that was, indeed, no higher than my ankle. In *The Darkening Age*, Catherine Nixey writes:

> The destroyers came from out of the desert. Palmyra must have been expecting them . . . These men moved in packs— later in swarms of as many as five hundred—and when they descended utter destruction followed. Their targets were the temples and the attacks could be astonishingly swift. Great stone columns that had stood for centuries collapsed in an afternoon; statues that had stood for half a millennium had their faces mutilated in a moment; temples that had seen the rise of the Roman Empire fell in a single day . . . The zealots roared with laughter as they smashed the 'evil', 'idolatrous' statues; the faithful jeered as they tore down temples, stripped roofs and defaced tombs . . .

Nixey described devastation, not by modern Muslim fanatics, but by Christian vandals in the third century. The Christians attacked the statue of the goddess Athena with particular ferocity, smashing "the back of Athena's head with a single blow so hard that it decapitated the goddess." They cut off her helmet and severed her arms. Seventeen centuries passed, as monotheism, first Christian and then Muslim, flourished. In the twenty-first century, Athena suffered another assault. "In Palmyra," Nixey wrote, "the great statue of Athena that had been carefully repaired by archaeologists, was attacked yet again. Once again, Athena was beheaded; once again, her arm was sheared off." IS was, in its exuberant annihilation of the past, heir to the impulse that had motivated Christian fanatics of the earlier time.

The Palmyra I visited in 1987 and again in 2017 had survived wars, rebellions, and massacres over centuries. Within the grounds of the ancient city, nothing was as I recalled it from thirty years before. The triumphal arch was gone, its plinths silhouetted against the bare sky. The Temple of Bel had become a sea of broken stone that archaeologists believe will take a generation to piece together. The agora was unrecognizable. Wandering through ancient Palmyra in 1987, I could reflect on Queen Zenobia of Palmyra, her rebellion against Emperor Aurelian and the destruction, as well as later restoration, of her city. Zenobia had inspired historians to embellish her image, Boccaccio and Chaucer to celebrate her stamina, nineteenth-century American sculptor Harriet Hosmer to immortalize her in stone, and the glamorous Anita Ekberg to portray her in the dreadful sword-and-sandal movie, *Sign of the Gladiator* (1959). The latest chapter of Palmyra's history offered no nobility to portray, to immortalize or to glamorize. The only consoling fact of the modern vandalism was that it could have been worse.

As IS prepared to abandon the site for the second time in March 2017, it placed so many charges throughout the ancient city that Russian and Syrian sappers needed months to remove them. The miracle was that the bombs did not explode. Like Hitler's order to destroy the historic heart of Paris before the German Army retreated in 1944, the demolition failed. Either there was no time or a local commander—a latter-day General Dietrich von Choltitz—refused the order to erase so much history and beauty from the face of the earth. Palmyra, despite the depredations to its monuments and its people, survived. For now.

CHAPTER THIRTEEN
ANOTHER CITY DEMOLISHED

Homs, January 2018

To see the consequences of war, go to Homs. Known to the Romans as Emesa, Syria's third-largest city is only a hundred-mile drive north of Damascus on the highway to Aleppo. A multitude of sects once shared the city, which spreads outward from its stone-built historic center into modern, high-rise suburbs. If you threw a shoe out the window, Homs' inhabitants used to say, it was bound to hit a doctor or an engineer. Now most of the doctors and engineers, like the buildings in which they dwelled, have vanished.

Homs boasts a sprawling university campus, magnificent mosques, towering church spires, parks, libraries, and hospitals. Before Syria succumbed to civil war, the old city and its covered bazaar housed a large Christian minority that thrived among its Sunni neighbors. The southern outskirts were the redoubt of urbanizing peasants, many of them from the Alawite sect of Bashar al-Assad, who wove themselves into the fabric of Homsi society. By the late twentieth century, the Alawites came to form about a quarter of the city's population.

The war transformed Homs in body and soul. As the cradle of the revolution, it was the first major city in Syria to follow the rural southern border town of Dera'a into peaceful, then violent, protests against the government. The old city and the Khaldiyeh, Baba Amr, and Wa'er quarters evolved into rebel fortresses, besieged by the government army outside and dominated by insurgents—most of them Islamists—within. It took the government four and a half years to force the rebels to surrender. Most relocated with their families and small arms to the country's largest insurgent concentration in Idlib province.

The landscape, more than two years after the fighters departed, evoked the devastation in Europe at the end of World War II. Hundreds of acres of what had been comfortable apartment complexes had become mangled mountains of deformed concrete. Homs was quiet, the war having moved to Idlib, Afrin, and other regions, but it had yet to recover. "Homs' population was about 650,000 before the war," a police source said. "It's now between one-quarter and 30 percent of that."

The humanitarian REACH initiative studied health conditions in Homs and concluded:

> All communities reported that they were unable to empty septic tanks and that connections to the sewage system were blocked, and 65 percent reported having insufficient water to meet household needs, including Zafaraniya [neighborhood]. Zafaraniya was also one of two communities that reported communicable diseases as a predominant health challenge.

Few people returned to the once quaint old city around the souqs. A friend of mine, a Christian born in Homs who lost his house in the old city, said that only about ten percent of the twenty thousand families who lived there before 2011 had moved back. As we walked through the area, we saw why. Few structures had escaped the destruction left by four years of battle: collapsed roofs, half-standing walls, burned apartments, and empty space where houses once stood. Yet many buildings were intact. The governorate restored the old souqs for the day when their customers would return. My friend and I had a delicious lunch of Homs food in a newly refurbished restaurant, while children played in the narrow street outside. A Greek Orthodox bishop came to gossip, and the waiters offered more food than we could eat.

The government, its treasury depleted by the conflict and under international sanctions, had little to offer residents to rebuild. The United Nations, whose own budget had shrunk amid a shortage of international donations, offered minimal assistance for restoring schools, hospitals, and housing. Inhabitants relied on their own meager resources to rebuild.

More glaring than the physical destruction, however, was the changed sectarian environment wrought by the war. Much of the trust that once existed among Sunnis, Christians, and Alawites had diminished. Fabrice Balanche, in his excellent report "Sectarianism in Syria's Civil War," wrote:

As early as fall 2011, for example, Sunni insurgents in Homs began daily bombing of the city's Alawi neighborhoods, with the aim of expelling Alawites from a city where many regarded them as intruders. Some observers speculated that the regime deliberately let the situation in Homs deteriorate so that sectarianism would fracture the local revolutionary movement. And in areas where the regime resorted to direct, violent repression, pacifist demonstrators were quickly overtaken by militarized opposition as people picked up weapons to defend themselves. These armed elements then organized by sect; as in many other conflicts worldwide, violence created stark dilemmas in which people had to make tough choices with group consequences.

One of the toughest choices the city's residents faced when the artillery fell silent was whether to return to a battered Homs or to make a new life elsewhere. Many Christians, for centuries an integral part of the city, chose the latter. Visas for Australia and Canada were not hard for the educated Christian middle class to obtain, and many Muslims also found ways out, possibly for good. My friend, who said that 90 percent of his friends were gone, decided to stay. "I can't leave it," he told me after lunch. "I don't know why. I've had many occasions to leave the city, but I can't. All of Homs is my home."

The city where he is raising his children no longer resembles the one in which he grew up. "Before 2011, we lived in real . . . what's the word? . . . harmony." And now? "It's all gone."

§

The war could have ended in 2017, a time when the opposition had lost the initiative and was incapable of deposing Bashar al-Assad. Yet it continued desultory fighting from its Turkish-sponsored enclave around Idlib, surviving until the moment when Assad became weaker or his allies abandoned him. The next phase had little to do with Syria, apart from the fact that it was taking place there. The antagonists were Turkish president Recep Tayyip Erdoğan, who escalated his anti-Kurdish war on Syrian soil, and the United States, which declared its mission was to keep American advisers with the Kurds and to suppress IS remnants. The US plan involved training and arming a thirty thousand-strong, mostly Kurdish border security force. Following the US announcement of the project on January 14, 2018, Erdoğan pledged "to strangle it before it's even born." He moved Turkish military units over the border and expelled Kurds from their western enclave of Afrin.

Aware that his opposition to the US-backed Kurdish force pitted him against his largest NATO ally, Erdoğan told members of parliament from his Justice and Development Party: "Hey, NATO! You are obliged to take a stance against those who harass and violate the borders of your members." His policy undermined the unity of the military bloc and obliged the United States to prolong its military presence in a country where it had no strategic interest on behalf of its Kurdish clients. Erdoğan saw the backbone of America's proposed border security force, the Kurdish People's Protection Units (YPG), as an arm of the *Partiya Karkeren Kurdistane* (PKK, Kurdistan Workers' Party). Turkish security forces had fought the PKK off and on since 1984. Turkey long ago persuaded the United States and European Union to join it in designating the PKK a terrorist organization. No one doubted the PKK's influence over the Syrian YPG or the role its fighters played, alongside other Kurdish groups, in defeating IS. The United States faced the options of removing the PKK from the register of terrorist groups or selling its NATO allies on the idea that the group is a terrorist organization in Turkey but not in Syria.

Erdoğan's resistance to a prolonged US presence in Syria under the guise of the new force received support from Turkey's adversaries in the Syrian civil war—namely Bashar al-Assad, Russia, and Iran. These three undoubtedly feared the US scheme was a pretext to keep a military presence in Syria, deprive Syrian authorities control over large swaths of the country, and gain leverage over the war's putative victors.

In his testimony to the Senate Foreign Relations Committee on January 11, 2018, David Satterfield, the State Department's senior official for Near Eastern Affairs, explained that the proposed border force's purpose was "to not only diminish Iranian foreign influence in Syria generally, but to protect our allies from the very real threat Hezbollah poses in southwest Syria to our allies." But that raised the question: How often have Hezbollah or other militias backed by the Syrian government attacked Israel across the cease-fire lines Henry Kissinger negotiated in 1974?

The answer is never. Israel is capable of protecting its border with Syria, where a UN disengagement force has been in place since 1974. A US presence in the form of a Kurdish-dominated militia, particularly one that was overextended in areas with Arab majorities, was unlikely to increase border security miles away. It would, however, have presented a tempting target for attacks by groups loyal to the Syrian government.

One of the leading American experts on Syria, Joshua Landis at the University of Oklahoma's Center for Middle East Studies, wrote:

> By controlling half of Syria's energy resources, the Euphrates dam at Tabqa, as well as much of Syria's best agricultural land, the US will be able to keep Syria poor and underresourced . . . The US should be helping the PYD to negotiate a deal with Assad that promotes both their interests: Kurdish autonomy and Syrian sovereignty. Both have shared interests, which make a deal possible. Both see Turkey as their main danger. Both need to cooperate in order to exploit the riches of the region. Both distrust radical Islamists and fear their return. Neither can rebuild alone.

In the absence of US-Russian-Syrian cooperation to end the war, US troops on the ground faced the prospect of becoming hostages to guerrilla warfare against them. The precedent for successful Syrian covert action against the United States and Israel was Lebanon after Israel's 1982 invasion, when assassination, suicide bombings, and direct attacks drove the United States out in 1984 and forced a total Israeli withdrawal sixteen years later.

President Trump, however, attempted to spare US troops this fate by summarily ordering their withdrawal from the Kurdish areas of Syria in December 2018. That was a clear betrayal of America's Kurdish allies, who had done all the ground fighting for the US against IS. It became more heinous when US commanders were ordered to show Turkish officers where the Kurds' defenses were. Turkey easily defeated the Kurds, as it had in Afrin. After abandoning the Kurds along the Turkish border, Trump reversed course and kept nine hundred Special Forces troops to work with the Kurds and "protect" oilfields in the desert of eastern Syria.

CHAPTER FOURTEEN

TELL ME HOW THIS ENDS

Washington, D.C., May 2018

America in the Middle East: learning curves are for pussies.
—Jon Stewart

The Struggle for Syria, as Patrick Seale titled his 1965 classic, has escalated steadily since Britain seized the territory from Turkey in 1918. The British turned it over to France in 1920 and took it back from Vichy in 1942. Following nominal independence in 1946, Syria became an arena of Cold War rivalry between the United States and the Soviet Union. The stream of military coups between 1949 and 1970 concluded with the Hafez al-Assad putsch that left Syria in the Kremlin camp. Assad, however, proved anything but subservient to his superpower patron. The struggle for Syria continued in haphazard fashion as Syria irritated Moscow by flirting with the US in Lebanon and sending troops to support the American *Reconquista* of Kuwait in 1991. The relationship reverted to form, when the US labelled Syria a "terrorist state" and condemned both its support for Hezbollah in Lebanon and its alliance with Iran. In 2011, the struggle became a war. The US and Russia, as well as local hegemons, backed opposite sides, ensuring a balance of terror that devastated the country and defied resolution.

The Russians, having lost Aden, Egypt, and Libya years earlier, backed their only client regime in the Arab world when it came under threat. The US gave rhetorical and logistical support to rebels, raising false hopes—as it had done among the Hungarian patriots it left in the lurch in 1956—that it would intervene with force to help them. Regional allies, namely Saudi Arabia, Qatar, and Turkey, were left to dispatch arms, money, and men, while disagreeing on objectives and strategy.

Christopher Phillips's *The Battle for Syria: International Rivalry in the New Middle East* provided a refreshing contrast to works by most ostensible experts, who were partis pris, ill-informed or both. Phillips joined a short list of writers, among them Joshua Landis, Patrick Cockburn, Fawaz Gerges, Fabrice Balanche, and the late Anthony Shadid, who made original contributions to understanding the Syria war's causes and consequences. *The Battle for Syria* apportioned responsibility to all the countries whose lavish provision of weapons and money prolonged the war far beyond what Syria's own resources would have permitted. The estimated deaths of five hundred thousand people and the dispossession of half of Syria's estimated twenty-two million inhabitants testified to the lack of interest outsiders had in Syria itself and the priority they placed on their own competing goals.

"On the eve of civil war," Phillips wrote, "Syria and the Middle East appeared deceptively stable." It turned out that the region was static rather than stable. Hints of imminent change were few, but not invisible. President Barack Obama intimated that the United States, as Britain had done forty years before, was reducing its involvement in the region. America's Iraq invasion, like the Suez fiasco for the British and French in 1956, had stretched American resources and made similar ventures less appealing. Obama admitted to a Cairo audience in 2009, "America does not presume to know what is best for everyone." This should have opened a space for public participation in governance that all Arab leaders were resisting.

Tunisia led the way out of tyranny, when popular demonstrations forced the exit of a Western-backed Arab head of state whose corruption and brutality were on a par with those of his colleagues elsewhere in the Arab world. That success kindled hope that revolution was a viable option and made France particularly wary of further identification with untenable if hitherto compliant tyrants. The virus spread to other Arab countries, playing out differently in every infected state. In Bahrain, the Saudis and the local royal family crushed the protestors. In Egypt, a dictator departed, the voters elected and then disowned a religious Candide, and another military dictator restored the old order in a more vicious form. In Libya, unrest led to bloodshed and NATO intervention that replaced a dictatorship with virulent chaos.

Despite the failure of revolution everywhere but Tunisia (until President Kais Saied dissolved parliament), external powers seized with alacrity on Syrian dissent to bring down a regime whose cardinal sin was its affiliation with Shiite Iran, Hezbollah, and Russia. While Syrian protestors sought relief from a security system that denied them basic rights, the outsiders who rallied to them, notably Saudi Arabia and Qatar, hardly stood as paragons of freedom and elected government. Syrian activists at first demanded reforms within the system and later a change of leadership without destroying, as the US had done in Iraq, the state itself. The sheikhs of Riyadh and Doha, however, wanted to replace Bashar al-Assad with someone from the majority Sunni community who would enforce a style of dictatorship closer to their own Wahhabi beliefs and hostile to Iran.

By mid-2012, the opposition by Phillips's count was divided into no fewer than 3,250 armed militias. Other observers put the number at a mere 1,500, still too many to unify under joint command when local warlords sought loot rather than national victory and foreign paymasters refused to coordinate their policies. The traditional invaders of the Mideast—Britain, France, and the US—became, in Phillips's words, "prisoners of their own rhetoric." Phillips accused the US of a "significant historical knowledge gap on Syria" and branded as "inexcusable" Obama's reticence to consider contingency plans when his belief in Assad's imminent demise did not come to fruition. Saudi Arabia, in Phillips's view, overestimated the rebels' strength while underestimating Assad's. Saudi Arabia was not alone in that miscalculation. Yet, Phillips argued, Obama resisted the arguments of those, like Hillary Clinton, urging direct American military action that risked, not only a quagmire like Vietnam, Afghanistan, and Iraq, but war with Russia.

§

In January 2017, following Donald Trump's inauguration, his national security staffers entered their White House offices for the first time. One told me that when he searched for the previous administration's Middle East policy files, the cupboard was bare. "There wasn't an overarching strategy document for anywhere in the Middle East," the senior official, who insisted on anonymity, told me in a coffee shop near the White House. "Not even on the IS campaign, so there wasn't a cross-governmental game plan."

Rob Malley, President Barack Obama's senior Middle East adviser and Harvard Law School classmate, denied the charge. "That can't be true," the fifty-five-year-old scholar insisted when we met in his office at the International Crisis Group in Washington. "We provided comprehensive memoranda to the incoming team, though we can't know if they read them. We definitely had a long one on Syria, on all aspects of the conflict."

Although I covered the Syrian conflict off and on from the beginning, the story as seen from inside Syria seemed as incomplete as the Trojan War without the gods. In the conflagration's eighth year, I flew to the Olympian heights of Washington to ask the immortals what they were doing while an estimated half-million of Syria's twenty-two million inhabitants were dying, millions more fled the country and some of civilization's most precious monuments were destroyed.

The mandarins' disclosures, along with their published memoirs and position papers, made me sympathetic to the Trump staffer's claim that the Obama team had not clarified its Syria strategy. There was no strategy. There were debates, options, discussions, anguish, orders, counterorders, and actions. In his recent book on his years as Obama's deputy national security adviser, *The World As It Is*, Ben Rhodes portrayed White House deliberations as group therapy more than strategic planning. "I felt the burden on Obama," he wrote, one of many examples of his and his colleagues' *feelings* overshadowing strategic analysis. "He had to respond to this awful event in Syria while bearing the additional weight of the war in Iraq . . ." But wasn't that a president's job?

The men and women around Obama's conference tables and via video links claimed that, more than anything else, they wanted to do the right thing. In Rhodes's case, *anything*. "Even though I had misgivings about our Syria policy," he wrote, "I was glad we were doing *something*." Obama's strategists sought to make Syria better. As they admit now, they didn't.

The year 2010 had ended with the Middle East mired in stasis. The United Nations Human Development annual report for that year concluded that the Arab states suffered the world's greatest democracy deficit, the highest number of human rights violations, and the world's most pronounced "gender disparities in reproductive health, empowerment and labor market participation." Arab dictators had their populations under control, while they pillaged the public purse to purchase American weaponry and increase their personal fortunes. Palestinian-Israeli peace was going nowhere, and Iran appeared determined to acquire nuclear weapons to match Israel's.

Stasis shifted toward dynamism in December 2010, when the self-immolation of an unemployed and desperate young man named Mohamed Bouazizi inflamed Tunisia. Mass demonstrations forced the flight of President Zine El Abidine Ben Ali, inspiring similar protests elsewhere in the Arab world. "They were the heady days of the Arab Spring," said Michael Dempsey, Obama's deputy director of national intelligence and chief intel briefer. Citizens massed in the thousands in Egypt, Bahrain, Yemen, and Libya, exploding the myth of a supine Arab world.

The vulnerable regimes in early 2011 were in the American camp, a coincidence that the Syrian president, Bashar al-Assad, interpreted as proof that the Arab Spring was a repudiation of American tutelage. As Russia's and Iran's only Arab ally, he foresaw no challenge to his throne. An omen in the unlikely guise of an incident at an open-air market in the old city of Damascus in February 2011 should have changed his mind. One policeman ordered a motorist to stop at an intersection, while another officer told him to drive on. "The poor guy got conflicting instructions, and did what I would have done and stopped," recalled the US ambassador to Syria, Robert Ford, who had only just arrived in the country. The second policeman dragged the driver out of his car and thrashed him. "A crowd gathered, and all of a sudden it took off," Ford said. "No violence, but it was big enough that the interior minister himself went down to the market and told people to go home." Ford reported to Washington, "This is the first big demonstration that we know of. And it tells us that this tinder is dry."

The next month, the security police astride the Jordanian border in the dusty southern town of Dera'a ignited the tinder by torturing children who had scrawled anti-Assad graffiti on walls. Their families, proud Sunni tribespeople, appealed for justice, then called for reform of the regime and finally demanded its removal. Rallies swelled by the day. Ford cabled Washington that the government was using live ammunition to quell the demonstrations. He noted that the protesters were not entirely peaceful: "There was a little bit of violence from the demonstrators in Dera'a. They burned the Syriatel office." (Syriatel is the cell phone company of Rami Makhlouf, Assad's cousin, who epitomized for many Syrians the ruling elite's corruption.) "And they burned a court building, but they didn't kill anybody." Funerals of protesters produced more demonstrations and thus more funerals. The Obama administration, though, was preoccupied with Egypt, where Hosni Mubarak had resigned in February, and with the NATO bombing campaign in Libya to support the Libyan insurgents who would depose and murder Muammar Qaddafi in October.

Ambassador Ford detected a turn in the Syrian uprising that would define part of its character: "The first really serious violence on the opposition side was up on the coast around Baniyas, where a bus was stopped and soldiers were hauled off the bus. If you were Alawite, you were shot. If you were Sunni, they let you go." At demonstrations, some activists chanted the slogan, "Alawites to the grave, and Christians to Beirut." A sectarian element wanted to remove Assad, not because he was a dictator but because he belonged to the Alawite minority sect that Sunni fundamentalists detested. Washington neglected to factor that into its early calculations.

Phil Gordon, assistant secretary of state for European affairs before becoming Obama's White House coordinator for the Middle East, told me, "I think the initial attitude in Syria was seen through that prism of what was happening in the other countries, which was, in fact, leaders—the public rising up against their leaders and in some cases actually getting rid of them, and in Tunisia and Yemen and Libya, with our help."

Ambassador Ford said he counseled Syria's activists to remain nonviolent and urged both sides to negotiate. Demonstrations became weekly events, starting after Friday's noon prayer as men left the mosques, and spreading north to Homs and Hama. Ford and some embassy staffers, including the military attaché, drove to Hama, with government permission, one Thursday evening in July. To his surprise, Ford said, "We were welcomed like heroes by the opposition people. We had a simple message—no violence. There were no burned buildings. There was a general strike going on, and the opposition people had control of the streets. They had all kinds of checkpoints. Largely, the government had pulled out."

Bassam Barabandi, a Syrian diplomat who defected to Washington to establish an exile organization, People Demand Change, thought that Ford had made two errors: his appearance in Hama raised hopes for direct intervention that was not forthcoming, and he was accompanied by a military attaché. "So, at that time, the big question for Damascus wasn't Ford," Barabandi told me in his spartan Washington office. "It was the military attaché. Why did this guy go with Ford?" The Syrian regime had a long-standing fear of American intelligence interference, dating to the CIA-assisted overthrow in 1949 of the elected parliamentary government and several attempted coups d'état afterward. The presence in Hama of an ambassador with his military attaché allowed the Assad regime to paint its opponents as pawns of a hostile foreign power.

The State Department closed the US Embassy in Damascus in February 2012 following intelligence that the Salafist Jabhat an-Nusra group planned to bomb it. Syrian friends told me that, before he left, Ford had urged them to defect and return as part of a post-Assad government. Ford's recollection differed: "I remember the next-to-last day of our embassy—we closed on February 6—I told the Syrian staff . . . the embassy is going to close. They said, What are we going to do? I told them, there is going to be a horrible war. There's going to be bombs. The currency is going to plunge. I said, those of you who can, buy dollars, buy euros, any kind of foreign currency, because the lira is going to drop like Iraq. And get out if you can. I don't remember telling any Syrian opposition to go to Istanbul." One Syrian contact told me that the French ambassador, Éric Chevallier, had invited him to leave and come back "in two months" as part of the new order. He declined the offer.

Ford returned to Washington, where Obama's brain trust held endless conferences to forge a policy for Syria. Jake Sullivan, Vice-President Joe Biden's national security adviser, attended most of the sessions. "The question was why Qaddafi must go and not Assad," the slim forty-one-year-old Yale law professor told me in his office at the Carnegie Endowment. No one, he said, convinced Obama that attacking Assad would achieve a result better than the anarchy following NATO's bombardment of Libya. The debates continued throughout the spring, as open warfare erupted in Syria.

"By summer," Sullivan observed, "there was a divide within the administration, 'principals' versus those who worked the Syria file. Experts were more forward-leaning; principals, more cautious."

The leading experts were Fred Hof and Robert Ford; the principals, Secretary of State Hillary Clinton and Defense Secretary Leon Panetta. Ford said, "I wrote a memo to Clinton with a copy that went to the White House—this was in June 2012—that the Al Qaeda faction is taking over eastern Syria. And the Free Syrian Army doesn't have enough supplies, not enough money, to hold them off. If eastern Syria falls, they are going to link up with the people on the other side of the border in Iraq and create this gigantic entity." Two years later, the Islamic State would establish its caliphate on exactly that territory.

With the principals urging caution, the Obama Administration dispatched nonlethal aid—what Ford called "food, medicines, meals ready to eat, stuff like that"—to the ostensibly moderate Free Syrian Army (FSA) faction. It also worked through a diplomatic channel with Russia. When neither produced results, a senior administration official said, "The State Department, the agency [CIA] and some in the White House began advocating for providing arms to the Free Syrian Army. That summer, [CIA Director David] Petraeus and Clinton made a pitch. The president shot it down, 'for now.'"

Derek Chollet, who served Obama at Defense, State, and the White House, picked up the story: "The general view was, and I think even at this point, that Assad, one way or another, he would go. And so we need to, in order to have any chance to be able to shape an outcome on the other end, we should be for it." In the absence of doing something, Obama said something, on August 18, 2011: "For the sake of the Syrian people, the time has come for President Assad to step aside." Where Assad sensed a plot to depose him, the opposition envisioned American-NATO commitment, as in Libya.

Fred Hof told me, "Our view in the State Department was, fine, if this is the judgment the president comes to, that Assad should step aside, then what we should really have in place is an interagency strategy to make it happen." Hof regretted that the White House did not develop that strategy, on the assumption that "this guy [Assad] is toast."

Chollet described one effect of Obama's "step aside" statement: "It raises expectations on the ground . . . It means you're saying they should go at the tip of a military spear." Obama, while imposing tougher economic sanctions on Syria, was not providing the spear, "for now." Then, Phil Gordon recalled, White House perceptions altered: "That was the evolution from skepticism and 'not really our role' to a bit more optimism [that] maybe we can even assist this process along." The question was, what kind of assistance? Gordon did not believe Obama had in mind "providing military material support to Arab protesters." There was a view, he said, "It's just, well, this is the trend, and the people overthrew their dictators in Tunisia and Egypt and Yemen. And Syria will be next. And I think it was more hope than a policy." But that hope ignored the differences between Syria and the deposed dictatorships.

Tunisia's tiny army was not a decisive political actor and the country had experienced only one coup in its history, Ben Ali's in 1987. Government institutions could function without him. In Egypt, Mubarak was the face—called derisively by Egyptians "*la vache qui rit,*" "the laughing cow"—of a military regime that could survive with any general as its figurehead. In Syria, Bashar al-Assad *was* the regime. His father, Hafez al-Assad, had come to power in November 1970 as the survivor of nearly annual military putsches in the 1950s and '60s. At his death in June 2000, he bequeathed his son an edifice that had prevailed over thirty years of failed coup plots, assassination attempts, wars with Israel and Islamist insurrections. To depose the son, the opposition had to undermine a fortress state to which many Syrians were loyal or, at least, acquiescent.

Obama imposed economic sanctions, primarily on members of the regime's inner circle, and he asked the Russians to pressure Assad to leave. Phil Gordon, who accompanied Hillary Clinton to meetings with the Russian foreign minister, Sergey Lavrov, said, "Lavrov would say, 'It's not up to us.' . . . The Russian view was, 'Look, we don't love Assad. We don't care about him, but it's not up to us to determine Syria's fate.'" Lavrov also warned Clinton that removing Assad would lead to chaos and jihadism. "They had a fair point in saying we didn't have a plan for Syria if we got rid of Assad," Gordon admitted. "And, to be honest, I don't think we were ever in a position to convincingly say, 'No, no, no, if Assad falls, it won't be like Iraq or Afghanistan.'"

In Damascus and other Syrian cities, security forces fired live ammunition at the crowds. The United States had sided with security forces who shot Arab demonstrators in Israel and Bahrain, but its sympathies in Syria were with the protesters. Many Syrian activists argued that they should take up arms in the belief that the United States would match action to words. Others urged restraint, fearing that, force against force, they would lose.

"The beginning of militarization had started before the end of 2011," Fred Hof said, noting the transition from defending demonstrators to offensive operations. The door opened wide to outside meddling. Hof said that arms from Turkey, Saudi Arabia, and Qatar—three countries whose human rights records were no better than Syria's—to various, mainly Islamist, groupings had an unexpected consequence: "I think all of this inadvertently but quite decisively played into the hands of the regime." Assad's strategy for dealing with civil disobedience, popular mobilization and general strikes may have been ineffective, but the regime knew how to handle armed insurrection. And Salafist fighters terrified many Syrians who, while dismissive of Assad, did not welcome his replacement by religious fanatics with long beards.

Hof said, "I'm not just talking about the entourage and members of the [Assad] family, but ordinary Syrians, Syrians I've known for decades, who would tell me, 'Fred, we're going to stick with the regime.'" Hof said they stuck with Assad, despite having "no illusions about the corruption, incompetence, and brutality of the regime." Others who did not fight against the regime were the minorities—Alawis, Ismailis, Druze, Arab Christians, Armenians, and Yazidis, all of whom the jihadis wanted to eliminate—as well as Sunnis who preferred a secular dictatorship to a theocracy.

Hof pushed for supporting secular insurgents. Other officials, he told me, shared his viewpoint:

> In the summer of 2012, you had the incident of Clinton, Petraeus, Panetta, and [Chairman of the Joint Chiefs of Staff Martin] Dempsey going to the president and saying, in effect, Look, Mr. President, what Assad is doing is terrible, but now we're noticing something else. We're noticing some Al Qaeda elements beginning to establish themselves in Syria, and what we recommend is that the United States take the lead in arming and training vetted elements of the Syrian opposition, focusing, for the most part, on officers and soldiers who had defected from the Syrian Army, forces that would be able to fight in two directions—against the regime and against Al Qaeda. And the president turned that down. He turned it down.

In August 2012, a year and a half into the war, a question from NBC correspondent Chuck Todd produced a portentous response from Obama: "We have been very clear to the Assad regime, but also to

other players on the ground, that a red line for us is [if] we start seeing a whole bunch of chemical weapons moving around or being
utilized. That would change my calculus." As with his call a year earlier for Assad to step aside, Obama's chemical-weapons declaration
would haunt him. A former US ambassador to the Middle East told
me, "The 'red line' was an open invitation to a false-flag operation."
Robert Gates, secretary of defense from December 2006 to July 2011,
after leaving the department called the red line "a serious mistake"
that eroded American credibility.

On August 21, 2013, poison-gas canisters shattered the ear-
ly-morning quiet in eastern Ghouta, a populous rebel-held suburb of Damascus. Horrifying videos showed children gasping
for breath, victims frothing at the mouth, and discolored corpses
without visible wounds. Prior to this massive outrage, there had
been sporadic and small-scale use of chemical weapons by both
sides, for which each blamed the other. In Washington, the director of national intelligence, James Clapper, told Obama that the
case against Assad was not a "slam dunk," the term CIA Director
George Tenet used in December 2002 to affirm the fiction that
Saddam was hiding weapons of mass destruction. Nonetheless,
Obama declared that Assad had crossed his red line. "Whoever
actually used chemical weapons in east Ghouta," said a CIA analyst, "the blame went straight to Assad. He had crossed the red line,
and the rebels were not the only ones who expected him [Obama]
to do something about it."

Ben Rhodes wrote that General Dempsey urged Obama to act:
"Up to this point, he had argued that Syria was a slippery slope
where there was little chance of success. Now he said that something needed to be done even if we didn't know what would happen
after we took action." Obama decided to act, calling on Britain and

France to join an American air and missile assault on Syria. France committed at once, but the British Parliament voted not to take part. As French and American forces prepared to strike, Obama took a walk in the Rose Garden with his chief of staff, Denis McDonough. Suddenly, the order went out for the warplanes to stand down. "The next morning, there was a meeting in the Situation Room," said Jake Sullivan, who sat in. "[Secretary of State John] Kerry, [Defense Secretary Chuck] Hagel, the principals. Samantha [Power] was on the screen. McDonough, [National Security Adviser] Susan Rice. Susan objected. She said, Don't go to Congress. Obama went out later that day and gave a statement on asking Congress."

Morning in Washington was night in Syria, when I drove into Damascus expecting the American-French assault. The city looked as if it had been evacuated. Even the troops had gone into shelters. Syrians braced for a massive strike. Some told me they feared the jihadis would overrun the capital under cover of the Western attack. Then came the announcement from Washington that the raid would not take place.

A series of unscripted statements by Kerry and Lavrov led Russia to persuade Assad to acknowledge his poison-gas arsenal, sign the Chemical Weapons Convention, and allow the Organization for the Prohibition of Chemical Weapons (OPCW) to destroy his stockpiles. When the Islamic State later overran the government's chemical-weapons stores, they had been removed. Obama's threat had, with Russian help, succeeded. The crisis ended, but gases including chlorine and sarin would be used again—as before, with blame placed on each side by the other. As the war escalated, at least ninety-five percent of the casualties resulted from conventional weapons from Russia, the United States, Saudi Arabia, Qatar, the United Arab Emirates, Turkey, and Iran that no one was obstructing.

Debate continued within the administration on what to do. Obama listened to arguments for and against no-fly zones and safe havens. Robert Gates addressed the no-fly zone proposal in an interview with CBS's *Face the Nation* after he left office:

> You know, I oversaw two wars that began with quick regime change. And we all know what happened after that. And as I said to the Congress when we went into Libya, when they were talking about a no-fly zone, "It begins with an act of war." And haven't we learned that when you go to war, the outcomes are unpredictable? And anybody who says, "It's gonna be clean. It's gonna be neat. You can establish the safe zones. And it'll be, it'll just be swell"—well, most wars aren't that way.

No-fly zones required demolishing Syria's air defenses, which the Russians had installed and were committed to defending. "No-fly" also meant making targets of Russian planes in Syrian skies, risking a third world war.

The bleak history of safe havens in Bosnia, where civilians seeking safety were massacred while UN soldiers looked away, made their utility suspect. Safe havens and no-fly zones, however, dominated White House deliberations. One of Obama's Middle East advisers recalled, "Was the right approach to create safe zones? No-fly zones? Discussions on this issue continued well into 2016. Even as late as the assault on Aleppo [by the Syrian Army and Russia in 2016], questions returned about what we could do, whether to go after the regime directly or protect the city." I asked the adviser, "Then the decision was made not to?" He answered, "Right."

If the Obama people were to have done *something,* what would it have been? An acquaintance of John Kerry with Mideast expertise who asked not to be named recalled Kerry telling him in 2013, "Let's get serious. There is no more resolution to this Syrian thing without Bashar. He has to be brought in, and we have to negotiate with him." The consultant recalled that Kerry spoke later that day to a wealthy Syrian-British businessman, who argued that the United States had to depose Assad. The consultant saw Kerry the next day: "Kerry told me, completely oblivious to what he said before, 'Assad has to go. As long as Assad is there, he is a magnet for terrorists.' I said, 'Assad is a magnet for terrorists? What is it about Assad that attracts them to fight? What about the ones in Sinai? In Mali? In Yemen? In Kenya? In Somalia? What do they have to do with Assad?' . . . There was no policy. They were making it up as they went along." David Wade, former chief of staff for Secretary Kerry, disputed this account: "There was no 2013 meeting that altered his view."

One of the administration's more articulate Syria hawks was Antony Blinken, Obama's deputy national security adviser and then John Kerry's deputy secretary of state from 2015 to 2017. He recalled Obama's reaction to every proposal to deploy troops or air power in Syria: "I think from President Obama's perspective, when some of us would advocate to do more, take some more chances, he would regularly ask, 'Tell me how this ends.' No one could answer with confidence that we would not wind up on a slippery slope, getting in deeper and deeper than we intended."

A senior Mideast adviser to Obama explained the misgivings of the administration's anti-interventionists:

Many in the administration were in favor of some form of intervention, perhaps targeted strikes. But there was also significant skepticism about the wisdom of direct US military involvement, about the nature of the opposition, the risk of a slippery slope.

The compromise between direct military involvement and staying out was the route taken by many presidents before Obama: a covert operation to raise an insurgent army and train it in nearby countries; provide weapons, sustenance, and communications; and oversee the military campaign. It was high-risk for the locals and casualty-free for the Americans. A senior administration official told me, "Only a few were against arming the opposition. Obama commissioned a report on the history of arming groups."

The CIA produced a history that remains classified and which, says one of those who read it, showed "only one or two instances of successful proxy wars." Despite the failure of the CIA's secret wars, from Albania in the late 1940s through Angola in the 1970s and 1980s, Obama assigned the CIA to train militants in Turkey and Jordan under what is called a Title 50 program in defense of American national security.

§

What is the source of the fascination with arming foreign insurgents and proxy armies to fight wars that the US won't fight itself? "We're busily training, you know, local troops to fight local militants, why do we think we have this aptitude for creating armies?" Andrew Bacevich, a retired army colonel and author of *America's War for the Greater Middle East*, told me. "I don't know. It sure as hell didn't work in Vietnam." Two reasons stand out. One is that, as Bacevich explained, insurgencies are wars "on the cheap," not only in dollars but in assuring the public that American soldiers' lives are not in danger. It is also a midway point between invasion and doing nothing. And most American presidents, faced with an opportunity to undermine rival states, prefer to do something.

It all started in Syria, where Britain conducted a successful insurgency against Ottoman Turkey from 1916 to 1918. The famed organizer of the Arab rebels was Lawrence of Arabia, whose *Seven Pillars of Wisdom* remains required reading for clandestine warfare operatives everywhere. Lawrence became the inspiration for Britain's first secret warfare organization, Special Operations Executive (SOE). SOE came into being in the summer of 1940, when Britain lacked resources to fight on alone after the German conquest of Belgium, Holland, and France. Winston Churchill created the office of "ungentlemanly warfare" on July 19 "to coordinate all action by way of subversion and sabotage against the enemy overseas." The British trained, armed, and financed local insurgents to harass the Germans, as well as their Italian and Japanese allies, in all countries under Axis occupation.

SOE's first director of operations, Lieutenant Colonel Colin Gubbins, who became overall chief in 1943, wrote the *Art of Guerrilla Warfare* and the *Partisan Leader's Handbook*, based on what he called "Lawrence's epic campaign." What he instigated was, by SOE's admission, "terrorism" against the Axis.

SOE mobilized mountain tribes in Burma, communist and royalist rebels in Yugoslavia, and disparate anti-Nazis in France. It also encouraged the US to establish its own covert operations unit, which became the Office of Strategic Services (OSS). Gubbins assigned Major Bill Brooker to train the Americans at top-secret Camp X in the Canadian woods, telling him, "We think the Americans are going to come into the war and they have to learn all about this stuff." One American official wondered, "What type of training was required to make an American un-American enough to stick the enemy in the back?" Camp X, which opened three days after Pearl Harbor, instructed more than five hundred inexperienced Americans in the dark arts of partisan recruitment, sabotage, assassination, secrecy, and encrypted communications.

The entrance of the Soviet Union and the US into the war against Germany altered the balance in Britain's favor and changed SOE's covert mission in Europe from harassment to support of an Allied invasion of the Continent. When Britain and the US invaded Italy and then France, SOE-backed guerrilla units diverted German resources away from advancing Allied armies.

Resistance was not decisive, but it saved Allied lives and shortened the war. SOE and OSS claimed numerous achievements, due to effective leadership by men and women who knew the countries they worked in, spoke the language, lived among their fighters, and observed strict security. One of the best was George Starr, who set up operations in southwest France and slowly grew his WHEELWRIGHT resistance network from one small district to the entire region. His forces helped to impede Germany's Second SS Panzer Division from reaching the Normandy beaches, where the Allies landed on June 6, 1944, by seventeen crucial days. By the time the battered division arrived, the beachhead was secure. SOE critics, including George's brother and fellow SOE operative John Starr, recorded fatal errors. The most famous was succumbing to false German radio signals, supposedly from SOE operators, that lured scores of British agents to their deaths. In World War II, SOE was a partial success.

Although the British shut down SOE and the Americans dismantled OSS right after the war, the seductiveness of special operations à la SOE and OSS lingered. The British absorbed former SOE agents into its traditional spy agency, the Secret Intelligence Service

(SIS), also known as MI-6. OSS veterans formed the backbone of the CIA that President Harry Truman established in 1947. Both organizations existed to collect intelligence, but they nonetheless conducted operations that included assassination and clandestine warfare. Historian of espionage Phillip Knightley wrote that mixing the two "made it inevitable that intelligence also involved covert action, and covert action now meant American intervention in countries with which the United States was not at war."

Intervention never stopped. The British and Americans infiltrated guerrilla bands into the Soviet Union and its satellites, in Truman's words, to roll back communism. They sometimes employed former Nazis, notably in the Ukraine where they armed fascist nationalists against the Russians in a disastrous campaign that left most of its participants dead, wounded or captured. The joint Anglo-American Operation Valuable infiltrated rebels into Albania to overthrow dictator Enver Hoxha, a former SOE ally during World War II. Most of them were immediately killed or taken prisoner. Frank Wisner, the CIA point man in Albania, told Kim Philby, the SIS operative secretly working for the Soviets, "We'll get it right next time." They didn't.

Attempts to use insurgents in the three Soviet-occupied Baltic nations led not only to failure but to seventy-five thousand civilian casualties. The infiltration of guerrillas into North Korea likely affected the North's decision to invade South Korea in June 1950. CIA support of rebellious colonels in Indonesia five years later did not prevent their total defeat by the Indonesian Army. The 1961 Bay of Pigs disaster in Cuba is well known, as is the clandestine Contra war against the Sandinista government in Nicaragua. CIA director and OSS veteran William Casey ran that illegal war over Congressional objections using Saudi money and funds from the illegal sale of arms to Iran. The CIA covert war in Afghanistan led to a mujahideen victory over the Soviets, then chaos, civil war, the creation of the Taliban, the hosting of Osama bin Laden, 9/11, and the longest war in American history.

In 2011, a revolt erupted in Syria. The US, which was witnessing the tragic consequences of its intervention in Libya, was reluctant to use its military again. The halfway house between quick victory by Assad, backed by allies Russia and Iran, and American invasion was a covert operation. This was supposed to be different from the failed missions catalogued in the CIA study that Obama commissioned. It wasn't. The CIA's bid to emulate Lawrence on the master's old terrain failed. Why?

Lawrence had advantages that the CIA lacked. First, the British Army under General Edmund Allenby invaded Palestine and Syria from Egypt. Lawrence's ill-equipped tribesmen, who on their own could not have defeated the Ottomans, served as Allenby's right flank on his advance north. Nearly a century later, the CIA had no invading American army to support in Syria. Second, Lawrence fought alongside his men, while most CIA operatives remained at base in Turkey and Jordan. Third, Lawrence's strategy was not to hold territory that his irregulars could not defend. Syria's rebels did that again and again.

Lawrence, writing on guerrilla warfare in the *Encyclopaedia Britannica* in 1929, explained that a guerrilla force had to be "an influence, a thing invulnerable, intangible, without front or back, drifting about like gas . . . never giving the enemy a target." He felt that "battles were a mistake," a lesson the CIA neglected to teach the Syrian rebels. The next edition of the CIA's covert ops history will have to include its many-billion-dollar disaster in Syria.

Did that mean an end to secret wars? Two hints that lessons remained unlearned were Trump lawyer Rudy Giuliani's call for regime change in Iran and Secretary of State Mike Pompeo's establishment of an Iran Action Group to undermine the Tehran regime. Meanwhile, Saudi Arabia funded the Mujahideen-e-Khalq (MeK), an Iranian Shiite mirror image of Al Qaeda. The MeK was an ally of Saddam in the Iran-Iraq War, massacred Kurds in 1991, and was for more than two decades on the US State Department's list of terrorist organizations. If Syria was a disaster, Iran could be a catastrophe.

A century before Britain sent Lawrence into Syria, Wellington's army supported Spanish partisans against Napoleon's occupation of their country. The Spaniards won in 1814, returning King Ferdinand VII to his throne in Madrid. One of the monarch's first acts was to restore the Inquisition that had for centuries burned heretics at the stake.

§

After Obama approved the covert Title 50 program, rebels turned up with equipment they could not have looted from the Syrian Army. In summer 2012, Al Qaeda-linked gangs shared the bounty, prompting Secretary of State Hillary Clinton to fly to Istanbul, by then the unofficial capital of the Syrian opposition in exile. Jake Sullivan said that she wanted US allies Turkey, Saudi Arabia, and Qatar "to ensure the arms were provided with checks to make certain they were not going to Nusra or other terrorist groups." He recalled her asking, "'How are the controls implemented?' The steps were taken, but they were incomplete." Incomplete or nonexistent, as jihadis with weapons supplied by American allies flooded Syria through the Turkish border.

Charles Lister, who monitored insurgent groups from the beginning of the Syrian conflict and wrote *The Syrian Jihad*, told me:

By the summer of 2012, there was a pretty active effort on both sides of Syria's northern and southern borders to prop up and help to create a somewhat more organized opposition movement. But the fact that Qatar and Turkey and Saudi and the UAE and Jordan were all involved, as governments, and then there were separate private networks coming out of Doha, Kuwait City, Istanbul—every single one of them was working along their own chart.

Lister estimated that at one time there were as many as fifteen hundred insurgent groups with conflicting goals and no central command. It was a recipe for failure as much as for carnage.

A major source of weapons for the Syrian opposition was Libya, which after Muammar Gadhafi's overthrow became a twenty-four-hour arms bazaar. It furnished TOW anti-tank missiles and other war matériel with the help of the CIA station at the US consulate compound in Benghazi—despite White House denials. CIA director David Petraeus became so concerned that Al Qaeda affiliates were receiving the weapons that he flew to Turkey on September 2, 2012, to complain to President Erdoğan. The supply chain became public after the September 11 murder that year of US ambassador Christopher Stevens in the Benghazi compound. Media outlets, including Fox News, reported that ships delivered TOWs, surface-to-air missiles, and other high-tech weaponry from Libya to the port of Iskenderun in southern Turkey. After the publicity, Washington put full blame on Qatar for running a rogue operation without US approval. "That's bullshit," a CIA source told me.

Rebel training became the province of US and British agents, and the Turks allocated weapons. But there was no control over

216

fighters when they infiltrated Syria, where many joined Salafist brigades. A British trainer told me that the program was benefiting religious fanatics more than any moderate, secular oppositionists.

The TOWs from Benghazi shifted the balance on the ground in favor of the rebels, especially the better-armed and highly motivated jihadis. Assad's tanks and helicopters were no longer invulnerable. Phil Gordon refused to discuss the issue of covert assistance, but he noted that the administration "started to publicly say in the spring or maybe June of 2013 that we were providing direct support to the opposition, including military support." The support was a program, and the program had a name: Timber Sycamore. Speaking in his office at Washington's Middle East Institute, Charles Lister recalled,

Sometimes they [the insurgents] suddenly found themselves wearing nice uniforms, new camouflage fatigues. And it pretty quickly emerged that, at the end of 2012, weapons, mostly from [the] former Yugoslavia, had started to be shipped in through Amman into the south. And then some of that started to appear in northern Syria.

I don't know exactly when an open channel was established, but it wouldn't have been any later than the spring of 2013. Certainly [by] December of 2012, those first weapons appeared in the south. And it subsequently became clear the reason why that had started was because the CIA had received clearance, I assume from the White House, to run a pretty substantial Title 50 covert program of assistance to the vetted Syrian opposition. CIA operatives in Turkey and Jordan screened rebels to weed out fundamentalists.

Vetting, however, proved futile. The net effect was not, as Phil Gordon hoped, to "accelerate the process of Assad's departure." In fact, Gordon conceded, it was the opposite: "I think that what we saw was that the more we did for the opposition, the more the backers of the regime did for the regime." Iran's Lebanese surrogate, Hezbollah, sent more fighters from Lebanon to back Assad. The Russians came to Assad's rescue with troops and air power, while the Iranians introduced units of Iraqi and Afghan Shias.

On the opposition side, jihadis from Chechnya, Afghanistan, Algeria, China, and Europe joined the fight. Together with indigenous fundamentalists, they reduced the FSA to irrelevance. "We didn't have a great understanding of who was doing what on the ground," Phil Gordon said, "and couldn't control it. So, you would be running the risk that, almost the inevitable risk that, in a revolutionary situation, the worst guys were the ones that would take and use the weapons." The most extreme elements, the Al Qaeda offshoots Jabhat an-Nusra and IS, not only used the weapons but also advertised them in videos that included beheadings, the hurling of gay men off towers to their deaths, the murder of American journalists and British aid workers, and the rape of Yazidi women. Charles Lister said that "all of the opposition worked with Nusra, because they were very good on the battlefield. But what was the result of that in London and Paris and Washington and elsewhere? We began to look at the opposition like they were all jihadis."

Gerald Feierstein, the US ambassador in Yemen, before becoming deputy assistant secretary of state for Near Eastern affairs in 2013, underscored the Obama administration's naïveté in 2014, three years into the war: "There was a sense that the momentum was really with the opposition, the government was weak, and some hope that at least if not Bashar himself but that others within the regime might be interested in some kind of a face-saving way to get out of a jam. But they weren't." Others in the administration, he said, "were saying that we should just accept that Bashar was going to stay."

While administration officials debated, Syria descended deeper into the mayhem that was driving millions out of the country and thousands to their graves. By the summer of 2015, I could no longer reach Aleppo from Damascus because of the fighting. I called Armen Mazloumian, whose family had owned and run the city's famed Hotel Baron since 1909. He blamed the West for giving arms to the jihadis occupying the eastern half of the city. Mazloumian died shortly afterward, his health having given out amid the danger and privation of the war. How far away all that must have seemed in the cozy offices of the White House, not to mention the Kremlin, where self-described statesmen determined the fate of Armen and the rest of Syria.

Rob Malley believes Obama's primary motivation was humanitarian. The administration sent aid to refugees in Turkey and Jordan and deployed a USAID transition-and-response team, under the name START, to assist local administration in parts of Syria that the regime had evacuated. The problem in Syria, though, was not humanitarian; it was political, and the political dynamics were evolving. An official who took up his post at the White House in February 2014 observed a policy too entrenched to be reversed: "The opposition backed by the US was also backed from the outset by others—Saudi Arabia, Turkey, and Qatar, whose objective clearly was to overthrow the regime and remove Iran. That is what the war quickly came to be about."

By that stage, one faction in the administration got cold feet. Phil Gordon said, "I'll be honest, and I've written about this publicly, by then I had concluded that we had a strategy that just wasn't going to work." Gordon said that by 2015, the United States had "a means-ends gap. You have to change the means or the end." His conclusion was that the United States should change the objective, because "it wasn't realistic to get rid of Assad. I didn't see a path of doing so without a major US military intervention that would escalate the conflict. And even if it succeeded, [it] could be a version of catastrophic success, where you create a vacuum that extremists would fill."

Seeking continued US support, the FSA distanced itself from the Islamic State. "On January 1, 2014, the FSA collectively, in northern Syria, declared war on IS," said Charles Lister. "And in ten weeks, IS was expelled from four and a half provinces in northern Syria." IS concentrated its forces in northeast Syria along the Iraqi border, rampaging across western Iraq, much as Ambassador Ford and others had predicted. The Islamic State's "caliphate" threatened America's local allies, the Kurds in Erbil and Baghdad's Shia-led government. Obama had ignored the Islamic State in Syria, until it impinged on American interests in Iraq. "I think there was a period of time where again there was a certain amount of panic, particularly involved with the threat to the Yazidis," Feierstein said. "And I think things in Iraq were unraveling at a pace that was really extremely concerning and that we needed to respond."

Obama's attention shifted from Assad to defeating a force dedicated to worldwide terrorism. This led to an overt Title 10 program for the Defense Department to arm anyone who would fight the Islamic State. The beneficiaries were mainly the Kurds of northeastern Syria, who fought tenaciously but had no interest in confronting the Syrian Army. This was not without its complications. Turkey regarded all armed Kurds as terrorists, and many Syrian fighters refused to fight the Islamic State if they could not confront the Assad regime as well. A state of lunacy was reached when the respective insurgent bands of

TELL ME HOW THIS ENDS

the CIA's covert and the Defense Department's overt programs turned their American weapons on each other. Former deputy director of national intelligence Michael Dempsey told me, "Some of the training programs were options between doing nothing and military intervention." Dempsey, whose brother Martin, as chairman of the Joint Chiefs of Staff (JCS), resisted military intervention in Syria, echoed Ben Rhodes: "No one was sure it would work, but we had to do something."

The triumphs of the Islamic State caused a change in thinking at the White House. One of the Obama insiders I interviewed said, "When I left in 2014, it was game over for dealing with Syria outside of IS." The Islamic State's sometime rival, occasional ally, and fellow Al Qaeda offshoot Jabhat an-Nusra also provoked the administration's ire. Joe Biden spoke to Qatar's ruler, Sheikh Hamad bin Khalifa Al Thani, in April of 2013, about his support for the extremists. One of Biden's closest advisers said that the vice-president told the emir, "If you gave me a choice between Assad and Nusra, I'll take Assad." Biden famously went public in October 2014 with his condemnation of Turkey, Saudi Arabia, and the UAE for providing firepower and money to the Salafists of al-Nusra and Al Qaeda. US strategists underestimated Russia's commitment to Assad. Assad's survival was a test of Russian credibility. Syria was its only ally in the twenty-two member Arab League, and Russia had its sole Mediterranean naval base on the Syrian coast at Tartous. Russia's air force and army intervened in September 2015. By December 2016, they helped drive the rebels out of the eastern half of Aleppo. Many regarded that as the war's turning point, after which Assad could no longer lose.

Syria proved to be Russia's redemption in the Middle East. Putin became a regional power broker, for the first time selling antiaircraft systems to Turkey, a NATO member; sending military delegations to

Iraq; and organizing discussions about Syria among Turkey, Israel, and several Arab states.

More regime victories followed the triumph in Aleppo, as Russia enabled the Syrian Army, with Hezbollah and Iran, to advance into rebel territory. The insurgents either fought to the death or accepted "reconciliation" that allowed them to go with their families and small arms to their last redoubt in the northern province of Idlib. The negotiators deciding Idlib's fate included Russia, Turkey, Assad, and most rebel leaders—but not the United States.

The result of US meddling in Syria was failure on all counts. It did not depose Assad, who looked set to hold power for years. It did not expel Iran and Russia, whose influence and footprints in Syria expanded. It did not break the Syria-Hezbollah alliance. Nor did it ameliorate civilian suffering, as refugees either stayed in exile squalor or returned to demolished homes. It had the unintended consequence of turning Turkey from a traditional ally into a regional adversary. Syrian conspiracy theorists claim the US goal was to destroy Syria, as it did Iraq, to protect Israel. Only if that were true could the United States be said to have achieved any objective.

The American election of November 2016 appeared to presage disengagement from Syria. Trump canceled Obama's Title 50 program that armed Syrian oppositionists in July 2017. But one of his senior officials admonished me, "When everyone tells you it's over, it's not over. This has a long way to go." He added, "And it's still in our interests to try to bring an end to it. But not an end to it just at any cost." Trump withdrew most of the Special Forces troops Obama sent to oppose the Islamic State in northeastern Syria, leaving Turkey to decimate America's Kurdish allies in Syria and seize parts of their former autonomous region. The American withdrawal from Syria remained incomplete while a small Special

Forces team remained with the Kurds and in the eastern desert near the Al-Tanf border crossing to Jordan and Iraq. Trouble lurked among the area's tribes who had made peace with the government in Damascus. The chief of the Ta'i tribe in February 2020 called for resistance against "American forces occupying our land and a clear message to reject their occupation and presence on Syrian soil."

Some State Department officials I know refused to discuss the Trump policy, saying the administration was keeping a close eye out for leaks. Anyway, one said, he wasn't sure what the policy was. Trump's principal target remained Iran, and his advisers proposed hitting Iran in Syria while supporting the "former" terrorists of the Mujahedeen-e-Khalq in Iran itself.

I asked an Obama Mideast adviser what, in retrospect, he would have done differently. "There were serious risks in throwing in our lot with the opposition," he said. "We gave them false hope. We didn't control what they did with their weapons. We didn't control who they cooperated with. And no matter what, we were still on the hook." Phil Gordon is one of those who learned something from Syria. Speaking to me in his Council on Foreign Relations office, where he is the Mary and David Boies senior fellow, he reflected,

> I've obviously thought about this many, many times, because you can't look back at Syria and conclude anything but, you know, that it's a horrific tragedy on every level, for the Syrians, for the neighbors, for us. I've yet to find the path to a better outcome, other than not fomenting the insurgency in the first place. I think the original sin is getting on board for supporting an armed opposition that had little

prospect of actually bringing about a political transition in
a more stable Syria.

Ambassador Robert Ford testified to Congress in early 2018 that the
"US military and civilian costs in Syria over the past four years are
at least $12 billion." It was a high price for failure—failure to depose
President Bashar al-Assad, to break his alliance with Iran, to prevent Salafist jihadism from taking root in Syria for the first time, to
maintain the friendship of NATO ally Turkey, to save an estimated
half-million Syrians from death and to stem the exodus of nearly half
the Syrian population from their homes.

The "Vietnam syndrome" that produced America's aversion
to invading other countries following the April 1975 fall of Saigon
lasted until January 1991. General Norman Schwarzkopf's defeat of
Saddam Hussein's occupying army in Kuwait made invasion respectable again. The US armed forces invaded Afghanistan in 2001 and
Iraq in 2003. The prolonged warfare in Afghanistan and chaos in
occupied Iraq were decisive factors in deterring Obama from invading Syria.

Phil Gordon thought the United States Army could have defeated
the Syrian Army, but that would have been the beginning, not the
end, of the problem: "Once we topple the regime, are the stable mod-
erates going to come to power and govern Syria? I don't think so.
And then you've just got a different form of chaos that we're responsible for."

Obama's foreign policy team had advanced degrees from
Harvard, Yale, and Georgetown, as well as Rhodes scholarships, and
better credentials than most Fortune 500 boards, university faculties,
and think tanks. They were "the best and the brightest" of our time,

heirs to the *wunderkinder* John F. Kennedy brought to Washington in 1961. Kennedy's brain trust gave the country the mass atrocity that was the Vietnam War, while Obama's oversaw the devastation of Syria.

Like Alec Guinness's Colonel Nicholson in *The Bridge on the River Kwai,* Obama's best and brightest may look with shock at their handiwork and ask, "What have I done?" Colonel Nicholson's final act, after trying to save the bridge he built for his Japanese captors, was to fall on the detonator and blow it up. Then, he died. In Washington, they go on to think tanks and academe to await the call to serve again.

CHAPTER FIFTEEN

THE BLOOD CAVE

Damascus, December 2018

> And Cain said unto the Lord, My punishment is greater
> than I can bear.
> —Genesis 4:13

Mount Qasioun soars above the Damascus plain to a height of four thousand feet, a sheer escarpment that for millennia has borne witness to insurrection, invasion, siege, and annihilation.

Mankind's first, albeit legendary, murder occurred in Qasioun's Cave of Blood, where Cain crushed his brother Abel's skull with a stone. For many Jews, Christians, and Muslims, Abel is the original martyr, the prototype for millions who followed him into blameless death. Cafés on the summit used to afford a vista of the sprawling metropolis below, until the government banned visitors lest they act as artillery spotters for the rebels. In 2011, Damascus divided into hostile strongholds of the state and its armed opponents. Six and a half years later, the government restored its rule to all the areas visible from Qasioun, apart from two besieged, nearly leveled corners, one along the city's eastern fringe and the other in a tiny pocket to the south. Occasional artillery and mortar rounds testified to the insurgents' stubborn survival, but the rebellion no longer threatened the rule of Bashar al-Assad. For Damascus, if not for the provinces, the postwar era had begun.

"The regime stays," one diplomat in Damascus told me. "That's it. The time of regime change is over." Terms such as "regime change" and "transition" had disappeared from political discourse by that time. The government was establishing a new normal. Electricity had been restored from a few hours to twenty-four most days. Water flowed from the taps, garbage was collected, and taxi drivers moaned about traffic. Brides in white chiffon swayed and ululated as they rode in open convertibles to their wedding parties.

When the guns went quiet in Damascus in the spring of 2018, Damascenes began speaking of antebellum Syria with the dreamy yearning that Scarlett O'Hara had for Tara. They reminisced about driving along a 225-mile checkpoint-free road north past Homs and Hama to Aleppo. They recalled strolling, day and night, without fear of robbers. Women did not suffer harassment in the streets. There were no potholes in the roads. No one asked about your religion. Visitors arrived from all over the world to see Syria's ancient treasures and shop in its vaulted souqs. Business was good. And on and on. Government supporters and those who wished that the war had had another result shared the conviction that life was better before.

"I think in the first six months of 2018 there will be a new constitution for Syria," a Syrian security source hoped, "but nothing will change." Nothing? "The structure will stay the same. Rami Makhlouf and the Alawis are secure. Everything else can change, but it's decoration." Makhlouf, Assad's fabulously rich first cousin, symbolized the financial chicanery that inspired resentment and protests against the regime in 2011. "The sad thing is that corruption-wise, things are worse," said a Syrian businessman in 2018 who struggled to remain neutral throughout the war. "As a regime, if they are worried about the country, they should stop the corruption. If they stay like that, there won't be any reconstruction. Five or ten people have ninety percent of the cake."

Syrian malfeasance is paltry compared to that in neighboring Lebanon and Iraq, where rampant bribery and official theft have crippled their economies, and lags behind the plundering by Assad's oil-rich patrons in Russia and Iran. But it remains a grievance. Drivers on the twenty-five-mile road between the Lebanese border and Damascus, for example, had to tip soldiers a dollar at one checkpoint and two packs of Marlboros at another to avoid lengthy inspections of their cars and documents. Small sums add up, and thousands of cigarettes found their way to the black market to benefit officers and supplement soldiers' modest salaries.

In society's higher reaches, the illicit gains were greater. By evading international sanctions during the war, a new breed of entrepreneurs enriched itself through arms deals, smuggling, and trading between government and opposition zones—including, many insist, brokering the sale of wheat and oil from areas then controlled by the Islamic State. Friends told me that war profiteering created so many *nouveaux riches* that they no longer recognized the clientele at the once-exclusive Aleppo Club. One can almost hear Lady Bracknell: "My dear, who *are* these people?"

When the government's position became more stable, it craved international legitimacy. It asked the United Nations to switch its vast wartime program of humanitarian aid to one of development, which would entail moving money from individual victims of the war to state institutions—a move the US opposed. The United Nations, one UN official explained, "gives cash for work, things like removing rubble. The cash goes to the local community in exchange for their work. It's happening everywhere [in Syria], but not on a large scale. But there is no development aid to build hospitals, schools, etc."

Wary of the US's veto power, the UN has so far maintained its humanitarian effort, albeit on a sharply reduced budget, as if the war were still raging everywhere, rather than commit to reconstruction. The switch to development, while bolstering the regime's international image, would nevertheless require it to submit to oversight and transparency. The government, along with most of the populace, wants the US and Europe to lift economic sanctions, arguing that they do more harm to civilians than to the senior officials they are intended to punish. Sanctions also encourage the corruption that accompanies sanctions busting everywhere.

Some European Union member states, most of whose ambassadors fled when the US closed its embassy in February 2012, send diplomats back on regular visits to discuss assisting Syria's reconstruction with or without the UN. "We have our papers and our statements on reconstruction, but only to implement when real political transition is on the table," one western diplomat told me. Transition implies the replacement of one regime with another, but Syria's victorious government is staying put. Even without a transition, American and other Western intelligence agencies resumed contact with Syria's forbidding military intelligence chief, Ali Mamlouk, seeking information on foreign jihadis to prevent their return home undetected.

Idlib was especially troubling to the West, Russia, and the regime. It held the greatest concentration of jihadi forces, many of whom were transferred there when they agreed to surrender other areas to the army. One international aid staff member, who has worked on both sides of the battle lines, admitted that "when you group three thousand rebels in one area, they will fight each other." A Moscow-trained security expert in Damascus believed that Assad could wait for Idlib's fighters to destroy themselves or flee the country: "Idlib is not strategic. It has no petrol. Let it take another year."

In 2018, the Turkish Army invaded Idlib province, to the annoyance of the Syrian government but with the acquiescence of Russia and Iran. Its stated purpose was to control the Islamist jihadis it once armed, but Kurds sensed the real goal was to prevent them from creating a contiguous Kurdish-controlled region along the Turkish border between Afrin in the west and the Iraqi border zone they held in the east. After Turkey expelled the Kurds from both areas, it kept its army in Syria alongside about seventy thousand Syrian and foreign militants with nowhere else to go. Many jihadis fought for Turkey against the Kurds, and Erdoğan deployed about two thousand of them in his subsequent foreign military gamble in Libya. He has used them as the US did the Kurds, and they may in the end suffer the same fate.

One senior Syrian official blamed the US for prolonging the conflict by keeping the Syrian Army out of the eastern desert with its oilfields: "It does not want the Jordanian and Iraqi borders in government hands." Jordan came to recognize that American strategy entrenched rather than broke the "Shiite crescent" that King Abdullah predicted in 2004. Syria's and Baghdad's victories over the Islamic State, as well as the defeat of Iraq's Kurds by the Iraqi Army and Shiite paramilitaries, allowed Iran's influence to run across Iraq and Syria to Hezbollah's enclaves in Lebanon. Persia, in effect, was reestablishing the direct route to the Mediterranean that the Byzantines denied it in the seventh century. The value to Iran of a little Silk Road is doubtful, given how expensive it is to secure and how easily Iran sends weapons to Hezbollah by air and sea.

The perceived Iranian-backed northern arc of Shiism across Iraq and Syria to Lebanon unsettled the Sunni monarchs in Saudi Arabia, the United Arab Emirates, Kuwait, and Bahrain. They saw Iran displacing them in the heart of the Arab world. Iran emerged victorious in Syria over dissidents the Sunni monarchs supported and became a more consistent and vociferous champion of Palestinian rights than Saudi Arabia.

While Saudi Crown Prince Mohammed bin Salman raged against Assad, Iran, and the Shias, Jordan's relations with Syria took "a positive turn." King Abdullah's bridge to Assad offered a degree of Sunni Arab amity to offset Iran. The strategy of Saudi Arabia, the jihadis' major financial benefactor, was less clear. The Saudi regime cut arms supplies to the most extreme jihadis, conceding defeat in Syria; but it escalated its challenge to Iran in both Yemen and Lebanon. When Saudi Arabia forced Lebanon's Sunni prime minister, Saad Hariri, to resign on November 5, 2017, many Lebanese feared that Saudi Arabia was signaling its encouragement of an Israeli attack or invasion of Lebanon to destroy Hezbollah and thus deprive Iran of its most valuable foreign military asset.

With Syria locked into a war of attrition in the north, the government and those who failed to bring it down blamed each other for the devastation that they—with foreign-supplied armaments—had wrought since 2011. The war's toll has been at least as high as those from the epochs of Sumerians, Persians, Greeks, Romans, Mongols, Turks, or French. Fighting between 2011 and 2020, according to the best if unverified estimates, has killed half a million human beings and left far more crippled, blind, limbless, or otherwise scarred in body and mind. The fratricidal struggle forced nearly half the country's pre-war population of twenty-two million out of their homes, drove five million out of the country, and left thousands of orphans. Historic monuments vanished; the country's wealth was looted. Mass exodus and distrust unraveled the social fabric.

Many Syrians abroad, including the respected human rights lawyer Anwar Bounni, demand a reckoning for wartime murder, rape, and torture. Dossiers on the behavior of both the government and the insurgents, especially the Islamic State, grew thicker as evidence mounted. But the testimony was likely to remain of more use to scholars than to courts of justice, which could not apprehend elusive jihadis and would be constrained from prosecuting government officials with whom most of the world—led by Russia, Iran, India, and China—does business.

Someone is to blame for the country's devastation, but neither side would take responsibility. Both bear the mark of Cain while claiming the unblemished cloak of Abel.

§

"Phase one is over," a Syrian security source, who studied his craft in Russia, told me. "Phase two is sharing the cake." Most of Syria's populated areas—the Mediterranean coast and the spine from Damascus north through Homs and Hama to Aleppo—was in government hands. "The government is on two paths," the source added. "One, it is building up the areas it has, providing electricity, water, schools, and all that. Two, it is taking back the areas it can." Three of the areas that the Syrian Army—aided by its Russian, Iranian, and Lebanese allies—remained determined to reconquer were the provinces of Idlib, Afrin, and the northern Aleppo countryside. Areas outside government control, while vast, contained a small percentage of the population. "What do people in Damascus care about Manbij or Afrin?" the security source asked. "They can live without them."

Soon after he spoke, the US pulled out of Manbij and the Syrian Army moved in.

The Turkish conquest of Afrin, a northern province that the war had left untouched until January 2018, did not affect daily life in Damascus and had nothing to do with regime change. Turkey crushed Afrin's US-supported Kurdish fighters and denied their colleagues in the Kurdistan Workers' Party access to the border. Afrin, an isolated pocket where Kurds had lived for generations, was separated from the main Kurdish areas of the northeast by regions under government and jihadi control. "We were talking to the Kurds before Turkey came in," said a Syrian senior official in 2018. "We offered to bring in our army. They said no. Now they are begging us to come to Afrin." The Syrian Army allowed Kurdish weapons and fighters to traverse its territory on their way to Afrin; it later joined the Kurds in the anti-Turkish campaign.

"Even if we have differences with the Kurds, they are Syrian," explained Fares Shehabi, a member of Syria's parliament for Aleppo. Turkey's Orwellian-sounding Operation Olive Branch expelled the Kurds, both fighters and civilians, from Afrin. The Kurds then braced themselves for the Turkish offensive in the northeast. The United States had vacillated between Turkey, a NATO ally, and its Kurdish surrogates. Past experience—from Henry Kissinger's abandonment of Iraqi Kurds to Saddam Hussein's murderous onslaught in 1975 to expulsion of the Kurdish governor of Kirkuk in 2017—indicated that US policy favored larger powers over Kurdish clients. Predictably, the US left Syria's Kurds to be removed by Turkey.

Syria's fate, like Lebanon's following the Israeli invasion of 1982, rested in foreign hands. Russians, Iranians, Americans, Turks, and, to a lesser extent, Saudis and Qataris, determined the course of events. In Sochi, Astana, and Geneva, the Syrian government's

THE BLOOD CAVE

supporters and opponents argued about their future—while Russia and the United States made the significant decisions.

Rather than encourage US-Russian agreement to end the war, the deep thinkers in Washington and Mar-a-Lago urged the United States to wade deeper into the swamp. Kenneth Pollack, a former CIA analyst and Bill Clinton's director for Persian Gulf affairs at the National Security Council, became one of the few commentators to admit that Syria was little more than a means to an end. In a strongly argued series in 2018 on the American Enterprise Institute's website, Pollack advocated using Syria to hurt Iran. He distinguished between, "(1) places where they [the Iranians] are vulnerable and where we can cause more harm to them than they can do to us, [and] (2) places where our allies are vulnerable and need help to fend off an Iranian challenge." Noting that "Syria is the best example of the first category," Pollack proposed "ramping up American covert assistance to the Syrian opposition to try to bleed the Assad regime and its Iranian backers over time, exactly the way that the United States backed the Afghan Mujahideen as they bled the Soviets in Afghanistan—or as the Russians and Chinese did to the United States in Vietnam."

Pollack's examples, however, undercut his case for deeper involvement. The Russians and Chinese bled the United States in Vietnam, but the benefits to them were few. The United States is now doing at least as well in Vietnam as either Russia or China. "US-Vietnam bilateral trade has grown from $451 million in 1995 to nearly $52 billion in 2016," notes the State Department website. "In 2016, Vietnam was America's fastest growing export market." In Afghanistan, the mujahideen proved more failure than success for both Afghans and Americans. Although the Soviets withdrew, the mujahideen's relentless civil wars reduced Kabul to rubble, brought in the Taliban to impose order, and produced Al Qaeda and its 9/11

235

attacks. If that is what Washington wants from Syria, it should take Pollack's advice.

The urge to hit Iran in Syria calls to mind an argument made, and heeded, in 2003, that "the option that makes the most sense is for the United States to launch a full-scale invasion of Iraq to topple Saddam, eradicate his weapons of mass destruction, and rebuild Iraq as a prosperous and stable society for the good of the United States, Iraq's own people and the entire region." Americans know where that advice led. The author? Kenneth Pollack.

President Donald Trump hedged his bets, keeping a small force in Syria ostensibly to protect a not particularly productive oil reserve at Tanf beside the Jordanian and Iraqi border triangle while harassing Iran in other places: in Baghdad with the assassination of Iran's Quds Force commander; in the economic sphere with ruinous sanctions; and in the Persian Gulf with periodic demonstrations of force. If the goal was to topple Iran's mullahs, it had yet to bear fruit.

By the time the Treaty of Westphalia ended the Thirty Years' War in 1648, the French, Danes, Swedes, and Ottomans had all joined the fray—and eight million people were dead. Syria has lost half a million to date, but further squabbling among outside powers threatens to dwarf that number and leave the country—and possibly the region—as devastated as Central Europe in the seventeenth century.

§

In March 2018, the jihadi revolution was dying in the eastern suburbs of the Syrian capital, Damascus. Syrian government forces, supported by aerial bombardment and heavy artillery barrages, split the opposition-held territory of eastern Ghouta into two bastions and ate away at both. The farmlands on which civilians and fighters in the besieged zones depended for food fell to the Syrian Army and its related militias. Threatened with starvation and braving the government onslaught, some residents defied army bombardment and rebel ire with public protests calling on the insurgents to leave. They claimed that it was the only way to end the hunger, privation, casualties, shelling, and chaotic jihadi governance they had endured for years.

The major jihadi groups remaining in eastern Ghouta were Hayat Tahrir al-Sham, an insurgent coalition of the former Jabhat an-Nusra, Jaish al-Islam (Army of Islam), and Faylaq al Rahman (Legion of Mercy). At that time, an aid worker who was dealing with them said many rebels wanted to depart under security guarantees similar to those that permitted the evacuation of Homs and rural eastern Aleppo. "Jaish al-Islam wants to go to Dera'a," the worker said, "Faylaq wants to go to north Aleppo [province]." Other jihadis, however, wanted to stay and fight at whatever cost to the area's civilians. Russian-sponsored discussions on "reconciliation," the government's term for rebel surrender, continued against the background of the loyalists' offensive and the insurgents' mortar shelling of central Damascus.

The outcome in eastern Ghouta was not in doubt, but the cost depended on whether and when the rebels departed. They fought among themselves, and they held many of each other's fighters prisoner. One intelligence source told me that Jaish al-Islam handed its captives from the former Jabhat an-Nusra to the government, something that was bound to embitter relations further. Wounded civilians languished without medicine, and in 2018, the International Committee of the Red Cross said that more than twelve hundred patients could not be evacuated until the insurgents and the government came to terms.

The same year, the UN estimated that four hundred thousand civilians remained in eastern Ghouta, although its previous estimates of populations under siege proved excessive. "In east Aleppo, they said forty thousand, but there were only eleven thousand in fact," one humanitarian official said. "In Daraya [suburb of Damascus], we said eight thousand. At the end, there were only two thousand." However many people remained in eastern Ghouta, they were paying a huge price: as many as one thousand died in one month of fighting. Clean water and electricity were nowhere to be found. Families slept underground in makeshift shelters. There was no gas for cooking, and firewood was in short supply. One of the few ways out was a humanitarian corridor from eastern Ghouta's largest town, Douma, across 2.5 miles of rubble and fields under the gaze of snipers. Many died trying to leave. Among the few who succeeded were two children whose parents were killed before the family reached the first government checkpoint.

More than ten thousand civilians fled Hammouriyeh on March 15, 2018, during a lull in the fighting in eastern Ghouta—a rare and chaotic flight that presaged others in the days that followed. While the international aid agencies that had been attempting for months to arrange evacuations were not involved, the government received the displaced families in makeshift reception centers.

Government troops occupied eastern Ghouta, securing the capital. The end of random shelling came as a relief to Damascenes, but the "victory" in eastern Ghouta did not end the war. The government turned its attention to other rebel-held territories with the repeatedly declared aim of restoring its rule over the entire country. "Our fear is that after eastern Ghouta we may see tremendous battles now in and around Idlib and, in the south, Dera'a," Jan Egeland, Norwegian Refugee Council director and UN adviser, correctly predicted. Egeland, one of the most conscientious and determined of the many nongovernmental organization chiefs involved in Syria, pressed the

Russians and Syrians to spare medical facilities in their attacks. No party, including US forces during their expulsion of the Islamic State from towns in eastern Syria, heeded such advice.

Tens of thousands of insurgents from scores of factions stayed in Idlib, many of them having retreated there with their families under agreements with the government to evacuate eastern Aleppo, Homs, and suburban Damascus. Idlib became, in Egeland's words, "a gigantic refugee camp." A further complication was the presence in Idlib of the Turkish Army, which responded forcefully to Russian and Syrian attacks on its troops and their allied insurgent forces.

The insurgents had relied on outside powers, including the United States and Saudi Arabia, for weapons, training, and financing. Their backers did not encourage them to lay down their arms or to leave the battlefield. Nikolaos van Dam, a former Dutch special envoy to Syria and the author of two authoritative books on the country, asked pertinent questions in a lecture he gave March 7, 2018, to the Bruno Kreisky Forum for International Dialogue in Vienna: "Isn't it time to admit that the war against the Syrian regime is in a stage of being lost? And if the outcome is already quite clear, what is the use of continuing it, and shedding even more blood?"

§

The most rebellious people in Syria's modern history are the Druze, most of whom live in a region called the Druze Mountain, Jabal al-Druze, about seventy miles south of Damascus. Members of this syncretic, semi-Shiite Muslim sect battled the country's successive overlords, notably the Ottoman Turks in World War I and the French Mandate authorities in the 1920s and '30s. Syrian independence in 1946 did not dampen their enthusiasm for revolt, as they rose against nationalist regimes that they felt threatened their survival as

SYRIA

a distinct community. Yet when the biggest rebellion in the country's history broke out in March 2011, the Druze stayed out.

The traditional leader of Lebanon's Druze, Walid Jumblatt, called on his Syrian brethren to "join the Syrian rebels who are marking in blood heroic battles against oppression on a daily basis." Jumblatt explained to me in 2012 that Druze survival depended on joining the majority Sunni population in opposition to rule by Alawites, another minority with roots in Shiite Islam. Although some Druze took part in peaceful demonstrations for reform in 2011, they did not turn to violence. Hassan al-Atrash, a biology teacher and former communist, told me in the Syrian Druze capital, Suwaida, "As far as people were concerned, this was not meant to be a war. They made legal demands for their rights." They thus ignored Jumblatt's call to join the rebels, but they did not join the Syrian Army either.

Suwaida was one of the few areas in Syria—along with the Kurdish pocket of Afrin in the north until Turkey invaded in January 2018—unscarred by years of war. Many Syrians from battle zones like the Yarmouk Palestinian refugee camp in Damascus, eastern Ghouta, Aleppo, and Deir ez-Zour sought refuge among the Druze. Raed al-Atrash, a Druze who works for Syrian television in Suwaida, estimated that as many as forty thousand people had fled to the tranquility of the Druze Mountain. He pointed to the dozen or so lively restaurants and cafés on the street where we met as a sign of a kind of normality, albeit a precarious one.

Neutrality was not easy with government forces to the north, the Islamic State to the west, other jihadis in Dera'a province to the east, and rebels coming across the Jordanian border to the south. The Druze live astride the Golan Heights, half of which has been occupied by Israel since 1967. According to Druze officials in Suwaida, some Israeli Druze encouraged them to cut themselves off from Bashar al-Assad's regime and establish an autonomous region similar to the US-backed Kurdish zone in northeastern Syria. One source said a Druze religious leader from Israel, Sheikh Muaffaq Tarif, offered them twenty million dollars to declare a Druze republic. "He gave us the money," he said, "but we used it to buy weapons to defend ourselves, and we did not separate."

Cousins Hassan and Raed al-Atrash are descendants of Sultan Pasha al-Atrash, the legendary, mustachioed tribal chieftain who led his people against the Ottoman Empire in 1916 and raised the Arab nationalist flag over Damascus when the Turks retreated in September 1918. He also led the Great Syrian Revolt, which nearly ended French rule over Syria in 1925 but resulted in massive destruction. Al-Atrash fled the country, returning to harass the French and, later, Syrian governments in Damascus. That legacy should have put the Druze at the forefront of rebellion for the last eight years, but it didn't.

Sultan Pasha's granddaughter, a retired French teacher named Rim al-Atrash, told me her grandfather had written a letter to his followers during the 1925 revolt that said, "It's necessary not to destroy public property. It's important not to kill." She added, "That's a real chief of a national revolution." She contrasted his words favorably to the jihadis who destroyed Palmyra, executed Christians, and enslaved Yazidis.

An additional obstacle to Druze participation in the uprising from 2011 onward was that minorities feared the rebels. Raed al-Atrash recalled, "At the mosques in Damascus suburbs and Dera'a, the sheikhs said it was *halal* [legitimate] for the jihadis to take Druze women and houses and to kill the men." How could the Druze support religious zealots who sought to destroy them as they did the Yazidis in Iraq? The Druze defended themselves against the Islamic

State, Hayat Tahrir al-Sham, and other Salafists; but they neither encroached on Sunni territory nor joined the Syrian Army.

The frontier between Druze Suwaida and Sunni Dera'a turned into a zone not so much of battle as of crime. Brigands on both sides took advantage of wartime lawlessness to profit from kidnapping, car theft, and extortion. "There were 137 kidnappings in three months in Suwaida," said one aid worker from the area. "We know this from Facebook posts that people have placed looking for their relatives." The hostages were taken to rebel-held parts of Dera'a until their families paid ransoms. The aid worker continued, "There are too many weapons. Children at schools are killing each other. Drugs. Stealing cars. If you catch them before they get to Dera'a, you can buy your car back."

The proliferation of weapons in private hands resulted from the government policy of arming young Druze men. "Because we were afraid of the jihadis, we asked the government for weapons to defend our areas," said Raed al-Atrash. "They were very effective. We stopped the jihadis from entering Suwaida." The long-term effect, however, was negative. "There was a time when they [the government] needed everyone to have a weapon," said a Syrian security source. "That time has passed." Yet restoring government authority over the Druze Mountain, let alone over Dera'a while jihadis remained a potent force, and removing the weapons awaited the war's end.

The outside powers that sought to upend Assad's rule by arming hundreds of factions misunderstood the dynamics of Syrian society and the loyalties of its communities. The strongest and most effective elements of the rebellion excluded the Druze, Alawites, Ismailis, Christians, and Yazidis on principle and sought to expel or annihilate them. Many of the Sunnis who resented Alawite minority rule feared a Sunni fundamentalist takeover more than they feared Assad. If all the Sunnis, who constituted at least seventy percent of the population, had risen up to fight against Assad, he would not have lasted ten days, let alone ten years.

§

Workmen throughout Syria have erected bronze, stone, and concrete statues in what the government calls "liberated areas." Some of the monuments were newly cast, while others had been in storage since the conflict began in 2011. At that time, protesters in rebellious cities like Dera'a and Homs were desecrating the sculptures of longtime president Hafez al-Assad, his successor Bashar, and Bashar's older brother, Bassel, the designated heir who died before ascending the throne. It was perhaps an omen of the rebellion's destiny that popular legend had a massive bust of Hafez in Idlib killing two demonstrators as it crashed to earth. The effigies, like the regime they embody, were back.

Outright victory remained elusive. With the Syrian Army controlling more than sixty percent of the land and eighty percent of the resident population, three sectors of the country remained to be "liberated":

- Northern Aleppo province and the adjoining provinces of Afrin and Idlib near the Turkish border in the north, where the Turkish Army and an estimated seventy thousand insurgents rule about three million Syrians.
- The northeast beyond the Euphrates River, where the Kurds cling to American-protected autonomy.
- A twenty-one-square-mile "red zone" the US declared around its military base in the southern desert at Tanf village, near the intersection of Syria's borders with Jordan and Iraq.

The Assad regime faced two tasks, neither easy: stabilizing, governing, and reconstructing the regions under its dominion; and clawing back the rest of the country. While waiting for the Turks, Americans, and jihadis to leave, the state is concentrating on the first objective. "The big victory is not in war," a professor at Damascus University told me, "but in peace."

The government must rebuild more than statues with money it does not have if it is to secure peace and a semblance of the status quo ante 2011. Foreign powers who backed Assad's opponents could be convinced to provide some funding, but only if he accepts reforms that would make him vulnerable to being replaced. "Assad didn't step aside for peace when he was losing, and he is not going to step aside for money now," observed an ambassador with long experience in Damascus. United Nations special envoy Staffan de Mistura, before the Norwegian diplomat Geir Pedersen succeeded him, conveyed Western conditions for aid that include a new constitution, internationally supervised elections, and an end to corruption. The opposition voiced the same demands. Assad, however, was not listening, and economic sanctions hit his population hard.

When the UN asked Assad whether a proposed Constitutional Committee should have thirty or 150 delegates, he opted for 150. One diplomat asked me with a smile, "Can you imagine 150 Syrians agreeing on anything?" Arguments over the committee's composition make Britain's Brexit negotiations with the European Union look like tic-tac-toe. The delegates, whenever they assemble, must write a document that would allow the US, the EU, and the financial institutions they control to release funds for rebuilding. In any case, as a Syrian defector from the regime said, "You can make the best constitution in the world, but no one will apply it."

The Arab states that dispatched jihadis to Syria observed none of the niceties of constitutional government in their own countries.

Thus it was not difficult for them to reabsorb Assad into the community of Arab autocrats. Jordan, site of command and control for much of the insurgency, reopened its border with Syria. The United Arab Emirates, which followed the lead of Saudi Arabia in assisting jihadi fighters attempting to overthrow Assad, reopened its embassy in Damascus in 2018. Iraq and Egypt remained friendly, and the other dictators of the Arab League at last welcomed Syria back into its ranks.

Meanwhile, some six million people, officially designated "internally displaced persons," are without permanent shelter. For them as for about five million in exile, homecoming awaits the rebuilding of houses and roads as well as restoring water, sanitation, and electrical infrastructure demolished in the fighting. In former battlefields, unexploded ordnance—land mines, booby traps, mortar shells, and cluster bombs—takes lives, limbs, and eyes, mainly of children, and must be removed. So too, millions of tons of mangled concrete to make way for new water conduits, sewage channels, electricity pylons, schools, and clinics. Rebuilding a country requires more money than destroying it. Countries that provided billions in weaponry have become parsimonious about rebuilding—this applies as much to Russia and Iran on the government's side as to the US, Britain, France, Turkey, Saudi Arabia, and Qatar on the opposition's.

"Everyone wants to come here, but they don't know how," said a European official who attended meetings with potential donors. Since US sanctions forbid donations and loans for reconstruction, some countries, including Germany, propose to channel aid to Syria by calling it "rehabilitation and not reconstruction." At the same time, in a sign of schizophrenia not exclusive to Germany, State Secretary of the Federal Foreign Office Walter Lindner admitted that his ministry had paid €37.5 million to Syrian rebels in Idlib. Italy, while officially backing the American position on Syria sanctions, has opened channels to the Syrian government. Syrian security chief Ali Mamlouk, a target of US and EU sanctions, visited Rome in January 2018. Mamlouk also paid calls on his counterparts in Saudi Arabia and Egypt. The Czech Republic, whose embassy remained open throughout the war and represents US interests, is establishing a school in Damascus. Several European diplomats in Beirut told me that their countries want a face-saving formula to reopen the embassies they closed in Syria when the US ambassador departed in 2012. "Europe has lost the battle" to unseat Assad, said one EU representative, "and still we don't know what to do."

Resident and expatriate Syrian businesspeople are filling the vacuum left by the International Monetary Fund, the World Bank, and overseas commercial banks prevented by US sanctions from assisting the Syrian economy. Shopkeepers have cleared rubble from their premises in Aleppo's majestic old city, and new hotels are going up in Damascus to welcome the entrepreneurs the government imagines will descend on the capital to cash in on a promised building boom. Syria may eventually benefit from the disappearance of its archaic industrial plants, as Germany's coal and steel industries did after World War II, by starting anew with modern machinery.

One of the largest obstacles to development, apart from Western distaste for Assad, is corruption. Already endemic before the war, it has ballooned thanks to arms smuggling and sanctions dodging. The government has sporadically sponsored anti-corruption "drives" that few take seriously, given the popular belief that corruption starts at the top. When the minister of the interior, Major General Mohammed al-Sha'ar, arrested a civil service clerk named Riyyad al-Batal in Aleppo for pocketing fifty Syrian pounds, about ten cents, the whole country laughed. The man's son wrote on Facebook that "no one dares to take bribes without directions by chairmen." The son, it turned out, had been serving in the army since the start of the war. Three weeks later, Assad reshuffled his cabinet and appointed a new interior minister, demoting Sha'ar to a largely ceremonial post in the National Progressive Front, the Baath Party-led coalition of legal Syrian political parties. Al-Batal was eventually released without charge.

Damascus is a mixture of normal and abnormal. Regime loyalists and opponents alike are relieved that mortars from the suburbs that the rebels evacuated no longer explode in the metropolitan area. The army has dismantled many of its checkpoints. Schools and businesses are functioning, albeit below pre-war capacities. The National Museum, with its historical treasures from several millennia, has reopened to the public. Restaurants and bars, for those who can afford them, are thriving. Some young people have turned away from politics to open music venues, art galleries, and cafés. Many exiles from rural areas who took refuge in Damascus to escape violence are returning to their now peaceful, if damaged, houses.

On the capital's outskirts, where the rebels reigned for six years, the landscape resembles another planet. The UN reckons that in some areas up to ninety percent of the structures have been destroyed. The estimated 350,000 inhabitants who stayed in Eastern Ghouta following the insurgents' departure for Idlib are free of the heavy government bombardment that leveled their homes, hospitals, schools, and businesses. But their ravaged neighborhoods lack basic services, and they must deal with contaminated water, which causes diarrhea and other ailments, while only half the schools and just one hospital are functioning.

Leaving a nightclub in Damascus on foot one night, I was stopped by young soldiers who asked for my passport. Beside them, a half-dozen youths in leather jackets and jeans stood in a circle while two older men inside a covered jeep inspected their identity cards. One, avuncular in rimless glasses slipping down his nose, tapped ID numbers into a cell phone and waited for a response from headquarters. The boys who had already served in the army or were exempt from service as the only sons in their families were free to go. The rest had to report to recruiting stations later in the week. Fear of conscription keeps thousands of young men outside the country, even when their families return.

Continued conscription is one sign that the government has not abandoned the military option of reclaiming occupied territories from the Turkish Army and as many as seventy thousand rebels. About half of Idlib province's population of about three million, as estimated by the International Committee of the Red Cross and Refugees International, are original inhabitants. The other half, mostly women and children, are exiles from other Syrian regions. Turkey, having ethnically cleansed Kurds from Afrin, has injected its culture, governance, and economy into the lives of north Syrian Arabs. Schools have begun teaching Turkish. Bilingual Turkish and Arabic signposts appeared on the roadways. Posters in the Turkish-occupied town of Azaz declare, "Brotherhood has no limits." Turk Telekom has replaced the Syrian cell phone network. In the formerly Kurdish town of Afrin, the Turkish Post Telephone and Telegraph (PTT) has moved into the old Syrian post office, and letters are sent with Turkish stamps. Turkey is exporting to Idlib and Afrin the foodstuffs, furniture, and textiles that previously came from other parts of Syria.

"The Turks have always pursued an unhappy policy in regard to native populations," wrote German Gen. Erich Ludendorff of his World War I Ottoman allies. "They have gone on the principle of taking everything and giving nothing. Now they had to reckon with these people (Kurds, Armenians and Arab tribes) as their enemies." The Turkish Army, driven out of Syria after four centuries in 1918 by the British and "native populations," returned on the orders of Turkish president Recep Tayyip Erdoğan. His involvement in Syria reverses the policy of the republic's first president, Mustafa Kemal Atatürk, that kept Turkey out of the Arab world. Atatürk looked westward in the belief that returning to lands that had rejected Turkish rule was futile.

That arrangement worked for Turkey until 2011, when the uprising in Syria opened the way to foreign interference. The United States, the United Kingdom, France, Saudi Arabia, Qatar, and the United Arab Emirates were backing assorted militias in their effort to depose Syrian president Bashar al-Assad. Erdoğan would not be left out. His border with Syria offered the most extensive terrain for infiltrating fighters and war material. Moreover, his Justice and Development Party had a long friendship with Syria's Muslim Brotherhood, whose attempt to depose Assad's father, Hafez al-Assad, in 1982, ended with the infamous massacre in Hama. Erdoğan looked to the Muslim Brotherhood and its offshoots to play a leading role in the resistance to the younger Assad. In 2012, a Syrian former Cabinet minister told me that Erdoğan had asked Assad to put Muslim Brothers into his Cabinet. When Assad refused, the former minister said, Erdoğan made clear that he would back all efforts to remove the president and replace him with Islamists.

One of the stated reasons for excluding the Muslim Brothers, in addition to their history of violent opposition to the regime, was that Syria had not legalized religiously based political parties. The divisive effects of sectarian parties had played out badly in Lebanon after 1975 and had done little to benefit Iraq after the US invasion in

2003. Assad countered Erdoğan's support for his opponents by allow-
ing Turkey's Kurdistan Workers' Party (PKK) to threaten Erdoğan
from Syria. The PKK was instrumental in the formation of the Syrian
Kurdish People's Protection Units (YPG) that fought with the United
States against the Islamic State without joining the US-backed
anti-Assad opposition.

Erdoğan went step by step into Syria, opening the border to
jihadists, facilitating weapons deliveries, and, when needed, backing the rebels with firepower—as when Turkish artillery shelled the
Armenian Syrian village of Kassab before the Islamists conquered
it in March 2014. Barely one year later, Erdoğan sent Turkish troops
over the border on an innocuous mission, code-named Operation
Shah Euphrates, to rescue the remains of Suleyman Shah, an ances-
tor of the first Ottoman sultan. Erdoğan's next venture into Syria was
an all-out invasion, Operation Euphrates Shield, ostensibly to combat Islamic State militants but effectively to force the YPG to retreat
from the border zone in the northwest.

Then came Operation Olive Branch from January to March 2018
in the largely Kurdish province around Afrin. In that onslaught into
a hitherto peaceful corner of northwestern Syria, Turkey relied on
about twenty-five thousand Free Syrian Army and other rebel fighters to occupy towns and villages. "Instead of protecting vulnerable
civilians' rights, these fighters are perpetuating a cycle of abuse,"
Human Rights Watch declared. The United States refrained from
assisting its Kurdish allies, a precedent for its behavior when, following his now-famous telephone conversation with President Trump,
Erdoğan ordered his army and its allied Islamist militia to advance
into northeastern Syria on October 9. Turkey's Operation Peace
Spring followed the Operation Olive Branch game plan that expels
Kurds, civilians and fighters, from the northeast; executes Kurdish

politicians; and gives Turkey control of a twenty-mile-wide belt from the Mediterranean to the Iraqi border.

Despite international outrage and sanctions, Erdoğan's decision to expand his military occupation of northwest Syria to the northeast and destroy the YPG is popular among all factions in Turkey. The new mayor of Istanbul, Ekrem Imamoglu, who won office on promises to resist Erdoğan's Islamist and anti-Kurdish policies in Turkey's most cosmopolitan city, backs the military operation. On Twitter, he called the YPG a "treacherous terror group," betraying the Kurds who helped elect him. A leading opposition daily, *Sozcu*, headlined its front page, "Americans, Europeans, Chinese, Arabs— all united against Turkey. Bring it on." The pro-war fever infecting Turkey replicates the parades, flag-waving, and oaths of allegiance that accompanied the country's entry into World War I in 1914. When the Ottoman fleet attacked Russia's forts along the Black Sea, Turkish political parties and media outdid each other to demonstrate support for an offensive that started well and ended badly. Turkey lost its empire, and the European Allies occupied Istanbul.

Turkey had much to gain if its Syria gamble succeeded—control of a large area it abandoned in 1918, removal of thousands of Syrian refugees from Turkey to parts of Syria they did not know, containment of the YPG and PKK to areas south of its so-called safe zone, and a voice in Syria's future. It also had much to lose—the lives of its soldiers, perpetual warfare along its border, and the undying animosity of Kurds in both Syria and Turkey.

Erdoğan's collaboration with Russian president Vladimir Putin—with whom he agreed at Sochi, Russia, on October 22 to deploy joint Russian-Turkish patrols in the twenty-mile security zone that he ordered the Kurds to evacuate—diluted his control in northeastern Syria. It also permitted Assad's Syrian Army to return to an area where Syria has a greater claim to sovereignty than has Turkey. One obstacle to ending the Syrian civil war remained Turkey's sole control of the northwestern Syrian province of Idlib and the rural areas around Aleppo and the estimated sixty thousand rebels, most of them jihadists, it controlled there and used as its mercenaries against the Kurds.

During his first term as president, Trump permitted the Turkish invasion, then decided it was not such a good idea and, while not sending the Turkish Army back into Turkey, imposed selective economic sanctions, which he lifted on October 23. Many Americans supported Trump's stated desire to end the "endless wars" in the belief that taxpayers' money is better spent on education, health and infrastructure at home than on military operations abroad. Trump, however, did not bring troops home. About two hundred American soldiers remained at al-Tanf military base, part of a fifty-five-square-kilometer (twenty-one-square-mile) area of oil-rich desert where the borders of Syria, Iraq, and Jordan meet. He redeployed a thousand special operations forces from Syria to western Iraq and kept another nine hundred with the Kurds in the northeast. He sent 1,800 soldiers to Saudi Arabia. He threatened Iran with war following his abrogation of the 2015 nuclear deal. He supplied weapons, intelligence, and logistical support to Saudi Arabia's relentless war in Yemen.

Ending the endless wars is not unlike decolonization, which Europeans undertook due to the bankruptcy of their economies during World War II. Most of the colonial withdrawals were as disastrous for the countries involved as the colonial conquests had been. Think of the massacres that followed the partition of India in 1947, the war in Palestine when the British withdrew in 1948, the French wars in Algeria and Vietnam, and Belgium's criminal actions in the Congo. Among the most irresponsible colonial retreats was Portugal's from lands it had occupied for four centuries: Angola, Mozambique, and East Timor. The first two suffered protracted civil wars, while Indonesian troops invaded East Timor in December 1975 with American approval and massacred a third of its population by the time they were forced to leave in 1999. More recently, the United States, after arming and earning the trust of Syria's Kurds, risked leaving them to face the Turkish onslaught.

Recall that President Barack Obama, when considering the covert Operation Timber Sycamore to train and equip Syrian rebels in 2013, asked his aides, "Tell me how this ends." As Syrians are aware, it doesn't.

CHAPTER SIXTEEN

A TOURIST IN SYRIA

Damascus, February 2023

Covid pandemic limits on travel and the Syrian Ministry of Information's mishandling of my many visa applications kept me out of Syria for four years. In February 2023, at last, I returned.

A battered old Mercedes taxi took me from Beirut to Damascus for my first visit to Syria at Easter 1973. We entered the city through Mezzeh, a semi-rural zone that was once a village with farms all around. Later, high-rise government offices, embassies, and apartments for a new class of military officers, civil servants, and merchants absorbed Mezzeh into the metropolis. I was a tourist then, an ignorant American graduate student on his way by land from Lebanon to Aqaba in Jordan, pausing long enough for lunch and a little sightseeing. When I returned the following October to cover the war with Israel, it was as a journalist on a visa approved by the Ministry of Information's obstructive, sluggish bureaucracy. Since then, I've had to apply to the ministry whenever I sought to return.

Because Syrian embassies in the United States and most of Europe are closed, applications must go through the Syrian Consulate in Beirut. I waited in Beirut for a full month in the spring of 2022, but the visa was approved as I was leaving for Pakistan. When I submitted a new request on October 16, 2022, the Syrian

Consulate informed me, "The visa process takes twenty to thirty days to get a response from Syria." Three months later the ministry had yet to deliver. Syrian and Lebanese friends with *wasta*—influence—in Damascus offered to obtain a visa for me through the more powerful Ministry of Interior. To my surprise, they succeeded. I took a taxi from Beirut to the Syrian border post at Jdaideh, where an officer behind the counter examined the visa and checked his computer. When my journalist status flashed up, he declared that I could not enter without the imprimatur of the Ministry of Information. My driver remonstrated with him, until a man in civilian clothes behind us offered help. He told the officer to admit me if I wrote a letter affirming that I had retired from journalism and would not be reporting from Syria. I did so, the official relented, and I paid 140 dollars for the visa stamp. When I turned to thank my savior, he had disappeared.

Relieved of my journalist status, I skipped interviews with officials in favor of meeting friends, visiting monuments and museums, lingering in coffeehouses, gossiping with shopkeepers, and hearing again and again that life is unbearable. Electricity is supplied one hour in every six. Gasoline and diesel to run cars, heaters, and kitchen stoves are in short supply and, when available, too expensive for the average worker. Iran has increased the price it charges Syria for seaborne deliveries of refined oil, only one of the reasons Syrians pay about ten times what the next-door Lebanese pay for a liter of gasoline. Oil traders point to the government's hoarding of gasoline and diesel in storage tanks near Baniyas harbor, which delays distribution to keep prices—and profits—high.

The value of the Syrian pound has dropped steadily, from 3,000 to the US dollar last year to 6,500 when I arrived, and it continued to fall while I was there. With the largest denomination note only five thousand pounds, men carry thick bricks of cash in handbags. Bread costs forty thousand pounds a kilo. A year ago, it was a mere five hundred. Meat, vegetables, olive oil, and other basics are beyond the means of most Syrians. The World Food Programme (WFP) estimates that twelve million out of Syria's estimated eighteen million inhabitants—6.6 million have fled the country since the civil war began in 2011—do not have enough to eat. More than a quarter of a million qualify for assistance to ameliorate what the WFP calls "acute malnutrition." The World Health Organization had recorded more than fifty thousand cases of cholera across Syria by the end of last year and warns of other epidemics due to the shortage of imported medicines.

Damascus reminded me of Baghdad on my many trips there between the war over Kuwait in 1991 and the American invasion in 2003. In those years the US, the EU, and the UN were enforcing similar restrictions based on their conviction that economic hardship would destabilize Saddam Hussein's regime or compel a hungry populace to depose him. In Iraq then, as in Syria in 2023, the regime flourished and people starved. I recall Iraqi teachers begging in the streets and middle-class married women turning to prostitution to feed their children. The reported deaths of half a million Iraqi children from malnutrition were, in the words of then US ambassador to the UN Madeleine Albright, "worth it." The failure of sanctions on Iraq to bring about regime change, as in Cuba over a longer period, has not persuaded Washington to conceive of an alternative for Syria.

Perfunctory US sanctions on Syria had been in place since 1979, but the all-out economic blockade went into effect 180 days after December 20, 2019, when Congress passed the Caesar Syria Civilian Protection Act—named for the photographer who documented murder and torture in government prisons. President Bashar al-Assad, assisted by Russia and Iran, had just secured his regime with the expulsion of his rebel enemies to a periphery in northwest Syria, near the Turkish border. The Orwellian preamble to the State Department's fact sheet on the legislation declared, "Our sanctions under the Caesar Act and Executive Order 13894 are not intended to harm the Syrian people." My daily promenades through Damascus's old and new sections suggested that the intention is belied by reality. The run-down flats and houses of the poor, who complain of the struggle to afford food and heat, coexist with the prosperous Abu Roummaneh and Malki quarters' neon-lit restaurants, cafés, and nightclubs.

Compounding the misfortune is the transformation of Syria into what *The Economist* calls a "narco-state" that produces and exports billions of dollars' worth of illegal, addictive, amphetamine-like Captagon pills in cooperation with Lebanese, Jordanian, and Saudi smugglers. Many a Ferrari and Maserati parked outside expensive restaurants was purchased with drug money. Scions of old but recently impoverished trading families speak with derision of the *nouveaux riches* who made their fortunes from the war and are increasing them by evading sanctions.

"The regime is still here, and the people are suffering," a diplomat tells me. "Reconstruction" remains a forbidden word, as international agencies are permitted to provide the drip-drip of humanitarian aid but not the means to rebuild. The Caesar Act threatens to penalize anyone from any nation who assists in reconstructing Syria's infrastructure, which has been devastated by years of war. Such is the logic of sanctions.

While the government and many citizens blame sanctions for the country's plight, the victorious president does not escape blame. "I don't dare say it, but I like him," an old friend confides. "Before the war, no one dared say he didn't like him. Now, it's the opposite." Over the following days more people, including those who supported him on my previous visits, criticize his performance, the blatant corruption, and the ostentatious wealth enjoyed by his inner circle. Another friend, who posted pro-Assad propaganda on social media during the war, is fed up. "He betrayed us," he says, sotto voce. Assad's critics do not pronounce his name. It is always "he" or "him." They never know who is listening. Their grievances are now more economic than political, as they were ten years ago. Disenchantment, however, does not imply another rebellion. Instead, there is resignation.

I meet the novelist Khaled Khalifa, a longtime friend, in an old city coffee shop deserted except for two waiters and us. Slivers of sun filtered through the dingy windows, exaggerating the exhaustion in Khaled's bearded, once-vivid face. His latest novel, *No One Prayed Over Their Graves*, like his previous works, is banned in Syria. He spent ten years writing it, conceiving the story after seeing a church in the region of Qamishli, near the Turkish border in the northeast of the country, that the Ottomans had desecrated in their genocide of the Armenians during World War I. "It explains everything now," he said over a tiny cup of sugarless Turkish coffee. He added, "All my friends have left Syria." We walked along a narrow, cobbled street toward his car. "Syria is finished," he told me. "Who knows what will happen to Syria now? No one." I remember when he had hope and could laugh about police breaking his arm during an early anti-regime demonstration. Now the laughter is gone. He tells me he is leaving the next morning for Zurich on a writing fellowship, and I wonder whether he will return.

I wander alone through the old city and the jammed Souq Hamadieh, finding my way through the ancient walls to the disused Hejaz railway station. From there I walk to the Fardoss Tower Hotel's ground-floor café. I remember the enthusiastic youngsters who gathered there in 2012 and 2013 to organize peaceful protests demanding reform. Most of them are gone, some arrested, others in exile. A few students gather there, but I see from their laptops that all they are doing is homework. A university degree will make it easier for them to do what most young Syrians want to do: emigrate.

"If a country like Canada agreed to admit any Syrian, the country would be empty," says another friend. Even without a visa, young men who can are fleeing in search of work and perhaps a semblance of normal life. Most of the Syrian capital's inhabitants must have forgotten the savage artillery and aerial bombardments that terrorized them for years. Otherwise they would not say, as they do, that life is worse now than it was during the war. "We miss the rocket times," a friend whose retail business has failed tells me. "If we died, we died. It was war. Now we don't know." What he doesn't know is how he will feed his children.

The war may be over in Damascus, but it still rages in outlying regions so far away that they seem to be on another continent. Syria, like Caesar's Gaul, is divided into three parts: the government-held center with about sixty percent of the land and nearly eighty percent of the population; the Turkish-occupied northwest, where unreconstructed jihadis and other rebels launch desultory attacks on government outposts; and the Kurdish-governed northeast under the protection of nine hundred American soldiers and American air power. The US keeps a twenty-one-square-mile "red zone" of oil-rich desert in the south near Tanf along the Jordanian and Iraqi borders.

Syria today is a multi-ring circus where armed forces from Turkey, the US, Russia, and Iran engage in an internecine conflict with no obvious objectives. US troops are never far from their

Russian counterparts in the government zone. The Turkish Army attacks the Kurds despite American presence. Iranian troops, augmented by Iraqi Shiite militiamen and Lebanese Hezbollah irregulars, harass the Kurds, the Americans, and Turkish-supported Sunni fundamentalist militias. The Israelis regularly bombard the Iranians, Iraqis, and Hezbollah from the air.

"Syria is the stadium," a businessman whom I have known for years laments. "We are the grass. All the players play on us: Russia, the US, Iran, and Turkey." While outside powers keep the conflict simmering, they are attempting to win through negotiations what they cannot achieve by force. Moscow sponsors talks between Turkey and Syria aimed at persuading Turkey to withdraw from the northwest to allow Damascus to disarm the Kurds and police the border for Turkey. The US seeks a compromise between Turkey and the Kurds to prolong the Kurds' autonomy and keep Damascus from threatening them. Neither diplomatic push has succeeded.

Meanwhile the US feels betrayed as its Arab allies welcome Assad back into the fold, just as they did Egypt's Anwar Sadat after his "treachery" of making peace with Israel in 1979. Jordan, the UAE, and to a lesser extent Saudi Arabia have reopened relations with Assad in the hope of reducing Iranian influence. Most of their diplomats are back, their intelligence services have resumed cooperation, and trade delegations are booking Damascus's hotels.

I visited the newly opened Golden Mazzeh Hotel, a ten-story reminder that some Syrians are surviving America's economic sanctions better than others. Its 111 suites and rooms, ten restaurants and bars, two outdoor swimming pools, ballroom, meeting rooms, theater, gym, and conference center make it a formidable competitor to the older Sheraton and Four Seasons. Guests can sip martinis in its two rooftop bars while contemplating a 360-degree panorama of the sprawling Syrian capital: suburban apartment complexes and parks to the west, Mount Qasioun to the north, and to the east the ancient walled city where Saint Paul eluded his persecutors and which tradition says the Prophet Muhammad bypassed in the belief that man could enter paradise only once. An Italian architect, Massimo Rodighiero, designed the hotel, whose manager, Patrick Prudhomme, is French. In the eucalyptus-shaded public garden across from the entrance, mothers watch their children as traffic rumbles along the nearby Mazzeh Highway toward Beirut. Most Syrians, however, cannot afford to go inside and pay for a drink, let alone dinner.

§

On February 6, 2023, soon after my return from Damascus to Beirut, the violent shaking of my bed woke me around 3:15 a.m. I got up and stood in a doorway, as I was advised to do during my youth in earthquake-prone California. My eleventh-floor flat oscillated for a few minutes and stopped, then swayed again with less force for another minute and stopped for good. Later that morning I read that the quake had devastated southern Turkey and northern Syria. To war and hunger can be added the blind cruelty of nature.

At last count, although the figure continues to rise, the toll from the magnitude 7.8 earthquake, and the smaller one that followed on February 20, 2023, was at least fifty thousand people killed, more than six thousand of them in Syria. Turkey, where the epicenters of the quakes were located, suffered the most casualties and buildings destroyed. In Syria, the ancient city of Aleppo, the country's commercial capital, was the worst hit. Much of it had yet to be rebuilt following the government's December 2016 conquest of rebel strongholds in the eastern half.

Many residents had moved back rather than become refugees or lose title to their properties. Their homes remained so precarious that the earthquake knocked them down for good. A woman I know in Aleppo sent me pictures of her apartment. It had scars in the walls so wide you could walk through them, and ceilings had collapsed into rooms below. Men, women, and children shivering outdoors needed not only blankets but food. Aid was slow to arrive in both Aleppo and the Turkish rebel territory north of it.

The regime and its jihadi opponents blamed each another for blocking deliveries of desperately needed earthmovers, food, blankets, tents, and medicines. The UN accused the largest jihadi coalition, Hayat Tahrir al-Sham, of delaying supplies over "approval issues." Although one of Hayat Tahrir al-Sham's predecessors, the Al Qaeda-affiliated al-Nusra Front, used to kidnap and torture foreign journalists, its leader, Abu Mohammad al-Jolani, granted an interview to *The Guardian* in which he claimed that the regime could not be trusted and that it had turned the region "into an ongoing earthquake the past twelve years." He eventually withdrew his objections to receiving aid, no doubt under pressure from his Turkish protectors and the thousands of civilians among whom he and his fighters live.

After the earthquake, President Assad, who had insisted for years that Syrian sovereignty required the UN to provide assistance only through Damascus, belatedly agreed to permit the UN to send aid to rebel areas from Turkey through two border crossings. The US also softened its hardline stance on February 9, 2023, and lifted some of its sanctions for 180 days to allow agencies to send earthquake relief, but it has not responded to appeals from Pope Francis, the World Council of Churches, the Norwegian Refugee Council, and Syria's Christian bishops for further easing of the embargo. While the US remains firm, some EU countries—notably Italy, which sent ambulances and the navy ship *San Marco* to Beirut with equipment for Syria, and the Czech Republic—are breaking ranks and demanding that more be done to allow Syrians some measure of dignity and self-reliance. The Syrians deserve better than what their government, the foreign powers who have meddled in their affairs, and the rebels have offered them. And yet their suffering goes on. And on.

DEATH IN DAMASCUS

> [Hafez al] Asad's rule in Syria began [in 1970] with an immediate and considerable advantage: the regime he displaced was so detested that any alternative came as a relief.
> —Patrick Seale, *Asad: The Struggle for the Middle East*, 1988

Florence, Italy, December 2024
I applied for visas at the Syrian Consulate in Beirut in October 2023 and July 2024. My appeals to the Ministries of Information and Foreign Affairs in Damascus went unanswered, and no visas were granted. This left me to follow Syria from Lebanon when Lebanon was preoccupied with the border conflict between Israel and Hezbollah.

On Tuesday July 5, 2024, an ambulance rushed an attractive, forty-eight-year-old woman to Damascus's elite Al Shami Hospital. The woman, suffering a brain hemorrhage, was unconscious. Witnesses said that an unidentified car had rammed her silver BMW, forcing her driver to swerve into traffic that caused further damage. Police seized the BMW and detained the driver.

The accident, as common in Syria as in the rest of the world, would have gone unremarked but for the identity of the injured party: Luna al-Shibl, media advisor to President Bashar al-Assad. Born in 1975 in Suweida, capital of the Druze region in the south, she studied at Damascus University. She left Syria to work as a news presenter for Al Jazeera television at its headquarters in Doha, Qatar, where she met and married a co-worker, Lebanese journalist Sami Kleib. Her green eyes, mousey blond hair, and pleasing voice made her one of Jazeera's many popular women anchors in the early 2000s.

In May of 2010, Shibl and seven other female journalists at Al Jazeera publicly protested the behavior of a senior executive who, they said, made "repeated offensive remarks" about what he called their immodest on-air clothing. Reporters without Borders and the International Federation of Journalists supported the women's stand against "sexual harassment." The network investigated itself and concluded the women were mistaken. Five of them, including Shibl, resigned. She returned to Syria, where she presented the news on Syrian television. While there, she came to the attention of the presidency, which hired her as a media consultant.

She emerged as a fervent advocate of the government's crackdown on protestors demanding democracy in early 2011. Journalists seeking interviews with Assad found that their requests went through her rather than the Ministry of Information. All indications were that she and Assad grew close. Rumors circulated that the first lady, Asma al-Assad, became jealous of the young woman working daily with her husband. The rumors may have been false, but Syrians who believed them referred to her as "the second lady." A western television crew that interviewed Assad in the early phase of the civil war told me that Shibl fussed over Assad during the interview and went so far as to coach him. They believed, rightly or wrongly, that she exerted considerable influence over her boss.

Shibl and her Lebanese husband, who lived between Beirut and Paris, spent less time together and divorced in 2014. Two years later, she married the head of the National Union of Syrian Students, forty-nine-year-old Ammar Saati. The Syrian news website *Enab Baladi* reported, "Saati was known as 'an active member of Syria's cruel shabiha militia.' 'Shabiha' means 'ghosts', and it is a term for 'pro-government militias and supporters'." The Shabiha, drawn largely from unemployed Alawite youth in the Latakia region, suppressed protestors and fought alongside government troops against Assad's opponents. *Enab Baladi* also claimed that Saati was involved in business with Assad's brother Maher, commander of the fearsome Fourth Armored Division. Shibl's brother, Brigadier Mulham al-Shibl, was assigned to the Republican Guard that protected the president. Her husband and brother were alleged to have used her position to enrich themselves.

In August 2020, the US Treasury placed Saati and Shibl, along with other regime functionaries, under economic sanctions. The Treasury's ruling prohibited "all dealings by U.S. persons or within (or transiting) the United States that involve any property or interests in property of blocked or designated persons." Britain followed suit in March 2011. This did not inhibit Shibl's rise to prominence in Assad's inner circle. Assad included her in his delegation to the Geneva peace talks in January 2014. She subsequently accompanied him on state visits to China and Russia.

Her influence waned following Israel's bombardment of the Iranian Consulate in Damascus on April 1, 2024, which destroyed the diplomatic mission and killed two Iranian generals and two other officers. Suspicion grew that she or her brother provided the time of the Iranian Revolutionary Guards' meeting in the consulate. With Assad's two external benefactors, Russia and Iran, vying for influence in the country, Shibl was seen to be closer to the Russians. If she did tell the Russians about the meeting, the Russians let the Israelis know.

Four days after being admitted to Al Shami Hospital, Shibl died of her injuries. The Presidential Palace allowed only a two-hour mourning period, and she was buried in Damascus without ceremony. Her husband and her brother, according to reliable reports from Syria, were arrested. Syrian social media were rife with speculation about the ostensible killer's identity: Iran and Hezbollah; Russia; jealous courtiers; Asma al-Assad with the help of her son; and Bashar al-Assad himself. No proof was provided, and no one allowed for the possibility that her death was an accident. In a regime as opaque as Syria's, it was unlikely that the truth would be known.

Shibl's death and the speculation surrounding it were signs of fissures within the regime, which was maneuvering between its Russian and Iranian backers to obtain maximum leverage with both. It turned out to be a game not worth playing. Russia pulled most of its air force from Syria to bomb Ukraine. Israel's decimation of Iran and its proxies in Lebanon and Syria over the course of 2024 led the Iranians to withdraw vital military assets. Without Russian and Iranian support of the kind that led to Assad's "victory" in 2016, he was liable to defeat in 2024 if the jihadis in Idlib attacked. And attack they did.

Led by their largest militia, Hayat Tahrir al-Sham (HTS), with the aid of the Turkish-supplied Syrian National Army, they targeted the nearby regime-held city, Aleppo. Hezbollah had already withdrawn from western Aleppo to concentrate on its battle for survival against Israel in south Lebanon. Poorly paid Syrian Army units there were insufficient to mount meaningful resistance. The jihadists, having been expelled from the city in 2016 in what appeared to be victory for Assad, advanced from the west. They killed the Iranian commander in Aleppo, Brigadier General Keyomarth Pourhashemi, and seized villages on the city's periphery. Three days into their offensive, the jihadists had conquered the western half of Aleppo and were flying their flag over the ancient Citadel in the city center. As they completed their occupation of the city, Israel launched air strikes on Syrian and Hezbollah forces all over Syria. Israeli prime minister Binyamin Netanyahu issued a warning to Assad not to allow Hezbollah weapons into Lebanon from Syria and declared, "Don't play with fire."

The warning was superfluous. Assad's forces were falling back everywhere. On December 3, Hayat Tahrir al-Sham moved south to Hama, the lovely town on the River Orontes with its famed Roman aqueducts and giant water wheels. It was in Hama that the Muslim Brotherhood raised the flag of Sunni Islamist insurrection in 1982. Inspired by the Iranian revolution's success in establishing the region's first Islamic republic, the Brothers had fought to end secular, Baathist Party rule. Hafez al Assad crushed their rebellion, killing ten thousand or more people in the process of restoring his control of the mostly Sunni city. For HTS, Hama represented a reversal of the prior Islamist defeat—neglecting the irony that, far from taking Iran as the inspiration its predecessors had, it was driving Iran out of Syria.

On other fronts, Kurdish forces about three hundred miles to the east, backed by American air strikes, seized Deir ez-Zour on the River Euphrates from the Syrian Army. Hayat Tahrir al-Sham would capture the town and its oilfields from the Kurds four days later. In the south near the Israeli-occupied Golan Heights, Druze militias from Suweida joined the revolt. In nearby Dera'a, where the uprising began in 2011, Sunni rebels expelled government forces. The Kurds and the Druze, who had fought the Islamists earlier in the war, found themselves aiding HTS—perhaps with a view to claiming a stake in the new order.

With speed that shocked not only Assad and the outside powers, but the rebels themselves, they advanced into Homs the next day. Assad promised a counter-offensive that failed to materialize. A friend of mine, who left Homs ahead of the rebel breakthrough, told me over the telephone that he watched government soldiers fleeing the front with their tanks, armored personnel carriers, and artillery intact. The rebels he saw had only small arms that were no match for the army's firepower. In a matter of four hours from 6 p.m. to 10 p.m., he said, the regime lost the war. He could not understand why the army did not fight, one of many puzzles surrounding the old regime's final days. One theory had it that the rebels paid senior officers, who earned only forty dollars a month, hundreds of dollars to disappear.

On December 7, Hayat Tahrir al-Sham's irregulars assumed control of Homs. Their leader, Ahmed al-Sharaa—using his nom de guerre Abu Mohammed al-Jolani—told his followers, "Damascus awaits you." Damascus lay only a hundred miles south through sparsely populated farmland and desert. His men made it there in a day.

As the rebel forces raced south from Homs on Sunday, December 8, the Syrian Army abandoned Damascus. Bashar al-Assad, whose family had ruled Syria for fifty-four years, fled to Moscow. The city gates were open, as they had been when Ottoman forces pulled out in 1918 before the invading British Army with its Arab nationalist auxiliaries under Prince Feisal of the Hejaz and T. E. Lawrence. The British betrayed the Syrians, denying them their promised independence. When Damascus fell to Hayat Tahrir al-Sham in 2024, Jolani was making promises of his own. They contrasted with the strict governance he had enforced for years in Idlib: to preserve state institutions, protect private property, and respect the rights of minorities.

Jolani marched into Damascus's ancient Omayyad Mosque that Sunday in triumph. The former Byzantine Cathedral of Saint John the Baptist, which had fallen to the original Muslim followers of the Prophet Muhammad in AD 634, was a prized symbol of Sunni Islam and its early victories over the Shiites. To his enthusiast supporters, Jolani declared, "A new history, my brothers, is being written in the entire region after this great victory."

Jolani granted amnesty to Syrian Army conscripts and pledged to prosecute those responsible for mass torture and murder under the Assad regime. The veteran jihadist with a ten-million-dollar price on his head from the US, over his prior affiliation to Al Qaeda and the Islamic State, seemed to be transforming himself from Osama bin Laden to Thomas Jefferson. Alastair Crooke, a British former diplomat and spy who monitors jihadism closely for his Conflicts Forum consultancy, said, "Well, I just don't believe it." Others do. Take your choice.

As thousands of Damascenes celebrated the end of the dictator's rule, others feared that dictatorship in another guise would replace it. Turkey, Israel, and the US aggravated the country's plight with an escalation of air bombardment throughout the country. Turkey intensified its attacks on Kurdish forces in the northeast, despite the Kurds' alliance with the US. American forces with the Kurds bombed Islamic State fighters in the eastern desert, as they had for the previous five years without notable success. Israel, taking advantage of the demise of the Syrian Army, moved troops into the Syrian Golan Heights and seized the summit of Mount Hermon—abrogating the Syria-Israel ceasefire accord that then-US Secretary of State Henry Kissinger negotiated in 1974. The Israeli Air Force struck Syrian naval ships in Latakia harbor and weapons depots in Damascus. The Syrian Observatory for Human Rights on December

9 "documented 176 attacks in 2024: 150 airstrikes and 26 rocket attacks by ground forces, during which Israel targeted several positions in Syria, destroying nearly 326 targets, including buildings, weapons and ammunitions warehouses, headquarters, centres and vehicles." Russia declared it would maintain its naval base at Tartous and its Hmeimim airfield in northern Syria, pledging to defend them against anyone attempting to remove them.

With so many external actors, whose interests conflict more than coincide, and internal antagonists hostile to one another—Sunnis, Druze, Alawites, Ismailis, Arab and Armenian Christians, fundamentalists, and secularists—the disappearance of the Assad regime may presage not so much the end of the war as the beginning of a new one.

ACKNOWLEDGMENTS

MY DEBT TO THOSE WHO OVER MANY years have taught me about Syria is greater than I can ever repay. I am particularly grateful for the education I received from the late Patrick Seale, John Cooley, and Peter Jennings, all of whom wrote presciently about Syria throughout their illustrious careers. I must also thank the Agence France Presse correspondent in Beirut, Rana Moussaoui, for her insights into a conflict she has been reporting from Syria since its birth in March 2011; Jim Muir of the BBC; David Hirst, formerly of the *Guardian*; and Jonathan Steele of the *Guardian*.

Most of those I need to thank are Syrian friends who have endured with patience the slow destruction of their country while giving of their time to explain it to this outsider: Georges Saliba, Tony Touma, Georges Antaki, Ghaith Armanazi, Colette Khoury, human rights lawyer Anwar Bounni, Samir Khaterji, Bishop Armash Nabaldian, Monsignor Boutros Marayati, Ambassador Sami Khiyami, Jihad Makdissi, Lina Sinjab and Jack Barsoum of the BBC, Roulla Rouqbi, Nabil Sukkar, Nashwa Mraish, Orwa Nyarabia, Zaidoun al-Zoabi, Nora Arissian, Missak Baghboudarian, Razek and Maia Mamarbashi, Maria Saadeh, Yazan Abdallah, Zeinab Al Basha, Dr. Maamoun Abdelkarim, Louai Hussien, Rim Al Attrache, Hassan Al-Attrache, Raed Al-Attrache, Bouthaina Shaaban, Reem Haddad, Emma Abbas, and Rana Al Khayrat. I wish that I could repay the kindness of the Greek and Syriac Orthodox archbishops of Aleppo, Boulos Yazigi and Gregorios Yohanna Ibrahim, who were kidnapped by jihadists in April 2013 and whose fates remain unknown. They did all they could to prevent the spread of hatred and fanaticism in their country and became two of among millions of victims in a war that should never have begun.

My thanks must also go to countless staff of the United Nations staff, International Committee of the Red Cross, and aid agencies, who have been unfailing in their courtesy in difficult circumstances. I think particularly of Moktar Lamani, Yacub El Hilo, Emilio Tamburi Quinteiro, Matthew Hollingworth, Tamara Zayyat, Hussam El Saleh, Karin McLennan, George Comninos, Stephanie Khoury, Juliette Touma, Pawel Krysiek, Adnan Hizam, Ingy Sedki, and Andreas Kruesi. This list is anything but exhaustive. I would also like to thank Walid Bey Jumblatt for his many insights into Syrian history and his caustic observations on its political life, as well as his wife Nora, a loyal Syrian of whom her country can be proud. With the change of regime in Syria, Nora reclaimed her family house in the old city of Damascus—like thousands of other Syrian exiles who returned to rebuild their homes.

I am unable to thank the Syrian friends who have sadly died since they gave me valuable insights into the nature of their country: Armen Mazloumian of the famed Baron's Hotel in Aleppo, Magdy Jubaili, and Khaled Khalifa. Armen, like his father before, always made me at home in Aleppo and introduced me to that great city's leading Armenian and Arab families. It is my hope that his wife, Rubina, reopens their grand old hotel and restores it to its former glory. Magdy Jubaili, a patrician of Aleppo, generously guided me through his country's labyrinthine political structure and helped me to meet many of the people who enliven this book. Khaled Khalifa, one of his country's finest novelists who can justifiably be called Syria's biographer, never disappointed in his sharp analysis and his optimism that, somehow, Syrians would pull through their long tragedy. His indefatigable humor sustained me through some of the darkest hours. I miss them all.

For my understanding of American policy in Syria under the Barack Obama administration, I must thank Lisa Shields of the Council on Foreign Relations, Seymour Hersh, Christopher Ross, Jake Sullivan, Anthony Blinken, Paul Salem, Rob Malley, Robert Ford, Fred Hof, Phil Gordon, Bassam Barabandi, Derek Chollet, Charles Lister, Michael Dempsey, Gerald Feierstein, and Ray McGovern.

Without the support of the late Robert Silvers at the *New York Review of Books*, I would not have been able to spend as much time as I have in Syria after 2011. He was as gracious and conscientious an editor as any writer could hope to please. To Michael Shea, who succeeded Bob as my editor and benefactor at the NYRB, goes a special thanks. The same thanks must go to Rick MacArthur, Ellen Rosenbush, and Chris Carroll at *Harper's*, and to Sigrid Rausing at *Granta*. I must also express my gratitude to Jamie Stern-Weiner at OR Books for his meticulous editing of my often unwieldy text and to publisher Colin Robinson for suggesting this book and bringing it to fruition. I owe Patrick Cockburn and Aaron Maté many drinks for their unjustifiably laudatory forewords.

—December 2024

ABOUT THE AUTHOR

Charles Glass was ABC News Chief Middle East Correspondent from 1983 to 1993. Since 1973, he has covered wars in the Middle East, Africa, and the Balkans. He is the author of *Syria Burning, Tribes with Flags, The Tribes Triumphant, Money for Old Rope, The Northern Front, Americans in Paris, The Deserters, They Fought Alone,* and *Soldiers Don't Go Mad: A Story of Brotherhood, Poetry, and Mental Illness During the First World War.* His website is www.charlesglass.net.

www.ingramcontent.com/pod-product-compliance
Lightning Source LLC
Jackson TN
JSHW081150100325
80347JS00002B/2